P. 62

138
163

YEATS
Coole Park
&
Ballylee

YEATS
Coole Park
&
Ballylee

DANIEL A. HARRIS

The Johns Hopkins University Press

Baltimore
&
London

Manufactured in the United States of America

The Johns Hopkins University Press, Baltimore, Maryland 21218
The Johns Hopkins University Press Ltd., London

Library of Congress Catalog Card Number 74–5185
ISBN 0–8018–1576–2

Library of Congress Cataloging in Publication data
will be found on the last printed page of this book.

This book has been brought to publication
with the generous assistance of the
Andrew W. Mellon Foundation.

Contents

ILLUSTRATIONS

Acknowledgments

I wish to thank the people who taught me how to read: William K. Wimsatt, Martin Price, Thomas M. Greene, and Cleanth Brooks. My debt to Deborah Harris is measureless; only she and I can know how much assistance she has given. Michael Harper, Marshall Ledger, and Robert Ross generously criticized various portions of the manuscript and saved me from many follies; those that remain are my own. I have benefited greatly from my students in classes on Yeats and Jonson; they have contributed more to this book than they may suspect. Constance Sekaros typed the manuscript with care; Jane Green and Cady Olney proofread it patiently. Aida DiPace Donald and Nancy Middleton Gallienne, at The Johns Hopkins University Press, were particularly helpful in preparing the manuscript for publication.

A research grant from the University of Pennsylvania (1969) and, most especially, a postdoctoral fellowship from the Andrew Mellon Foundation (1971–72) gave me time to think and write.

I am grateful to Mr. Michael Yeats, the Macmillan Company of New York, the Macmillan Company of London and Basingstoke, the Macmillan Company of Canada, and A. P. Watt & Son for permission to reprint material from the following works of W. B. Yeats: *The Collected Poems of W. B. Yeats* (© Macmillan Publishing Company, Inc., 1956); *The Collected Plays of W. B. Yeats* (Copyright 1934, 1952 by Macmillan Publishing Company, Inc.); *A Vision* (Copyright 1937 by W. B. Yeats, renewed 1965 by Bertha Georgie Yeats and Anne Butler Yeats); *Explorations* (Copyright 1962 by Mrs. W. B. Yeats); *Mythologies* (Copyright 1961 by Mrs. W. B. Yeats); *Essays and Introductions* (Copyright 1961 by Mrs. W. B. Yeats); *The Autobiography of William Butler Yeats* (Copyright 1916, 1935 by Macmillan Publishing Company, Inc., renewed 1944, 1963 by Bertha Georgie Yeats); *The Vari-*

orum Edition of the Poems of William Butler Yeats, eds. Peter Allt and Russell Alspach (Copyright 1957 by Macmillan Publishing Company, Inc.).

For permission to reproduce illustrations of Coole Park and Thoor Ballylee, I wish to thank the following: Mr. Michael Yeats (W. B. Yeats's pastel of Coole House); Bord Fáilte Éireann (the illustrations of Coole House); Manchester University Press (Robert Gregory's painting of Coole Lake [D. J. Gordon, *W. B. Yeats: Images of a Poet* (Manchester: Manchester University Press, 1961)]; Miss M. Frances Mac-Nally (the photographs of Thoor Ballylee); Mr. Robert Ross (the photographs of the stone carving on Thoor Ballylee's west facade).

Philadelphia
December 15, 1973

Note: Unless otherwise indicated, I have accepted Richard Ellmann's dating of the poems (*The Identity of Yeats* [1954; rpt. London: Faber, 1964], pp. 287–94). In dealing with the longer poems whose stanzas Yeats did not number, I have designated the stanzas with Roman numerals, e.g., "A Prayer for My Daughter" (VI). For poems which Yeats divided into sections by Roman numerals, I have used lower-case Roman numerals to indicate the stanza within the section, e.g., "The Tower" (II.iii).

YEATS
Coole Park
&
Ballylee

All things fall and are built again,
And those that build them again are gay.
                    ["Lapis Lazuli"]

CHAPTER

ONE

Introductory:
The Myths of Place

In 1896 Yeats visited Coole Park, Lady Gregory's Georgian estate in the West of Ireland. The new environment—near Gort, Kiltartan, the austere Burren Hills—altered his life and generated "metaphors for poetry"[1] commensurate with those in *A Vision,* and more humane. In 1917 he purchased Thoor Ballylee, the gaunt fourteenth-century tower four miles from Coole, and tightened his hold on a territory he had already begun shaping into a self-coherent world. His intensified awareness of place—precise boundaries—flowered in a self-dramatizing language whose force was intimately specific: "Beyond *that* ridge lived Mrs. French" ("The Tower," II.ii). Yet Yeats wore many masks: he was a Celt, a Renaissance courtier-poet, an Anglo-Irishman by turns; the identity of his territory changed with his consciousness.

Initially, despite his Anglo-Irish birth and the Gregorys' prominently Anglo-Irish tradition, Coole for Yeats was not Coole at all, but Kyle, a Celtic terrain. Why? The tremendous task Yeats undertook after Parnell's death in 1891—the reformation of Ireland's literature, its literary history, and its national consciousness—demanded his opposition to Anglo-Ireland, and not simply because Yeats despised his kinship with seven centuries of English oppression. He had adopted the difficult, potentially condescending role of a nationalist Anglo-Irishman trying to purify Irish culture from within, and his nationalism was critical as well as devout. If he glorified "the Celtic intensity, the Celtic

---

[1] W. B. Yeats, *A Vision* (New York: Macmillan, 1961), p. 8.

fire, the Celtic daring,"[2] he also abhorred the conventions of maudlin patriotism, divisive stereotypes, and abstract simplification of complex historical problems which had prevailed since Davis founded the Young Ireland movement in 1848: "All the past had been turned into a melodrama with Ireland for blameless hero and poet; novelist and historian had but one object, that we should hiss the villain, and only a minority doubted that the greater the talent the greater the hiss."[3] Thus, "If I must attack so much that seemed sacred to Irish nationalist opinion, I must, I knew, see to it that no man suspect me of doing it to flatter Unionist opinion"; he antagonized his father's friends "by deliberate calculation,"[4] and prided himself on being denied entrance to aristocratic houses.[5]

The strategy, if self-conscious, was sincere. "A writer or public man of the upper classes," Yeats wrote in 1901, "is useless to this country till he has done something that separates him from his class."[6] But Anglo-Ireland, unionist, self-serving, had rejected Ireland with "cynical indifference."[7] Although he needed English models for his verse, he defended much second-rate Irish writing, in addition to the ancient epic cycles, and attacked Anglo-Irish scholars like Dowden and Mahaffy for smugly denying the merits of indigenous Irish culture:

> Here in this very library, called National, there are Greek grammars in profusion and an entire wilderness of text-books of every genera and species, and but the meagrest sprinkling of books of Irish poetry and Irish legends. . . . As Dublin Castle with the help of the police keeps Ireland for England, so Trinity College with the help of the schoolmasters keeps the mind of Ireland for scholasticism with its accompanying weight of mediocrity.[8]

Even after Yeats embraced the eighteenth-century Anglo-Irish tradition in the twenties, he continued to criticize its modern failures: Protestant

---

[2] W. B. Yeats, *Uncollected Prose by W. B. Yeats: First Reviews and Articles, 1886–1896,* ed. John Frayne (New York: Columbia University Press, 1970), p. 201.

[3] W. B. Yeats, *The Autobiography of William Butler Yeats* (New York: Macmillan, 1938), p. 177.

[4] Ibid., p. 200.

[5] Ibid., p. 201.

[6] W. B. Yeats, *Explorations* (New York: Macmillan, 1962), p. 83.

[7] *Autobiography,* p. 201.

[8] *Uncollected Prose,* pp. 232–33.

Ireland in the nineties had "lacked hereditary passion,"[9] the will and perspicuity to serve the national interest. When the landowning class ignored Lord Salisbury's call to reform estate management, he recalled:

> There was deep disappointment. Protestant Ireland had immense prestige, Burke, Swift, Grattan, Emmet, Fitzgerald, Parnell, almost every name sung in modern song, had been Protestant; Dublin's dignity depended upon the gaunt magnificence of buildings founded under the old Parliament; but wherever it attempted some corporate action, wherein Ireland stood against England, the show, however gallant it seemed, was soon over. It sold its Parliament for solid money, and now it sold this cause for a phantom.[10]

That violation of the true Anglo-Irish legacy reflected the notorious corruption of nineteenth-century landed culture: "Ireland's 'dark insipid period' began. . . . [A] new absenteeism, foreseen by Miss Edgeworth, began; those that lived upon their estates bought no more fine editions of the classics; separated from public life and ambition they sank, as I have heard Lecky complain, 'into grass farmers'."[11] Lady Gregory's childhood home was not exempt from judgment: "Roxborough Protestantism was on the side of wealth and power"—a society of "soldiers, farmers, riders to hounds" that had "lacked intellectual curiosity until the downfall of their class had all but come."[12] For Castle Dargan Yeats barely muffled his contempt; its violent, hypocritical rituals of family pride epitomized "the reckless Ireland of a hundred years ago in final degradation." Once a year its squireen "drove to Sligo for the two old women, that they might look upon the ancestral stones and remember their gentility, and he would put his wildest horses into the shafts to enjoy their terror."[13] Yeats's general indictment of Anglo-Ireland was stiff, a bitter castigation of his own ethnic identity.

No wonder Yeats in 1896 translated Anglo-Irish Coole into Kyle in order to appreciate its virtues—Lady Gregory's friendship, moral energy, and generous patronage among them. The notion that he "was turning to a still celebrated family out of the eighteenth century"[14]

---

9 *Autobiography*, p. 358.

10 Ibid., pp. 357–58.

11 *Explorations*, p. 350.

12 *Autobiography*, pp. 337, 335.

13 Ibid., p. 49.

14 Donald T. Torchiana, *W. B. Yeats and Georgian Ireland* (Evanston: Northwestern University Press, 1966), p. 43.

misrepresents both his vaunted Celtism and his politics, based upon avoiding all taint of complicity with Anglo-Ireland. He saw Coole out of context. What mattered to Yeats in Lady Gregory's comment—"I defy any one to study Irish History without getting a dislike and distrust of England"[15] —was its Irishness, not its Anglo-Irish disinterest. While he plainly found Coole a noble exception to a debased culture, he did not simultaneously consider that transcendence a validation of the historical Anglo-Irish ideal. There was little in Coole's Anglo-Irish heritage Yeats did not eventually amalgamate into his own aristocratic vision: the study of family history, the consciousness of dwelling on a traditional land consecrated by significant acts committed in time, the intimate reciprocity of aristocrat and peasant, the assumed symbiosis between art, personal excellence, and national welfare—the sense, finally, that the house itself symbolized those "lovely intricacies"[16] in permanent, organic form. But Coole was not a ready-made, static emblem of those values; *Purgatory* (1938) shows Yeats manipulating the house and its traditions for a theme which hardly represented his feelings about the actual estate: final aristocratic degeneration.

The history of Yeats's conception of Coole is therefore one of gradual discovery. It reflects both his evolving quest for aristocratic perfection and his habitual responsiveness to public issues. The exploration is evident in Yeats's reactions to the house itself, which he shunned as a poetic symbol until "Upon a House Shaken by the Land Agitation" (1909). The earliest poems, the preface to *The Shadowy Waters* (1900) and "In the Seven Woods" (1902), remake the estate into a natural realm of Celtic myth; it made no difference that those woods, planted by the first Robert Gregory to "change the face of the district," had been praised by the eighteenth-century agriculturalist Arthur Young.[17] He balked at the house's classic Georgian interior, a manifestation of "that hated century."[18] When he first came to Coole, Lady Gregory told May Morris in 1923, he was so dominated by Morris's insistence on plain wood that he could not restrain himself from criticizing Coole's

---

15 Isabella Augusta Persse, Lady Gregory, *Our Irish Theatre* (1913; rpt. New York: Capricorn, 1965), p. 55. Lady Gregory was "still a Unionist" when Yeats met her and had written an anonymous pamphlet against Home Rule (W. B. Yeats, *Memoirs*, ed. Denis Donoghue [New York: Macmillan, 1973], p. 117 and n. 2); as she edited *Mr. Gregory's Letter-Box* (1898), her attitudes rapidly changed.

16 "In Memory of Major Robert Gregory," X.

17 Lady Gregory, *Lady Gregory's Journals*, ed. Lennox Robinson (New York: Macmillan, 1947), p. 15.

18 *Autobiography*, p. 148.

old mahogany, painted in *faux marbre*.[19] He did not connect the furnishings with the traditions of aesthetic discrimination they reflected. He could not grasp, there, the fundamental metaphoric equation between self and architecture he had already used in "The Lake Isle of Innisfree" (1890) and would handle so brilliantly in his country house poetry and the poems about Thoor Ballylee. He later wondered at his initial distaste: "I was so full of the medievalism of William Morris that I did not like the gold frames, some deep and full of ornament, round the pictures in the drawing-room; years were to pass before I came to understand the earlier nineteenth and later eighteenth century, and to love that house more than all other houses."[20] Fed on Dante, Blake, and Shelley, he spurned all enemies of imagination, acknowledged eighteenth-century influences on his life only after elaborate disguisings. The speaker of the *Rosa Alchemica* (1897) transforms the Dublin row house of his Augustan ancestors into an exotic, occult world, replaces their portraits with a Crivelli Madonna; lurid candlelight illumines "the gods and nymphs set upon the wall by some Italian plasterer of the eighteenth century, making them look like the first beings slowly shaping in the formless and void darkness." In this aesthete's paradise which transmutes all neoclassical elements, the speaker can admit memories of Swift "joking and railing" on the "wide staircase."[21] Yeats could not similarly metamorphose the house at Coole; and so he disregarded it.

In 1907 Lady Gregory took Yeats to Italy, read him Castiglione's *The Courtier*,[22] and thus sparked the analogy between Coole and courtly, humanistic Urbino. He had reread Shakespeare in 1901, Spenser in 1902. Most important, he had absorbed Ben Jonson (1905–6):

---

[19] Lady Gregory, Unpublished Journals, TS, Book XXIII, May 15, 1923, Gregory Papers, Henry W. and Albert A. Berg Collection of the New York Public Library, Astor, Lennox, and Tilden Foundations.

[20] *Autobiography*, p. 332.

[21] W. B. Yeats, *Mythologies* (New York: Macmillan, 1959), pp. 271–72. Yeats had excluded Swift from his *Book of Irish Verse* (1895) for not being sufficiently Irish.

[22] See Yeats, "Discoveries: Second Series," ed. Curtis Bradford, *Massachusetts Review* 5 (1964): 297–306. These essays leave no doubt that Yeats did not read Castiglione until 1907. Lady Gregory dated Yeats's dictation of them "May 24, 1908" (p. 297, n. 1); section [VI] begins: "Every summer I have some book read out to me, and last year I brought into the country *The Courtier* by Castiglione, in Hoby's translation" (p. 305). There are no definite allusions to *The Courtier* prior to 1907, at which point there is a plethora. See also W. B. Yeats, *The Letters of W. B. Yeats*, ed. Allan Wade (London: Hart-Davis, 1954), pp. 532–33. Cf. A. Norman Jeffares, *W. B. Yeats: Man and Poet*, 2nd ed. (London: Routledge, 1962), p. 170, who suggests that Yeats first read Castiglione in 1904; and Corinna Salvadori, *Yeats*

Courtesy of Bord Fáilte Éireann

COOLE HOUSE, front
"The house itself was plain and box-like . . ."

the country house became his chief symbol of aristocratic excellence. He now studied the Arundel prints of Renaissance masters in his room at Coole: Botticelli, Benozzo Gozzoli, Giorgione, Girolamo dai Libri, Melozzo da Forli, Mantegna, the Van Eycks.[23] Sir William, Lady Gregory's husband, had founded the Arundel Society, believing that proper aristocracy and aesthetic sensibility should conjoin in courteous behavior. When Robert Gregory died in 1918, he was "Our Sidney and our perfect man";[24] Coole remained for Yeats a Renaissance house until "A Prayer for My Daughter" (1919). With "Coole Park and Ballylee, 1931" and *Dramatis Personae* (1934) Yeats publicly acknowledged what he had increasingly understood since the Civil War (1921–23): Coole's Anglo-Irish identity. He lauded its inherited Georgian vitality, sense of form, commitment to excellence. Although "The house itself was plain and box-like," Richard Gregory (Sir William's

---

and *Castiglione: Poet and Courtier* (Dublin: Figgis, 1965), p. 18, who argues for 1903. Both Jeffares and Salvadori base their dates (more or less) on Yeats's comments in *The Bounty of Sweden* (*Autobiography*, p. 463).

[23] Yeats, *Memoirs*, p. 189; cf. *Autobiography*, p. 428.

[24] "In Memory of Major Robert Gregory," VI.

Courtesy of Bord Fáilte Éireann

COOLE HOUSE, rear

"... except on the side towards the lake where
somebody, probably Richard Gregory, had enlarged the
drawing-room and dining-room with great bow windows."

grand-uncle) had "substituted for the old straight avenue two great
sweeping avenues each a mile or a little more in length" and "enlarged
the drawing-room and dining-room with great bow windows."

> Every generation had left its memorial; every generation had been
> highly educated . . . Richard had brought in bullock-carts through
> Italy the marble copy of the Venus de' Medici in the drawing-room,
> added to the library the Greek and Roman Classics bound by
> famous French and English binders.[25]

Sir William Temple's library, by which Yeats thought Swift so influenced, now approximated the library at Coole[26] where Yeats received
his neoclassical education ("Mad as the Mist and Snow"). The break-
fast-room, which Lady Gregory considered a guide to Ireland's late
Georgian and Victorian history,[27] was lined with

[25] *Autobiography*, pp. 334, 333, 332.

[26] Lady Gregory, Unpublished Journals, Book XXXVIII, August 26, 1928.

[27] Lady Gregory, Holograph MS. to *Coole*, Book VIII, Gregory Papers, Henry W.

mezzotints and engravings of the masters and friends of the old
Gregorys . . . Pitt, Fox, Lord Wellesley, Palmerston, Gladstone,
many that I have forgotten . . . and amongst them Lady Gregory
had hung a letter from Burke to the Gregory that was chairman of
the East India Company saying that he committed to his care, now
that he himself had grown old, the people of India.[28]

The bust of Maecenas in a corner of the walled garden, gracing nature
with intimations of artistic and civil order, epitomized the deliberate
link between Coole and Augustan Rome on which the Gregorys had
founded their tradition. "There is no country house in Ireland with so
fine a record," Yeats told Lady Gregory in 1921.[29]

Although Yeats violated Coole's historical—Anglo-Irish—context
until the twenties, the span of the poetry shows a profound historical
orientation. Through this sequence of historical myths, he made the
estate embody his most pressing historical concerns and gained crucial
images of temporal glory. Most remarkably, the mythic sequence parallels that in the poems about Thoor Ballylee which Yeats began two
decades later. "Ego Dominus Tuus" (1915), "A Prayer on Going into
My House" (1918), and "The Phases of the Moon" (1918) have the
same medievalism as his first poems about Coole. "In Memory of Major
Robert Gregory" (1918) and "A Prayer for My Daughter" (1919) mark
the Renaissance phase which, in the Coole poems, includes "Upon a
House Shaken by the Land Agitation" (1909), "The New Faces"
(1912), the epilogue to *Responsibilities* (1914), and "Shepherd and
Goatherd" (1918). Yeats at the tower explored his eighteenth-century
Anglo-Irish heritage in "Meditations in Time of Civil War" (1921–22),
"The Tower" (1925), "Blood and the Moon" (1927), and "Coole Park
and Ballylee, 1931," which finally joins the two sequences. "The Black
Tower" (1939), Yeats's last poem, is so lost in the gigantic shadows of
Ireland's heroic age that it all but transcends time.

That Yeats recreated the same evolutionary pattern twice, and
incorporated it into the two architectural symbols he valued most,
demonstrates its extraordinary magnetism. As a personal quest for
identity, the mythic sequence measures his grave difficulty in grappling
with his Anglo-Irish birth. The masks of medieval legend and occult
fantasy, Renaissance passion and courtesy, simultaneously evade the
eighteenth century and herald the Anglo-Irish pride of his supremely

---

and Albert A. Berg Collection of the New York Public Library, Astor, Lennox, and
Tilden Foundations.

28 *Autobiography*, pp. 333–34.

29 Lady Gregory, *Journals*, p. 17.

powerful, racist Divorce Speech (1925); this is one of the great unspoken tensions of the sequence. Concomitantly, the successive historical myths register his increasingly direct confrontation with modern Ireland and the modern world. With the temporal distance always decreasing, the constant interplay between past and present, historical myth and actual history, is rich. The sequence is Yeats's abbreviated version—poetic, historical, psychological—of the biological proposition, ontogeny repeats phylogeny. "Every child in growing from infancy to maturity," Yeats wrote in 1925, "should pass in imagination through the history of its own race and through something of the history of the world."[30] The historical identities with which he endowed his territory enabled him to recapitulate Western culture and thus become a self-transcending, encyclopaedic man. Eliot, Joyce, Pound sought the same goal; none achieved it so personally as Yeats. The poems are an intricate unity, Yeats's most sustained effort to dramatize the panoramic complexities of *A Vision*.[31]

Yeats's historical myths of self-explanation were also myths of possession. They reveal an incessant, often tortured quest to gain an "original relation" to Ireland. "Have not all races had their first unity from a mythology, that marries them to rock and hill?"[32] From *John Sherman* (1890) and the multitudinous early reviews to "The Municipal Gallery Revisited" (1937), the same message dominates:

> All that we did, all that we said or sang
> Must come from contact with the soil, from that
> Contact everything Antaeus-like grew strong.

Through his myths he appropriated a concrete physical space that was no mere picturesque landscape: it was a microcosm of Ireland and a mediatory ground between himself and the Ireland of plaster saints he so often derided. Yeats was acutely sensitive to the dangers of a local poetry. Allingham, he wrote in 1891, was "the poet of Ballyshannon, though not of Ireland." Although Yeats respected the Anglo-Irishman's melancholic affection for provincial life and his avoidance of cosmopolitan condescension, he also understood the consequences of provin-

---

30 W. B. Yeats, *The Senate Speeches of W. B. Yeats,* ed. Donald Pearce (Bloomington: Indiana University Press, 1960), pp. 173–74.

31 There is no finer study of the general relation between Yeats's poetry and *A Vision* than Thomas R. Whitaker's *Swan and Shadow: Yeats's Dialogue with History* (Chapel Hill: North Carolina University Press, 1964). See especially pp. 3–11 and pp. 133–35.

32 *Explorations,* p. 235; *Autobiography,* p. 169.

cialism: dessicated language and emotion, the breakdown of poetic form. Allingham had failed to make his territory an exploratory device: "One can only reach out to the universe with a gloved hand—that glove is one's nation, the only thing one knows even a little of." Lacking "national fire," he had failed to transfigure Ballyshannon into a symbol of "heaven and earth."[33] Yeats, by compacting his historical myths into the space between Coole and Thoor Ballylee, possessed a spiritualized realm, a defined place where in theory he could realize all moments in time simultaneously and, in practice, meditate upon chosen historical epochs until they yielded him their secret knowledge. His space was a memory, a "spot of time."

The quest for a sanctified ground which will vouchsafe redemptive self-knowledge and joy is a central myth in the poems about Coole and Thoor Ballylee. Logically extending Wordsworth's concept of epiphany, the self-consciousness of blessedness within the space-time continuum,[34] Yeats insisted on a permanent "spot," not random "spots." He needed not only a temporal continuity between moments of revelation but a continuity of location. While Wordsworth recognized his "spots of time" after they had occurred and narrated them as recollections, Yeats compulsively created poems whose speakers seek revelation in the same place and enact those moments in the present. The seminal poem about Sligo, "The Lake Isle of Innisfree" (1890), anticipates Yeats's obsession with a numinous place. The poem is a memory of place now revivified to inspire the future, yet with such intensity that expected happiness becomes present joy:

And I shall have some peace there, for peace comes dropping slow,
Dropping from the veils of the morning to where the cricket sings;
There midnight's all a glimmer, and noon a purple glow,
And evening full of the linnet's wings.

[II]

---

33 *Uncollected Prose*, p. 209; W. B. Yeats, *Letters to the New Island*, ed. Horace Reynolds (Cambridge: Harvard University Press, 1934), pp. 174, 163. Torchiana (*W. B. Yeats*, p. 6), citing another of Yeats's essays on Allingham (*Uncollected Prose*, pp. 258–61), believes that Yeats "highly praised" him "for evoking a local rather than an abstractly national feeling." But as Whitaker notes (p. 137), Yeats's attitude toward Allingham was always ambivalent, although there is little question of his influence in guiding Yeats toward possession of Thoor Ballylee. See *Uncollected Prose*, p. 211: "those songs of his may have turned Ballyshannon into one of the spots held sacred by literary history." Dwight Eddins, *Yeats: The Nineteenth Century Matrix* (University, Alabama: The University of Alabama Press, 1971), pp. 57–64, discusses Allingham's influence on Yeats's ballads.

34 Wordsworth, *The Prelude*, Book XII, 11. 208ff. For a fine discussion of Wordsworth's idea, see Geoffrey H. Hartman, *Wordsworth's Poetry, 1787–1814* (New Haven: Yale University Press, 1964), p. 212.

Everything here generates a magical stasis in time. "I *shall have* some peace" rapidly changes to "peace *comes*": the shift eliminates the spatio-temporal dichotomies between London and the present, the island and the future. Chronological time vanishes: morning midnight, noon, and evening swirl in reverie. Midnight and noon, their colors reversed, interpenetrate in unearthly irridescence. "Peace," linked with dew, lapping water, the throb of blood, is less an absolute tranquillity than a tremulously slow ecstasy.[35] Like the "small cabin ... of clay and wattles," Coole and Thoor Ballylee were situated near water, Yeats's traditional symbol of the lunar imagination: they too were places of potential revelation. The equilibrium of nature and artifice had magical power:[36] to go West was to seek visionary self-realization. Yeats's historical myths, themselves sacramentalizing his space, finally transcend their origins to participate in his overarching quest for the "Profane perfection of mankind" ("Under Ben Bulben," IV). The heroic figures populating his world become talismanic models of imitation whereby the quester may achieve the ahistorical knowledge that "We are blest by everything, / Everything we look upon is blest" ("A Dialogue of Self and Soul," II.iv).

Yeats's myth of perfection was also communal. His ideal pastoral society of aristocrat, peasant, and poet actualized the idea of unified culture whose emblem, created through distanced speculation, he made Byzantium. Because Byzantium could never be possessed, it could never be lost: a safe utopia. With Coole and Thoor Ballylee, Yeats attempted something more difficult: his territory was an incipient Eden, perpetually awaiting imaginative redemption, perpetually endangered by chaos. The twin myths of paradise regained and paradise lost go hand in hand to produce the emotion of tragic joy which Yeats, through Blake and Nietzsche, so relentlessly pursued. The vast majority of these poems celebrate innocence, aristocratic self-perfection, and momentary sanctity in the face of imminent disaster. Yeats's serpent was not simply the imagination's failure to sustain its unifying vision. He included in his territory the West of Ireland's own psychic nemesis, the dread of physical invasion; the West had resisted English domination and thus retained its Irish character intact. Yeats's theme of incursion surfaces in "Upon a House . . ."—as soon as he left the Seven Woods of Coole for its house. It reappears shortly after he purchased the tower, in "A

---

35 See Bernard Levine, *The Dissolving Image: The Spiritual-Esthetic Development of W. B. Yeats* (Detroit: Wayne State University Press, 1970), pp. 31–32, for an account of the fusion of visual and aural imagery.

36 See Yeats, *W. B. Yeats and T. Sturge Moore: Their Correspondence*, ed. Ursula Bridge (London: Routledge, 1953), pp. 109, 111. On the occult significance of Coole's location, see *Autobiography*, pp. 315–19.

Prayer on Going into My House." During the twenties, as the nemesis
became fact, "a place set out for wisdom" became "this tumultuous
spot" and compelled hard self-awareness ("The Phases of the Moon";
"Meditations in Time of Civil War," II.iii). Black and Tan brutalities
near Kiltartan, the burning of many aristocratic country houses, the
assassination of Kevin O'Higgins, the inevitable destruction of Coole—
all marked the poetry of a man prepared to risk exposure to the bitter
confusions of his time rather than court the alluring dangers of poetic
isolation. Embattled against the last invasion, death's, he refused to
surrender the space he had made, swore allegiance to an invisible lord,
and committed an epic suicide:

> Say that the men of the old black tower,
> Though they but feed as the goatherd feeds,
> Their money spent, their wine gone sour,
> Lack nothing that a soldier needs,
> That all are oath-bound men:
> Those banners come not in.

> ["The Black Tower," I]

CHAPTER

TWO

The West of Ireland:
Early Explorations

In "The Shadowy Waters" (1900) and "In the Seven Woods" (1902), Yeats rode roughshod over Coole's Anglo-Irish history to superimpose his own context, Celtic myth imbued with traditional religious imagery. The realities which made his transformation feasible—Coole's woods were reputedly magical, he had collected local folklore with Lady Gregory and just rewritten *The Shadowy Waters* at Coole[1]—obscure Yeats's psychological need to possess Coole personally. He could not employ foreign modes to express his consciousness of a ground he already felt sacred: the ancestral trees he later loved for harboring memories of an eighteenth-century Gregory and his bride[2] now belong to ancient "immortal, mild, proud shadows." As in the Gregory tradition, the actual land insures continuity with the past and intimates ideals to be observed; but Yeats's speakers bypass Coole's Augustan mythology for Eden and Tara, seat of the ancient Irish kings. The perfection Coole symbolizes is not that of purposive public activity but of divine grace and poetic illumination.

Yeats's central mythological concern in "The Shadowy Waters" is Eden's relation to Coole. Edenic "shadows" have given the speaker knowledge of Forgael and Dectora, the legendary Celtic figures in his play; where is the source of his ideal images? By designing a set of

[1] W. B. Yeats, *The Letters of W. B. Yeats*, ed. Allan Wade (London: Hart-Davis, 1954), pp. 320–22.

[2] W. B. Yeats, *The Autobiography of William Butler Yeats* (New York: Macmillan, 1938), p. 333.

unanswerable questions, Yeats tactfully created an ambiguous realm
where the collocation of Eden and Coole becomes poetically plausible:

> Is Eden far away, or do you hide
> From human thought, as hares and mice and coneys
> That run before the reaping-hook and lie
> In the last ridge of the barley?
>
> [11. 30–33]

Both the either/or construction and the naturalizing simile pull Eden
earthward, subject it to a temporal imagination which destroys what it
seeks. Against that dangerous immanence, the speaker wonders if
Coole's visible woods "cover" (1. 34), reflect a chthonic Eden whose
degree of beauty, but not its kind, surpasses the world's. Finally, "Is
Eden out of time and out of space?" (1. 36).[3] The speaker's meditations all depend on Coole's woods as the indispensable medium of
inspiration. Their "sudden fragrances" induce a tranced receptivity like
that in "Byzantium":

> Dim Pairc-na-tarav, where enchanted eyes
> Have seen immortal, mild, proud shadows walk;
> . . . .
> I had not eyes like those enchanted eyes,
> Yet dreamed that beings happier than men
> Moved round me in the shadows, and at night
> My dreams were cloven by voices and by fires;
> And the images I have woven in this story
> Of Forgael and Dectora and the empty waters
> Moved round me in the voices and the fires . . .
>
> [11. 11–12; 17–23]

Immemorially a place of vision, the Seven Woods redeem spiritual
blindness; walking there, the speaker discovers his poetic ancestors, the
"enchanted" bards of Ireland's heroic age.

Yet this lush evocation of past insight confesses failure as it claims
victory. Coole may be Edenic, but he comes there fallen from visionary
innocence: "I had not eyes like those enchanted eyes." Thrall to
illusion—except when, so briefly, knowledge beyond his power is
granted—he now discovers no more than tantalizing concealment:
"hazel and ash and privet blind the paths" (1. 8). He foists his

---

[3] Cf. George Mills Harper, "Yeats's Quest for Eden," in *The Dolmen Press Yeats
Centenary Papers*, ed. Liam Miller (Dublin: Dolmen Press, 1968), p. 308. Harper
assumes that the question is merely rhetorical.

frustrations upon the audience by assuming the enticing mask of a magus:

> And more I may not write of, for they that cleave
> The waters of sleep can make a chattering tongue
> Heavy like stone, their wisdom being half silence.
> [11. 24–26]

But the pose trips him up. At the poem's dramatic center, he admits his blank ignorance: "How shall I name you, immortal, mild, proud shadows?" (1. 27). The Miltonic echoes,[4] defining the Seven Woods as an epic realm, brilliantly emphasize the paradox of fallen Adam in the Garden, unable to name the "high invisible ones" (1. 44), agonized by having created *The Shadowy Waters* without knowing the source of his creativity. His question, phrased not to pay homage but to escape a self-demeaning ignorance, transforms the normative function of invocation: personal quest undertaken *after* creation supplants the conventionally *prior* request for inspiration. The heterodox invocation signals the poem's Wordsworthian time-scheme: the speaker seeks, now, to recapture in the same place the initial trance which generated his play. The epic catalogue of the Seven Woods (11. 1–16), no picturesque indulgence, constitutes sympathetic magic: by evoking the sacred woods he will evoke the "shadows" who once aided him.

As in "The Tower" (II), the delicate meditation on place develops a highly dramatic relation between land, self, and myth; without it, the intense questions concerning Coole's Edenic nature cannot be asked. In stressing that drama, Yeats broke sharply from his earlier methods. The ballad form, for all its naming of place, forestalls the elaboration of landscape on which subjective response depends: "The Hosting of the Sidhe" (1893) didactically assumes the connection between land and myth; "The Stolen Child" (1886), spoken by the Sidhe, blocks personal involvement in the mythologized geography. Except for "The Lake Isle of Innisfree," none of the earlier poems has a speaker whose private experience of place is the principle of poetic unity, nor does the grounding of myth in the soil proceed organically from the speaker's emotion. In "In the Seven Woods," however, Yeats appropriated Coole with even greater dramatic force than in "The Shadowy Waters," exchanging mystery for concreteness:

> I have heard the pigeons of the Seven Woods
> Make their faint thunder, and the garden bees

---

[4] *Paradise Lost*, I.6–12; III.1–8; VII.1–2.

Hum in the lime-tree flowers; and put away
The unavailing outcries and the old bitterness
That empty the heart. I have forgot awhile
Tara uprooted, and new commonness
Upon the throne and crying about the streets
And hanging its paper flowers from post to post,
Because it is alone of all things happy.
I am contented, for I know that Quiet
Wanders laughing and eating her wild heart
Among pigeons and bees, while that Great Archer,
Who but awaits His hour to shoot, still hangs
A cloudy quiver over Pairc-na-lee.

As the half-remembered landscape of "The Shadowy Waters" assumes present existence, the language of soliloquy reflects a known world from which the speaker can select details at will. "Faint thunder" sounds familiar. The pigeons are *"of* the Seven Woods"—the partitive presupposes his long acquaintance with Coole's traditional bonds between animal and vegetable kingdoms. He recognizes—again—the expected appearance of Quiet and the Great Archer. The place, consequently, offers a different type of refuge. The speaker returns from the "streets" anticipating a particular solace: the regathering of heroic energy. The spatial dichotomy, foreshadowing the epilogue to *Responsibilities,* corresponds to fierce political and intellectual opposites. "In the Seven Woods," introducing a volume originally subtitled "Being Poems chiefly of the Irish Heroic Age,"[5] remakes Coole into the symbolic seat of ancient royalty, a mythical realm where knowledge of "Tara uprooted" seems a fictional disaster: heroic Irish civilization still flourishes in the West. Outside Coole lies an artificial world as "charter'd" as Blake's London where "New commonness," the coronation of Edward VII, reinforces the old Irish bitterness: the interminable hatred of English power which drains the heart of vitality to resist.

As in "The Shadowy Waters," Yeats showed uncanny tact in mythologizing an actual landscape without offending credibility. Knocknarea, near Sligo, was the hallowed burial place of Queen Maeve, but no such customary belief supported his linking of Coole with Tara. Yeats the realist also knew that myths of political victory based on heroic periods in Ireland's dismal history, although grist for propaganda, required ironic qualification in poetry. Thus, instead of dogmatically yoking Coole and Tara, he made the mythic relation depend upon organic imagery and psychological drama. He naturalized Tara

---

5 Yeats, *The Variorum Edition of the Poems of W. B. Yeats,* eds. Peter Allt and Russell K. Alspach (New York: Macmillan, 1966), p. 198.

into a tree "uprooted," surrounded his speaker with Coole's ancient trees (which again induce amnesia of temporality), and posited the illogical but poetically persuasive conclusion: if Coole's woods remain permanently rooted, so must Tara's. Paralleling "I have heard" (1. 1) with "I have forgot" (1. 5), he indicated the psychology: natural sounds displace both the speaker's cacophonous turmoil and the re-membered noise of base royalty proclaimed. Tara's permanence, trans-planted to Coole, thus results from an intense perception of landscape. Yeats substantiated that mythic bond through daring maneuver: he took hold of the skepticism his analogy would generate and, deflecting criticism, created a speaker too tormented to accept the myth he most desires to believe. The speaker's vehement assertion of Tara's survival (11. 5–9) hardly suggests that he has forgotten Tara's destruction, Irish servitude, the sleazy present. How can you enumerate what you have forgotten? Current history wars on myth; the struggle, proving the myth numinous, confirms it. Yeats made his myth, in short, through antimythological means.

The struggle breeds new faith. Wittily misnamed, Quiet personifies the psychic wholeness the speaker craves. Heroic rather than maso-chistic, she feeds on her own passionate autonomy; as Coole's *genius loci,* she represents not a Lethean escape but a self-delighting joy sprung from conflict. This ideal of personal renovation, typically female for Yeats, complements a male symbol of Ireland's imminent cultural recrudescence, the Great Archer. As Apollo, he signifies poetic rebirth; as a warrior, political independence.[6] His poised calm above the Seven Woods, reproving the speaker's self-destructive anxiety, designates Coole the center of that rejuvenation. The authority of his silence hushes into expectancy a poem filled with sound: the coming rain will strengthen ancestral roots. Unlike the equally ennobling comparison of Coole with Tara, these personifications are free from Irish history and geography: the speaker can thus name them with casual confidence. Although derived from European mythology, they appear spawned from the speaker's own brain, yet superimposed upon the landscape in such a way that they seem traditionally associated with the spot. This is not simply Yeats remaking Coole in the manner of "The Shadowy Waters": the speaker himself actively creates new myths and becomes conscious of inhabiting the self-reflecting world he has made. Whereas

[6] Richard Ellmann, *The Identity of Yeats* (1954; rpt. London: Faber, 1964), p. 103, associates the Great Archer with Jupiter Pluvius. For the poetic connotations of archery, see "The Arrow," immediately following "In the Seven Woods"; for the political ramifications of the image, see Yeats's memories of the apocalyptic storm which occurred during Parnell's funeral ("Commentary on A Parnellite at Parnell's Funeral," section IV, *Variorum Poems,* p. 834).

the images of Eden and Tara have a received content which circum-
scribes the speaker's response, the periphrasis of the Great Archer
mythologizes the territory as the newly created objectification of a
subjective mental state. Upon the sky the speaker projects his desires
for heroic power, serenity, Irish liberty. In the assured intonations of
"*that* Great Archer" you find the characteristic gestures of Yeats's later
poetry: the Adamic naming of a world, the self-dramatizing creation of
its population, the allusions to mythological or historical figures which
alter the environment so unexpectedly that you must think them the
common properties of the speaker's mind and universe.

II

Although "The Shadowy Waters" manipulates received traditions and
"In the Seven Woods" creates mythological self-projections, both an-
nexations of Coole rely upon private drama, "original relation," to
marry their speakers to the West of Ireland. Paradoxically, Yeats
consciously modeled that personal subjectivity on ancient modes of
pantheistic perception, in effect imitated the mythopoeic sensibility he
found maintained among the peasantry near Coole. "The Celtic Element in Literature" (1902) reveals the theoretical context from which
his use of the Great Archer springs:

> Once every people in the world believed that trees were divine,
> and could take a human or grotesque shape and dance among the
> shadows . . . . They saw in the rainbow the still bent bow of a god
> thrown down in his negligence; they heard in the thunder the sound
> of his beaten water-jar, or the tumult of his chariot wheels.[7]

Echoing Ruskin's attack against nineteenth-century mechanism ("We
have no belief that the clouds contain more than so many inches of rain
or hail"), Yeats sought to establish for himself at Coole the bond
between land and myth which the modern "profanity of temper"[8] had
willfully perverted. The mythopoeic imagination, evading the morbid
solipsism of pathetic fallacy,[9] had "once" vouchsafed a cultural awareness of harmonious universal order; the seminal essay on Spenser

---

[7] W. B. Yeats, *Essays and Introductions* (New York: Macmillan, 1961), p. 174.

[8] John Ruskin, *Modern Painters* (New York: Wiley, 1866), III: 257.

[9] See W. B. Yeats, *Uncollected Prose by W. B. Yeats*, ed. John Frayne (New York:
Columbia University Press, 1970), p. 103.

(1902) denounces the historical transition from pastoral community to urban impersonality: "Religion had denied the sacredness of an earth that commerce was about to corrupt and ravish, but when Spenser lived the earth had still its sheltering sacredness."[10] That "sacredness" is a large concept; Yeats explained it shortly after refurbishing Thoor Bally-lee as he commented on the philosopher Soloviev's doctrine that "no family has the full condition of perfection that cannot share in what he calls 'the spiritualisation of the soil' ": "I understand by 'soil' all the matter in which the soul works, the walls of our houses, the serving-up of our meals, and the chairs and tables of our rooms, and the instincts of our bodies."[11] Organic, alchemical, aesthetic, the metaphor of creation underscores the rejuvenation granted by proximity to earth. The stress on total environment, equating "soil" with the social and material artifacts of human organization, invokes the mythic sensibility which animates all "things."

Because Yeats thought peasant culture had perfected that sensi-bility, he made its values the basis of his ideal agrarian society; his meditations on the peasantry, peaking during these years, were of central importance to his exploration of the territory. The peasant, Yeats believed, inhabited a realm which his imagination perpetually and spontaneously consecrated. Revitalized by folklore, ancient myth flour-ished, producing sensuous fictions which brought the unknown into mediate relation with civilization. Dance, song, magic, the acceptance of fairies, and extrasensory perception—all reached easily into the unconscious world of the *anima mundi*, constantly renewed an earthly community in which, as Ribh says, "Natural and supernatural with the self-same ring are wed."[12] Like the Arthurian legend Yeats found among peasants speaking of Inchy Wood at Coole,[13] myth transformed landscape into a mnemonic device, a vast natural storehouse of Irish imaginative history. The peasant, though he may have been Lady Gregory's tenant, defined his world less by the estate's external bound-aries than by the mythological associations of the geography: he per-ceived location in the emotional, moral, and psychological terms given by a particular legend. This is the mythopoeic attitude Yeats imitated: Quiet and the Great Archer define Coole's spaces. He had praised Ferguson for restoring "to our hills and rivers their epic interest" and

10 *Essays*, p. 365.

11 W. B. Yeats, *Explorations* (New York: Macmillan, 1962), p. 273.

12 "Supernatural Songs," II ("Ribh Denounces Patrick").

13 W. B. Yeats, *Mythologies* (New York: Macmillan, 1959), p. 65.

had written enthusiastically to Katherine Tynan that "All peasants at the foot of the mountain [Ben Bulben] know the legend, and know that Dermot still haunts the pool, and fear it."[14] *The Celtic Twilight* (1893; additions concerning Coole, 1900 and 1902), whatever its skittish vacillations between intimate involvement and cosmopolitan reportage, was nothing less than Yeats's map of folklore and mythology in the West of Ireland, a delineation of the links between place and spirit.

Yeats's peasantry spoke their archaic myths in an Edenic tongue akin to the natural poetry Shelley believed "connate with the origin of man."[15] At Coole, and on the Galway Plains, he found "an old vivid speech with a partly Tudor vocabulary, a syntax partly moulded by men who still thought in Gaelic"; it retained the innocent playful delight "in rhythmical animation, in idiom, in images, in words full of far-off suggestion"[16] that had elsewhere faded into blankness. Like a mythologized landscape, its accumulated metaphoric resources were a memory of the nation's psychic history. Yet that language survived only in the West of Ireland; as much as the distinctively rough terrain, it shaped the area in Yeats's mind as the center of Irish culture. Galway itself already heard the dissonances of the London music-hall.[17] "One must not forget," Yeats criticized the disastrous effect of urbanized speech on aesthetic decay, "that the death of language, the substitution of phrases as nearly impersonal as algebra for words and rhythms varying from man to man, is but a part of the tyranny of impersonal things."[18] The poetry produced by peasant English reinforced Yeats's belief that the West of Ireland was the last heroic enclave of "ancient Ireland." The conviction, adumbrated in the first poems about Coole, dominates *The King's Threshold* (1903), whose hero, Seanchan, dying to "proclaim the right of the poets" to legislate cultural values, is master of a bardic college such as Yeats had studied around 1889–1900.[19] Setting the play in ancient Gort, near Coole, Yeats transformed the town he saw daily, and thus possessed it; manipulating his tortured passion for Maud into epic proportions, he became a public

---

14 *Uncollected Prose*, p. 90; *Letters*, p. 51. See also *Explorations*, p. 13.

15 Percy Bysshe Shelley, *A Defence of Poetry*, ed. H. F. B. Brett-Smith, The Percy Reprints, No. 3 (Oxford: Blackwell, 1953), p. 23.

16 *Essays*, pp. 513, 11.

17 *Explorations*, p. 203.

18 *Essays*, p. 301.

19 W. B. Yeats, *Collected Plays*, 2nd ed. (New York: Macmillan, 1953), p. 93. See *Letters*, p. 105; *Uncollected Prose*, p. 162.

visionary, possessing the direct knowledge of Ireland's heroic age that had eluded the speaker of "The Shadowy Waters." Nineteenth-century peasant balladists, preserving the exuberant instincts of their bardic forbears, had created a poetry "racy of the soil," yet marked by that "mysterious infinite of passion which is in so much of Gaelic poetry";[20] Wordsworth's leech-gatherer, also a type of the natural poet, never had the wildness Yeats attributed to his Irish peasantry. Through Raftery, who had loved and cursed near Ballylee, Yeats achieved his closest identification with the oral epic tradition. Singing for peasantry and nobility alike, Raftery became his Homer; and Mary Hynes, Helen—Yeats's Maud. Equating Irish poets and their myths with those of ancient Greece—as in "The Rose of the World"[21] —was a staple of nationalist propaganda in the nineties, but Yeats made the collocation a semi-private myth through which to explore the heroic legacy of his territory. The transposition of Greece to the West of Ireland meant, ultimately, that he could play out the genesis and death of Western civilization—not simply contemporary Irish culture—around Coole and Thoor Ballylee.

Yeats's conception of an Edenic peasant community was obviously a serviceable idealization, a displaced fulfillment of personal and political desires. His source was Morris, whose agrarianism and devoted medievalism were part of a systematic social vision. The perfect medieval world Morris portrayed in *News from Nowhere* had a romantic simplicity which allured a complex Yeats; it proposed, too, a more practical therapy than the fantastic, primordial Castle of the Heroes Yeats had planned with Maud. Ruskin's incisive complaint—"It is not . . . the labor that is divided; but the men"—had fed Yeats's hatred of industrialization; to Yeats, Morris's society exhibited "proper living ritual."[22] The patterns of life and work conformed with seasonal rhythms; infused like Morris's own wallpapers with a "passionate love of the earth," people gained joy and completeness from understanding "the life of earth and its dealings with men."[23] Art belonged to life: all objects in the daily environment were both functional and aesthetically

20 *Uncollected Prose*, pp. 218, 412.

21 See also *Essays*, p. 205: "The Greeks looked within their borders, and we, like them, have a history fuller than any modern history of imaginative events; and legends which surpass, as I think, all legends but theirs in wild beauty, and in our land, as in theirs, there is no river or mountain that is not associated in the memory with some event or legend."

22 John Ruskin, *The Stones of Venice* (New York: Wiley, 1865), II: 182; *Letters*, p. 278.

23 William Morris, *News from Nowhere*, in *Selected Writings of William Morris*, ed. G. D. H. Cole (New York: Random House, 1934), p. 194.

pleasing. The culture of personal relationships excluded the treacherous, tasteless middle classes Yeats despised—indeed, all modern notions
of "class" and a dehumanizing economics. Yeats absorbed Morris's
program and construed the peasantry in his terms. But he had different
political motives. Yeats, although his assiduous interest in the peasantry
alienated him from pragmatic nationalists, predicated his medievalism
on nationalist assumptions. Reviving medieval values in an ethnically
homogeneous country was not the same as exalting indigenous Irish
culture in the face of stubborn Anglo-Irish opposition or apathy: [24]
with Lady Gregory and Douglas Hyde, Yeats sought to reinstate the
true Irish identity so that, when English power was finally broken, the
Irish consciousness would not suffer a chaotic vacuum. Thus, tapping
the vocabulary of messianic nationalism, he admonished his drab,
hostile urban audiences to emulate the peasant's feel for consecrated
land:

> We Irish should keep these personages [i.e., Cuchulain, Emer,
> Deirdre, Fergus—the heroic figures in the epic cycles] much in our
> hearts, for they lived in the places where we ride and go marketing,
> and sometimes they have met one another on the hills that cast
> their shadows upon our doors at evening. If we will but tell these
> stories to our children the Land will begin again to be a Holy
> Land. [25]

Yet although he himself could journey backward in time from Dublin
to Coole, he doubted whether the invigorating bond between city and
country ideally symbolized in *News from Nowhere* by passage up the
Thames could be reconstituted in an urban world which had forfeited,
as if deliberately, its sense of historical origins.

Yeats's concern with peasant society, moreover, was abstract: he
focussed almost exclusively on the peasant's imagination. Despite his
commitment to Morris, he did not share his mentor's socialism. Unlike
Synge and Lady Gregory, he made no friends among the peasantry,
though he had informants. For all the vaunting of fieldwork in *The
Celtic Twilight*, Yeats spoke no Irish and found the peasantry close-
lipped; his knowledge of their customs often came from libraries, from
conversations with Lady Gregory, Douglas Hyde, Standish O'Grady. By
contrast, Lady Gregory managed an estate, saw the peasantry daily, and

---

[24] See Peter Faulkner, *William Morris and W. B. Yeats* (Dublin: Dolmen Press,
1962), p. 11; cf. Graham Hough, *The Last Romantics* (London: Duckworth, 1947),
p. 216.

[25] *Explorations*, p. 12.

preferred them to the local aristocracy, whose indifference to Irish culture she held in contempt.[26] And Synge on the Aran Islands found more than "a race / Passionate and simple like his heart."[27] Lacking Yeats's penchant for dogmatizing on the unity of all myth, he was free to experience "wonder" on hearing "this illiterate native of a wet rock in the Atlantic telling a story that is so full of European associations." He noticed different modes of keening, the absence of "feeling for the sufferings of animals";[28] he saw water shortages, rheumatism, evictions. In his reports on Connemara, he quashed his impulse to romanticize the peasantry: "One's first feeling . . . is a dread of any reform that would tend to lessen their individuality rather than any very real hope of improving their well-being. One feels then, perhaps a little later, that it is part of the misfortune of Ireland that nearly all the characteristics which give colour and attractiveness to Irish life are bound up with a social condition that is near to penury."[29] Yeats glorified precisely that penury: "the countrymen have made beautiful stories and beliefs, because they have nothing to lose and so do not fear."[30] Heroic "beggary," inducing the same detachment as abundant possession, generates the brilliant imaginative power of Hanrahan (*Stories of Red Hanrahan;* "The Tower," II.vi–vii), Lear on the heath, or Crazy Jane in old age. So quick to examine his own compensatory strategies, Yeats rarely questioned the social psychology which had produced such fecundity, though he once observed, with Synge's compassion, that "We too, if we were so weak and poor that everything threatened us with misfortune, might remember every old dream that has been strong enough to fling the weight of the world from its shoulders."[31] But unlike Synge, Maud, and AE, Yeats had nothing to do with land reform. When in 1911 he eulogized Lady Gregory's nephew John Shawe-Taylor for organizing the Land Conference of 1902, he praised

---

26 Elizabeth Coxhead, *Lady Gregory: A Literary Portrait*, 2nd ed. (London: Secker & Warburg, 1966), pp. 72–73: "She was careless of her position in Galway county society, and her carelessness gave offence . . . .. It is remembered that the door of Coole was always open to Kiltartan villagers and Gort townsfolk, but that county ladies, arriving in their carriages to pay a social call, would as likely as not be told that her Ladyship was not at home."

27 "In Memory of Major Robert Gregory," IV.

28 John Millington Synge, *The Aran Islands*, in *Collected Works: Prose*, ed. Alan Price (London: Oxford University Press, 1966), II: 65, 163.

29 Synge, *In Wicklow, West Kerry and Connemara*, in *Collected Works*, II: 286.

30 *Essays*, p. 251; see Louis MacNeice, *The Poetry of W. B. Yeats* (1941; rpt. London: Faber, 1967), p. 96.

31 *Mythologies*, p. 125.

his disinterested aristocratic courage, not the practical benefits of the conference.[32] For a man instinctively preserving the clarity of an ideal type, it sufficed that the Irish peasant imagination had richly fused sorrow and joy, pagan and Christian elements in the resolution of antinomies for which he battled interminably.

Even Yeats's attitude toward peasant speech remained symbolic rather than practical. While Lady Gregory transformed the local dialect into a workable literary language—"Kiltartan"—and used it in her plays and influential translations from Irish epic, Yeats employed it only occasionally, and then with her help. Although he respected its verisimilitude, he never felt Synge's elation in discovering "the dialect he had been trying to master."[33] If Lady Gregory, a Protestant aristocrat consciously writing *of* and *for* Catholic audiences,[34] used "Kiltartan" to achieve an important private reconciliation with the peasantry she loved and, thus, to alleviate the historical guilt which haunted enlightened members of her class, Yeats did not consider language part of a personal political dilemma. Despite his anxiety to be thought an Irish writer, or perhaps because of it, the regionalism of "Kiltartan" cramped him, and he was too resolute to submit to a language he had not crafted to project his own internal drama. Yet in "Upon a House . . ." he praised "Kiltartan" highly. An Irish English, it was the long-awaited answer to the revival of Gaelic which Hyde had demanded in order to de-Anglicize Ireland.[35] Defending "Kiltartan" against its detractors, Yeats implicitly asserted his privilege not to write in Gaelic.

Yeats's unswerving attention to the peasant imagination measures an intensity which his nationalism cannot fully explain. Long before he discarded his pre-Raphaelite style (around 1900), he conceived the peasant imagination as a model for his own development. He sought solid images of permanence, a structure of belief having traditional validity; his esoteric studies were but a lonely, underground attempt to assimilate circuitously "a phantasy that has been handed down for generations, and is now an interpretation, now an enlargement of the folk-lore of the villages."[36] He rejoiced to find a community which still possessed an instinctive comprehension of symbolic language yet whose

---

[32] *Essays*, pp. 343–45.

[33] Lady Gregory, *Our Irish Theatre* (New York: Capricorn, 1965), p. 124.

[34] See Lady Gregory, *Cuchulain of Muirthemne* (London: Murray, 1902), p. v.

[35] Yeats's response to Hyde's signal essay "The De-Anglicizing of Ireland" is printed in *Uncollected Prose*, pp. 254–56. Yeats later chastised Hyde for betraying "Kiltartan" ("Coole Park," II).

[36] W. B. Yeats, *A Vision* [A] (London: Laurie, 1925), p. xi.

earthiness forestalled limpid dreaminess. Timid, condemned to tortuous composition, he envied the peasant's capacious spontaneity. He had been almost engulfed by the introspective melancholy of the Rhymers' Club; his ethereal emotions in *The Wind Among the Reeds* (1899) disturbed him. When he revised his language, seeking a masculine self-dramatizing style which would appear effortless, he made a Connemara peasant symbolize his ideal:

> 'Before I am old
> I shall have written him one
> Poem maybe as cold
> And passionate as the dawn.'
>   ["The Fisherman"]

The peasant community was Yeats's first model of the perfect aristocratic audience he would find for *At the Hawk's Well* (1916). In "The Theatre" (1899), a plea under Blake's aegis for poetic drama, he excoriated the tasteless, ignorant complacency of urban audiences and then asserted: "We must make a theatre for ourselves and our friends, and for a few simple people who understand from sheer simplicity what we understand from scholarship and thought.[37] The "few simple people" were the peasantry; the value of their understanding, like that of cultures steeped in written tradition, Yeats defined in "Certain Noble Plays of Japan" (1916):

> A poetical passage cannot be understood without a rich memory, and like the older school of painting appeals to a tradition, and that not merely when it speaks of 'Lethe wharf' or 'Dido on the wild sea banks' but in rhythm, in vocabulary; for the ear must notice slight variations upon old cadences and customary words, all that high breeding of poetical style where there is nothing ostentatious, nothing crude, no breath of parvenu or journalist.[38]

The peasantry, because they revered their ancient traditions, were an audience whose attunement to his labors the poet could assume. The reciprocal relation increased his freedom of form, allusion, texture; he need not be alienated; he could write for an audience whose sensibility symbolized that larger cultural unity Yeats found so desperately lacking in contemporary Irish life. Firmly committed to Platonic recollection, Yeats surely exaggerated the degree to which the peasant memory

[37] *Essays*, p. 166.
[38] Ibid., pp. 227–28.

retained its heritage intact,[39] but the exaggeration underscores his desire for a world which integrated past and present in an eternal moment, a world whose "high invisible ones," if they could not be named, were constantly felt.

III

Sing the peasantry, and then
Hard-riding country gentlemen.

When Yeats's aristocrat first emerged into prominence (1900–07), he was the peasant's spiritual debtor; the sequence in "Under Ben Bulben" makes the subordination—ignored by critics—plain.[40] In "What is 'Popular Poetry'?" (1901) Yeats outlined the structure of his ideal medieval society prior to its catastrophic historical demise:

> Indeed, it is certain that before the counting-house had created a new class and a new art without breeding and without ancestry, and set this art and this class between the hut and the castle, and between the hut and the cloister, the art of the people was as closely mingled with the art of the coteries as was the speech of the people . . . with the unchanging speech of the poets.[41]

---

[39] See Lady Gregory's dedication to *Cuchulain of Muirthemne*, p. v; and Synge, *The Aran Islands*, in *Collected Works*, II: 171: "Both in English and in Irish the songs are full of words the people do not understand themselves, and when they come to say the words slowly their memory is usually uncertain." Alex Zwerdling, *Yeats and the Heroic Ideal* (New York: New York University Press, 1965), p. 46, has made a similar observation.

[40] Daniel Hoffman, *Barbarous Knowledge: Myth in the Poetry of Yeats, Graves, and Muir* (London: Oxford University Press, 1967), is the only writer to have taken seriously the role of the peasant in Yeats's social theory; I am grateful for his corroboration of my thinking. John R. Harrison, *The Reactionaries: A Study of the Anti-Democratic Intelligentsia* (New York: Schocken, 1967), and Torchiana both disregard the peasant and thus distort the evolution as well as the content of Yeats's celebrations of the aristocracy. Harrison's polemic against Yeats's politics seems hardly more rationally conceived than Maud Gonne's charge: "Yeats's aloofness and his intolerance of mediocrity, a spiritual pride which is dangerous, tended to keep him apart from the first person of the National Trinity, the People" ("Yeats and Ireland," in *Scattering Branches*, ed. Stephen Gwynn [London: Macmillan, 1940], p. 27). That the peasantry can be lumped together with the middle classes and then, all combined, dubbed "People" is a dubious practice. Yeats's words "folk" and "peasantry" are plain; the words "people" and "common people" may refer, as context dictates, either to the peasantry or the middle classes.

[41] *Essays*, pp. 10–11.

In this landscape symbolic of shared sensibility, unity of culture, the hut is the pivotal dwelling. Reconciling castle and cloister, it fuses secular and sacred into organic wholeness: the peasantry are the foundation of civilization. Yeats's claim meshes history and romanticism. As he asserted in reviewing Lady Gregory's *Poets and Dreamers* (1903), the peasantry were Ireland's lost nobility, the remnant of their Celtic and Anglo-Norman ancestors whom repeated English oppression had impoverished or destroyed.[42] By virtue of their mythopoeic imagination, moreover, they constituted a natural aristocracy. The concept was fundamental to Anglo-Irish literary activists seeking to exalt a people their forbears had downtrodden. The Aran Islanders, Synge observed, "seem in a certain sense to approach more nearly to the finer types of our aristocracies—who are bred artificially to a natural ideal—than to the labourer or citizen, as the wild horse resembles the thoroughbred rather than the hack or cart-horse."[43] And Yeats, after listening to peasant songs on the road to Kiltartan, pronounced folk-art "the oldest of the aristocracies of thought ... it is the soil where all great art is rooted."[44] The oral tradition, he wrote in 1901, "binds the unlettered, so long as they are masters of themselves, to the beginning of time and to the foundation of the world"; "the written tradition ... has been established upon the unwritten."[45] As with literature, so also with personal decorum: courtesy, that most distinguished virtue in Yeats's hierarchy of aristocratic attributes, originates in peasant society. In the same year as his first poem on courtesy, "Adam's Curse" (1902), he praised Lady Gregory's *Cuchulain of Muirthemne* for revealing "the courtly manners of the Irish country people."[46] Yeats's preoccupation with the debts of sophisticated, literate art and culture to the peasantry continued into his last years, as "The Municipal Gallery Revisited" shows. "Dream of the noble and the beggar-man" (VI), an unexpected pairing delivered as a commonplace, emphasizes the communal source of the aristocratic imagination; the brilliant conjunction of apparently disparate modes of speech in "(An image out of Spenser and the common tongue)" forces a sudden recession into immeasurable reaches of time, when nothing else can be normative except what Yeats called

---

42 W. B. Yeats, "A Canonical Book," *The Bookman* 24 (May 1903): 68.

43 Synge, *The Aran Islands*, in *Collected Works*, II: 66. The passage struck Yeats with peculiar force; see *Explorations*, p. 10, and "The Fascination of What's Difficult."

44 *Mythologies*, p. 139.

45 *Essays*, p. 6.

46 *Explorations*, p. 7.

"equality of culture."[47] "Coole Park and Ballylee" (VI) enunciates the same doctrines.

Yeats's ideal aristocrat recognized these debts. Anglo-Irish in blood, perhaps, but Irish in spirit (an image of Yeats himself), he rigorously assimilated peasant culture; the eighteenth-century aristocracy had degenerated because it had ignored the vigorous presence of a Celtic peasant "tribunal more ancient and august than itself."[48] In "The Galway Plains" (1903), Yeats admitted, uneasily, the possibility of a healthy Anglo-Irish aristocracy but damned the sterility of aristocratic indifference to its roots:

> The poet must always prefer the community where the perfected minds express the people, to a community that is vainly seeking to copy the perfected minds. To have even perfectly the thoughts that can be weighed, the knowledge that can be got from books, the precision that can be learned at school, to belong to any aristocracy, is to be a little pool that will soon dry up. A people alone are a great river.[49]

Yeats's countess Cathleen (1892), prepared to sacrifice her soul to save her peasantry from famine, anticipates his ideal image: "Lady Gregory, in her life much artifice, in her nature much pride, was born to see the glory of the world in a peasant mirror."[50] Understanding the debts of the "castle" to the "hut," she attributed her translations from epic and her "Kiltartan" style to the native Irish genius[51] and sought to "express" the culture that had shaped her mind. That the peasantry paid rents, in addition to having given the aristocracy their gift of imaginative innocence, did not concern Yeats; Lady Gregory herself, rather than raise rents, preferred to court financial disaster.[52] What Yeats

---

[47] The image—"No fox can foul the lair the badger swept" (V)—is taken from Spenser's poem on the deaths of Sidney and the Earl of Leicester, "The Ruines of Time" (11. 216–17); Yeats had earlier used the image to intimate the violent rise of the middle classes after Parnell's death and their corrupting infiltration of the nationalist movement (*Essays*, p. 260); *Explorations*, p. 203.

[48] Yeats, "A Canonical Book," p. 68.

[49] *Essays*, p. 214.

[50] *Autobiography*, p. 390.

[51] Lady Gregory, MS to *Coole*, Book II (Berg Collection, New York Public Library); see also Lady Gregory, *Visions and Beliefs in the West of Ireland* (London: Putnam, 1920), I: 3. Lady Gregory drew her support for "Kiltartan" from Ascham, who approved Aristotle's stipulation that good writing consists in fusing wise thought with the language of the common people (Unpublished Journals, Book XXIII, May 6, 1923).

[52] Lady Gregory, Unpublished Journals, Book XVIII, May 8, 1922. Coole was not

envisaged at Coole was a spiritual exchange: the reciprocal respect between aristocrat and peasant, deriving from mutual "contact with the soil," which was integral to his feudal vision.

The true recompense for the peasantry's legacy was the aristocrat's own passionate quest to recover, through self-conscious artifice, "radical innocence"—the Edenic condition of joyous simplicity which the peasantry possessed by nature. Yeats assumed the peasantry's pride in observing their culture reconstituted in its quintessential beauty:

> Certainly no simple age has denied to monk or nun their leisure, nor thought that the monk's lamp and the nun's prayer, though from the first came truth and from the second denial of self, were not recompense enough, nor has any accomplished age begrudged the expensive leisure of women, knowing that they gave back more than they received in giving courtesy.[53]

The achievement of that courtesy, the outward sign of "perfected" interior harmony and the generous virtue which bonds a community in human dignity, was Yeats's ultimate requirement of the aristocratic nature. In *The Tragic Generation* (1922), he would write of Henley's failure to understand "how small a fragment of our own nature can be brought to perfect expression, nor that even but with great toil, in a much divided civilisation."[54] But a demand less challenging could not have justified, ethically, a society based on unequal rights, unequal advantage. Yeats defined his attitude in metaphor: "Leisure, wealth, privilege were created to be a soil for the most living."[55] Soil is necessary for organic growth, the individual's flowering; should no flowering occur, the soil must be judged barren. To prove the social hierarchy fertile, the aristocrat must continually demonstrate, through the quest for personal radiance, the right to inheritance. Yeats never praised an aristocrat for the centuried possession of an estate, the great deeds committed by illustrious ancestors. These "gifts of chance," as Jonson called them,[56] far from redeeming ignoble behavior, could only publish in mute criticism an heir's betrayal of traditional excellence. The theme of violation—which erupts so ferociously in "Pardon, Old

---

a wealthy estate in Lady Gregory's time, although during the eighteenth century it had brought in annual rentals of over £7000 (Vere R. T. Gregory, *The House of Gregory* [Dublin: Browne & Nolan, 1943], p. 32).

53 *Explorations,* p. 274.

54 *Autobiography,* p. 251.

55 Ibid., p. 438.

56 Jonson, "Epistle. To Katherine, Lady Aubigny," l. 41.

Fathers" (1913) and recurs thereafter—has half its power from Yeats's nagging compulsion to subject himself to the same standards he demanded of the aristocracy.

In positing the aristocrat's indebtedness, Yeats guarded against his own shifting allegiances: as he discovered in Spenser, Jonson, and Castiglione unexcelled images of secular beauty, the concept allowed him to study Renaissance aristocracy without feeling that he was neglecting peasant culture. But by 1907 he had plainly moved from the "hut" to the "castle":

> Three types of men have made all beautiful things. Aristocracies have made beautiful manners, because their place in the world puts them above the fear of life, and the countrymen have made beautiful stories and beliefs, because they have nothing to lose and so do not fear, and the artists have made all the rest, because Providence has filled them with recklessness.[57]

Compare his vision a year earlier:

> The life of the villages, with its songs . . . its conversations full of vivid images shaped hardly more by life itself than by innumerable forgotten poets . . . grows more noble as he meditates upon it, for it mingles with the Middle Ages until he no longer can see it as it is, but as it was when it ran, as it were, into a point of fire in the courtliness of kings' houses.[58]

With its parallelisms, its logical clarity, the later passage rearranges the components of the ideal society from a fused organism to a balanced harmony of discrete units. The aristocrat, no longer the emblematic culmination of peasant culture, now possesses distinct creative attributes which reflect Yeats's long immersion in Renaissance thought. Though he had absorbed Pater and known Wilde, Yeats's preoccupation with the "beautiful manners" of courtesy is the nodal point of large-scale maturations. It involves a drastically sharpened conception of history, a new vision of the Fall and the self's redemption through personal artifice. Through his Renaissance studies, although they lured him from the West of Ireland, Yeats meditated indirectly on the poetic means of rooting a new mythology in Coole's soil. His country house poetry, the literary element in his love for Lady Gregory, and the transformed historical vision which marks "Upon a House . . ." are inseparable from his view of the Renaissance.

[57] *Essays*, p. 251.
[58] *Explorations*, p. 205.

IV

Yeats denied Burckhardt's cleavage between the Middle Ages and the Renaissance. His attitudes were Morris's: the Renaissance was "the fruit of the old, not the seed of the new order of things."[59] Its dominant ikon, symbolizing unity of being, was the "perfectly proportioned human body" Dante praised;[60] Castiglione but elaborated upon it. Alert to paradox elsewhere, Yeats blinked the doubleness of Renaissance life, the complicated intersection of medieval and modern values in its art, statecraft, and social organization. Even in *A Vision* he maintained the kinship of the Renaissance with its immediate past. Its difficulties were death-throes, not a gestation.

For Yeats the modern world—mechanization, mob rule, lack of education—began with inexplicable suddenness in the seventeenth century. The event was a Fall (Ruskin had dated it in the Renaissance itself): the "counting-house" broke the bonds between "hut," "castle," and "cloister." Like Eliot's "dissociation of sensibility," Yeats's pessimistic judgment was a breakthrough: if it doomed him to a degenerate epoch, his panoramic explanation for his own disharmony and contemporary confusions prevented the self-laceration of a solipsistic analysis. The problems he confronted had not always prevailed. The Renaissance, before the classical-Christian synthesis collapsed, was a historical period of individual and cultural perfection when "all but everything present to the mind was present to the senses"[61] —a model more visibly human in scale than Irish mythology, more concretely accessible than the Middle Ages. To recreate that world imaginatively was to slough off his martyr's temptation—so insidious in "Adam's Curse"—to deny the validity of temporal experience.

The true function of Yeats's dichotomy between sixteenth- and seventeenth-century worlds is that the Fall created analogies to his own dilemmas. His elegiac longing for an Edenic world did not blunt his recognition that the Renaissance also craved reinstatement of the Golden Age. Spenser in stating that the Blatant Beast had "got into the world at liberty againe" (*Faerie Queene*, VI.xii.38), Castiglione in opening *The Courtier* with memorials of the dead nobility whose excellence he would praise, Jonson throughout *The Forrest*—all warned of present corruption.[62] Shakespeare, according to Yeats, understood

59 William Morris, "The Beauty of Life," in *Collected Works of William Morris*, ed. May Morris (London: Longmans, 1914), XXII: 56–57.

60 *Autobiography*, pp. 247–48.

61 *Explorations*, p. 166.

62 Cf. William M. Carpenter, "The *Green Helmet* Poems and Yeats's Myth of the

that "The courtly and saintly ideals of the Middle Ages were fading, and the practical ideals of the modern age had begun to threaten the unuseful dome of the sky"; when he created the jarring contrast between Richard II, poet and contemplative, a delicate "vessel of porcelain," and Henry V, discourteous, known by "the gross vices, the coarse nerves, of one who is to rule among violent people,"[63] Shakespeare was really writing about his own time of transition. What impressed Yeats, a year before reading Nietzsche, was Shakespeare's unfluttered calm in depicting impending disaster. As Yeats had assimilated Ireland's heroic age by becoming Seanchan, he now assumed the historical character of men who confronted—and mastered—the epochal disorders he faced. Had they not attained their unity through a struggle which appeared effortless, they could not have so fascinated Yeats.

> Our present civilisation . . . reached its mid-point in the Italian Renaissance; just when that point was passing Castiglione recorded in his *Courtier* what was said in the Court of Urbino somewhere about the first decade of the sixteenth century. These admirable conversationalists knew that the old spontaneous life had gone, and what a man must do to retain unity of being, mother-wit expressed in its perfection.[64]

It was not the incomparable largesse of Renaissance courts in patronizing the arts which principally attracted Yeats, but the brilliant artistry of the self its men had practiced, their heroic will not to succumb.

Spenser, however, failed to overcome the Fall. His failure, together with his Anglo-Irish identity, magnetized Yeats. The essay on Spenser (1902) is intensely self-admonitory; combatting his own shadow, Yeats

---

Renaissance," *Modern Philology* 69 (1969): 54, and Salvadori, *Yeats and Castiglione* (Dublin: Figgis, 1965), p. 34. Both, considering Yeats's Renaissance his Golden Age, overlook Yeats's sense of the Renaissance's discomfort.

[63] *Essays*, pp. 106, 108. T. McAlindon, "Yeats and the English Renaissance," *PMLA* 82 (1967): 159, has interpreted Yeats's reading of Shakespeare similarly; I am generally indebted to his article for confirming my conclusions. Cf. J. Kleinstück, who oversimplifies Yeats's vision: "Yeats saw in Shakespeare a poet and playwright who happily lived before that filthy modern tide had set in" ("Yeats and Shakespeare," in *W. B. Yeats: Centenary Studies on the Art of W. B. Yeats*, eds. D. E. S. Maxwell and S. B. Bushrui [Ibadan: Ibadan University Press, 1965], p. 4).

[64] *Explorations*, p. 431. Yeats formally emphasized the analogies he felt with this aspect of Renaissance thought when, in *A Vision*, he placed himself in Phase Seventeen: "The *Will* is falling asunder, but without explosion and noise. . . . The being has for its supreme aim, as it had at Phase 16 (and as all subsequent *antithetical* phases shall have), to hide from itself and others this separation and disorder" (p. 141).

was constantly proposing alternative imaginative modes which might
have redressed the terrifying imbalance of Spenser's mind. Spenser,
compacting Richard II and Henry V in one self-divided personality, was
unfulfilled, hampered by a problem Yeats found new in English poetry—"the natural expression of personal feeling." Repressing his tem-
peramental affection for the courtly and fantastic, he "tried to be
... of the time that was all but at hand." Spenser showed Yeats the
tragedy, common in "a much divided civilisation," of submitting to a
false ideal: knowingly violating his own muse, he became "the first poet
struck with remorse"[65] —hardly, Yeats knew, the last. His Puritanism
nearly crushed his exuberant sensuality; his politics often warped his
celebrations of beauty into propaganda: both tendencies of the new
epoch reflected Yeats's own fears. Yeats condemned the first as "part
of an inexplicable movement that was trampling out the minds of all
but some few thousands born to cultivated ease."[66] The second produced Spenser's Artegall and "Cromwell's house"—a mock-dynasty of
the democratic mob.[67] When "Bunyan wrote in prison the other great
English allegory, Modern England had been born":[68] the real "prison"
was the post-Renaissance world.

Deep sympathy tempers the potential virulence of Yeats's criticism.
Henn's remark—"Spenser is approved as the first great representative of
the Anglo-Irish tradition"[69] —expresses what Yeats may have wished,
but not what he thought. Spenser in Ireland was Yeats's disturbing
predecessor, an Anglo-Irishman exiled from living tradition. Public
duties shut him off from his Elizabethan context, in which "Italian
influence had strengthened the old French joy that had never died out
among the upper classes."[70] If he had turned to Ireland—as a poet, not
a government agent compelled to hate his adopted country—he would
have recovered the Anglo-French tradition, fused with Celtic vitality.
But Spenser—committed to his public mask, afraid to buck history—refused to find the earth's "sheltering sacredness" around Kilcolman
Castle. To Yeats, making the West of Ireland his private world,
Spenser exemplified the poet's need for a mythology to marry him to

65 *Essays*, pp. 358, 370, 373. See McAlindon, "Yeats and the English Renaissance," p. 160.

66 *Essays*, p. 110.

67 "The Curse of Cromwell."

68 *Essays*, p. 365.

69 Thomas Rice Henn, *The Lonely Tower* (1950; rpt. London: Methuen, 1965), p.
38.

70*Essays*, p. 363.

rock and hill. Although he empathized with Spenser's unconscious urge to escape into Colin Clout's vision of the Graces, he recoiled from disembodied pastoral. Spenser could have escaped by embracing reality; and as Yeats set forth the Ireland Spenser rejected, he mythologized it, thus establishing the basis for "Shepherd and Goatherd":

> All about him were shepherds and shepherdesses still living the life that made Theocritus and Virgil think of shepherd and poet as the one thing; but though he dreamed of Virgil's shepherds he wrote a book to advise, among many like things, the harrying of all that followed flocks upon the hills, and of all the 'wandering companies that keep the wood.'[71]

Only Spenser's sense of courtesy saved him from complete disequilibrium. That Calidore, his ideal of courteous behavior, approved Artegall's ruthlessness must have bewildered Yeats, but he ignored Spenser's violent self-contradiction in order to salvage the humane: "One doubts, indeed, if he could have persuaded himself that there could be any virtue at all without courtesy."[72] Courtesy, the indispensable art which "spreds it selfe through all civilitie" (*Faerie Queene,* VI, Prologue), was Spenser's barrier against internal and cultural chaos, and it became Yeats's. From Castiglione he learned the stringent procedures of courteous self-development. Both corroborated the courteous fusion of aesthetic and social ideals he found in Celtic civilization: ". . . if we understand by courtesy not merely the gentleness the story-tellers have celebrated, but a delight in courtly things, in beautiful clothing and in beautiful verse, we understand that it was no formal succession of trials that bound the Fianna to one another."[73] He applied the Renaissance standard rigorously to himself—lamented the "harshness and roughness" which kept him from having "the manners of a Courtier," blamed himself for having failed to fight courteously, invoked courtesy to moderate fanatic nationalist debates over *The Playboy,* considered courtesy the ground of integrity: "Manhood is all, and the root of manhood is courage and courtesy."[74]

Yeats's courtesy was both the self's freedom from fallen nature and the technique of achieving it: "In life courtesy and self-possession, and

---

[71] *Essays,* p. 373.

[72] Ibid., p. 367.

[73] *Explorations,* p. 21.

[74] *Letters,* p. 827; *Autobiography,* pp. 34–35; *Explorations,* p. 228. See also ibid., p. 111.

in the arts style, are the sensible impressions of the free mind, for both arise out of a deliberate shaping of all things, and from never being swept away, whatever the emotion, into confusion or dullness." [75] Thus, in "Her Courtesy" ("Upon a Dying Lady," 1913), Mabel Beardsley refuses to let mere paltry death disrupt her intellectual pleasures:

> With the old kindness, the old distinguished grace,
> She lies, her lovely piteous head amid dull red hair
> Propped upon pillows, rouge on the pallor of her face.
> She would not have us sad because she is lying there,
> And when she meets our gaze her eyes are laughter-lit,
> Her speech a wicked tale that we may vie with her,
> Matching our broken-hearted wit against her wit,
> Thinking of saints and of Petronius Arbiter.

Playing "master of ceremony,"[76] the role Yeats thought Spenser should never have dropped, she selflessly designs a high verbal ritual to cheer her mourning friends, who are ironically more "piteous" than she for lack of joy. Behind her liberating heroic laughter—the speaker ultimately learns her gaiety—lies the exquisite self-discipline without which Yeats felt civilized discourse could not occur.

That oxymoronic compounding of "laughter" with courtesy (classically grave, as Yeats knew from Castiglione) is a recurrent motif; courtesy, if it was the most inclusive of virtues, was not for Yeats self-sufficient:

> The highest life unites, as in one fire, the greatest passion and the greatest courtesy.[77]

---

[75] *Essays*, p. 253. Cf. Salvadori, *Yeats and Castiglione*, p. 79. Yeats did not think style contained "moral implications" except insofar as it reflected, in the Arnoldian sense, the poet's self or the self he wished to project. Salvadori cites in her support a passage from *The Death of Synge:* "The element which in men of action corresponds to style in literature is the moral element. . . . The self-conquest of the writer who is not a man of action is style" (*Autobiography*, pp. 439–40). But Yeats's stress falls on the act of self-conquest, not on the application of moral principles in verse. Salvadori takes for praise of a moral style what in fact is not: Davis, Yeats wrote, "showed this moral element not merely in his verse—I doubt if that could have had great effect alone—but in his action" (*Autobiography*, p. 440). Davis's verses were "but an illustration of principles shown in action. . . . thought that is a little obvious or platitudinous if merely written, becomes persuasive, immortal even, if held to amid the hurry of events." How soon, Yeats implicitly asked, would Davis's poetry have faded from memory without the support of history?

[76] *Essays*, p. 360.

[77] *Explorations*, p. 162.

> —Pedant in passion, learned in old courtesies,
> Vehement and witty she had seemed—
>
> ["Upon a Dying Lady," III]
>
> ... this house,
> Where passion and precision have been one ...
>
> ["Upon a House ..."]

... Urbino, where youth for certain brief years imposed upon drowsy learning the discipline of its joy ...[78]

Persistently adding passion to Castiglione's courtesy, Yeats showed his suspicion—and reinterpretation—of an art which undervalued the emotions and considered the body, as Bembo says, "the earthly prison." [79] Although "courtesy" and "precision" were Yeats's frequent terms of approbation, he was initially unimpressed by the courtier's life of "continual schedule. The languages he should know, . . . the dances, the musical instruments, the games he should be master over."[80] What if the very discipline of magnificence sapped personal energy, degenerated into mere graceful habit? "Ben Jonson says in *The Poetaster* that even the best of men without Promethean fire is but a hollow statue." [81] Yeats wanted a "manhood" rougher, more heroic than Castiglione seemingly portrayed. His desire for the *"fascination* of what's difficult" indicates a romantic quest which was hardly Castiglione's major emphasis. The unity he sought by yoking passion to courtesy without denying the autonomy of either term was more paradoxical than Castiglione's subordination of elements into a Platonic-Christian hierarchy. Courtesy was the shaping restraint of energy which wrought passion to its uttermost intensity. Form created freedom, the self's transvaluation into a generic "manhood" which was also its greatest individuation.

Yeats's revision does not diminish his debt to Castiglione's conception of the completed self, in which the absolute concordance of thought and action emanates in "that kind of bodily beauty which Castiglione called 'the spoil or monument of the victory of the soul' "[82] —the redemptive incarnation of heavenly beauty in human-

---

78 *Autobiography*, p. 463.

79 Baldesar Castiglione, *The Book of the Courtier*, trans. Sir Thomas Hoby (1561; rpt., with an introduction by Walter Raleigh, London: Nutt, 1900), p. 345.

80 W. B. Yeats, "Discoveries: Second Series," ed. Curtis Bradford, *Massachussetts Review* 5 (1964): 305.

81 *Essays*, p. 278. See *The Poetaster*, V.i.11−16.

82 *A Vision*, pp. 292−93. Yeats misquoted slightly Hoby's translation: "Therefore

kind. Borrowing from Donne's *Second Anniversary* (1. 246), Yeats called that state "the thinking of the body," and later, "unity of being"; finally, it became the "profane perfection of mankind," for it owed nothing to divine intervention and everything to earthly struggle. Yeats's secularity does not violate Castiglione's meaning. Although Ms. Salvadori argues that "The spiritual formation and self-perfection of the courtier must be such that they will lead him to a final ecstasy comparable to that of a St. Paul or a St. Francis,"[83] Castiglione's real allegiances are with the Lady Emilia, who gently interrupts Bembo's rhapsodic contemplation of Venus Urania to reestablish the circle of human love—elegant conversation, mutual sorrow—he has nearly broken. The organic, earthly radiance Yeats found localized at Urbino is the subject of paired essays in *Discoveries* (1907). "The Looking-Glass" describes "a girl with a shrill monotonous voice and an abrupt way of moving," ignorant of beauty, tyrannized by modern mechanism. Against this image of rude, uncrafted nature, "A Guitar Player" poses another:

> Her voice, the movements of her body, the expression of her face, all said the same thing. . . . The little instrument is quite light, and the player can move freely and express a joy that is not of the fingers and the mind only but of the whole being; and all the while her movements call up into the mind, so erect and natural she is, whatever is most beautiful in her daily life.[84]

Like Helen in "Long-legged Fly," she is one of Yeats's Edenic innocents; like the peasantry, she possesses spontaneously the imaginative wholeness lost to the divided modern world except by diligent labor:

> 'To be born woman is to know—
> Although they do not talk of it at school—
> That we must labour to be beautiful.'
> ["Adam's Curse"]

The central art of courtesy, its labor, is *sprezzatura.* The courtier, Castiglione stipulated, should "use in every thyng a certain Reckelesness [*sprezzatura*], to cover art withall, and seeme whatsoever he doth and sayeth to do it wythout pain, and (as it were) not myndyng it"

Beawtie is the true monument and spoile of the victorye of the soule" (Castiglione, *The Courtier*, trans. Hoby, p. 350).

83 Salvadori, *Yeats and Castiglione*, p. 11.

84 *Essays*, pp. 268–69.

(Hoby).[85] Opdyke, translating *sprezzatura* as "nonchalance,"[86] conveys more satisfactorily the unobtrusive classical decorum Yeats admired. "To cover art withall": *sprezzatura* embodies the paradox which obsessed Yeats, the transmutation of fallen nature into an aesthetic perfection which appears natural—"An agony of flame that cannot singe a sleeve."[87] Were the artistry visible, the illusion would be destroyed:

> I said: 'A line will take us hours maybe;
> Yet if it does not seem a moment's thought,
> Our stitching and unstitching has been naught. [']
>   ["Adam's Curse"]

For a man distressed by his bodily awkwardness and public demeanor, subject to voices commanding him—as if he were some lame Hephaestus—to "Hammer your thoughts into unity,"[88] "nonchalance" had obvious attractions. When Yeats praised Gregory's utmost art in making an extraordinarily difficult feat seem natural, he was creating in his perfect aristocrat an image of his own desire:

> and where was it
> He rode a race without a bit?
> And yet his mind outran the horses' feet.
>   ["In Memory of Major Robert Gregory," VIII]

That public impression of unflawed self-possession, power held in reserve, paradoxically requires a modest self-regard—and not simply because a display of pride would betray the artifice to be concealed. Spenser's "bloosme of comely Courtesie" grows on a "lowly stalke" (*Faerie Queene*, VI, Prologue): the person who practices *sprezzatura* humbly understands all accomplishment as but a small progress toward complete perfection.

The essence of "nonchalance" is a delicate detachment, a self-distancing, ego-denying dramatic mask which frees the mind to judge the propriety of phrase or gesture. Yeats's aristocratic bird in "The Three Beggars" (1913), the "old crane" symbolically located in Gort, understands the function of this impersonal discipline:

---

[85] Castiglione, *The Courtier*, trans. Hoby, p. 59.

[86] Castiglione, *The Book of the Courtier*, trans. Leonard Eckstein Opdyke (New York: Scribner's, 1903), p. 35.

[87] "Byzantium," IV.

[88] *Explorations*, p. 263.

['] *It's certain there are trout somewhere*
And maybe I shall take a trout
If but I do not seem to care.'

This is a paradoxical self-trickery. Although the bird remains conscious both of its pretense and its concern, the mask itself, generating a relaxed detachment, will make achieved desire possible. As the violent farce of the bourgeois, self-centered beggars demonstrates, intense anxiety about achievement can only disrupt the quest. Many years later Yeats based a wholesale critique of Western desperation on the philosophy of time reflected in *sprezzatura*: "Our moral indignation, our uniform law, perhaps even our public spirit, may come from the Christian conviction that the soul has but one life to find or lose salvation in: the Asiatic courtesy from the conviction that there are many lives."[89]

The creative self-detachment Yeats found in the Renaissance aristocracy fostered a new epistemology. In section 27 of *Estrangement* (1909), as he compared the Renaissance with the dilapidated world of his youth, he saw that he had been sundered between false models of self-knowledge: the Irishman's "gradual absorption in some propaganda" and Pater's aestheticism, which could "only create feminine souls."[90] Dismissing obvious differences in social milieu and intellectual perspective, he charged them with a common fault: self-diffusion, externalization. "We grow like others through opinions":[91] Yeats's fearful contempt of propaganda was spawned in the nineties, when his nationalist activities made him "impassioned and fanatical about opinions, which one has chosen as one might choose a side upon the football field."[92] Prone to heated but superficial argument, he respected Lady Gregory's deliberate self-isolation "from all contagious opinions of poorer minds."[93] A cutting self-analysis underlies the snarling criticisms in "The Leaders of the Crowd" (1918–19): intolerant self-assertion only conceals an uncertain selfhood; "invention" sullied by self-interest replaces true imagination founded upon fixed principles; attraction to applause denies creative solitude; and the self disintegrates under the pressure of external affairs. Pater, too, had

[89] *Essays*, p. 436.

[90] *Autobiography*, pp. 406–7.

[91] *Explorations*, p. 237.

[92] *Autobiography*, p. 201. Phillip L. Marcus, *Yeats and the Beginning of the Irish Renaissance* (Ithaca: Cornell University Press, 1970), has described Yeats's propagandizing in detail; see especially Chapter III.

[93] *Autobiography*, p. 404.

rendered the self powerless, had made the soul a "mirror" of experience, "not a brazier."[94] Stressing the delectation of sensation, he had embraced flux rather than endure any system of observation which curtailed responsiveness. Thus, instead of tasteless opinions, tasteful discriminations without order; in place of aggression compensating for fear of solitude, an exquisite nurture of sensibility which paralyzed action; and, in "Ego Dominus Tuus," the underbelly of aestheticism:

> *Ille.*   by its light
> We have lit upon the gentle, sensitive mind
> And lost the old nonchalance of the hand;
> Whether we have chosen chisel, pen or brush,
> We are but critics, or but half create,
> Timid, entangled, empty and abashed,
> Lacking the countenance of our friends.

"The severest danger of Pater's aesthetic vision," Mr. Bloom remarks, ". . . is that you need to be a poet of genius and a moral titan fully to sustain it."[95] Quite right; but Yeats's objection, in 1909 and 1915, was that knowing what was "permanent in the world"[96] before knowing the self's eternal archetype inverted priorities. Pater had left no room for Coleridge's "shaping spirit of Imagination"; he had ignored the whole personality.

After detailing his objections to Pater in *Estrangement*, Yeats compared "the culture of the Renaissance, which seems to me founded not on self-knowledge but on knowledge of some other self, Christ or Caesar, not on delicate sincerity but on imitative energy."[97] That "imitative energy" is the "old nonchalance" which permits active creativity: the soul, "shaping" itself from an image beyond itself, becomes a "brazier." As Yeats roughened the Renaissance concept of

---

[94] Ibid., p. 407.

[95] Harold Bloom, *Yeats* (New York: Oxford University Press, 1970), p. 24. Bloom claims further (pp. 24, 30–31) that "Yeats himself came to misrepresent Pater," thinking perhaps of section 27 of *Estrangement* and "Ego Dominus Tuus" but specifically of Yeats's transformation (in *The Oxford Book of Modern Verse*) of Pater's description of the Mona Lisa. Surely Yeats used Pater to his own purposes, and especially when he sought to create dramatic contrast. Edward Engelberg, "He Too Was in Arcadia," in *In Excited Reverie*, eds. A. Norman Jeffares and K. G. W. Cross (New York: Macmillan, 1965), pp. 73–79, discusses only the affinities between Yeats and his Victorian master and neglects Yeats's intellectual quarrel with Pater concerning the ideal nature of the personality.

[96] *Autobiography*, p. 407.

[97] Ibid.

imitation into "imitative energy," it became a quest for the mask, passion given form by *sprezzatura,* the capacity to assume a role resembling the image desired. Renaissance men had "sought at all times the realization of something deliberately chosen, and they played a part always as if upon a stage and before an audience, and gave up their lives rather than their play."[98] To play a role would seem another self-diffusion; but when the role was chosen to fulfill all that a person lacked, playing became a concentrated energy which joined the self to that intuited self in the *anima mundi* whose existence Yeats thought Pater had disregarded:

> I know now that revelation is from the self, but from that age-long memoried self, that shapes the elaborate shell of the mollusc and the child in the womb, that teaches the birds to make their nest; and that genius is a crisis that joins that buried self for certain moments to our trivial daily mind.[99]

Classical *sprezzatura* suddenly verges very close to Romantic inspiration. Although Yeats did not identify nonchalance with joy,[100] he knew that without the capacity for play, the exultant tragic joy of momentary unity could not be felt.

In the Renaissance, knowledge of "some other self" was not so inaccessible. The ideal, a Platonic emblem of the individual's potentialities rather than of his deficiencies, was neither "buried" nor agonizingly "opposite": "Their generation had something present to their minds which they copied."[101] Yeats therefore thought himself back into the Renaissance, a time when, according to *A Vision,* Will and Mask all but coincided. Late in life he examined his urge to use not simply "half a dozen traditional poses"[102] but whole historical periods as masks: "We, even more than Eliot, require tradition and though it may include much that is his, it is not a belief or submission, but exposition of intellectual needs. I recall a passage in some Hermetic writer on the increased power that a God feels on getting into a statue. I feel as neither Eliot or Ezra do the need of old forms, old situations that . . . I may escape from scepticism."[103] Yeats's skepticism, bred

---

98 Yeats, "Discoveries: Second Series," p. 306.

99 *Autobiography,* pp. 233–34.

100 Cf. Salvadori, *Yeats and Castiglione,* p. 76.

101 Yeats, "Discoveries: Second Series," p. 306.

102 *Autobiography,* p. 77.

103 Quoted by Ellmann, *The Identity of Yeats,* p. 240.

out of Mill, exacerbated by Pater and his own self-criticism, involved fundamental questions about the possibility of poetry in a world lacking stabilized values. The Renaissance offered "old situations," definitude in the face of flux. Not only an "exposition of intellectual needs," it was a context for his emotions. He used it as Lady Gregory used Coole, an image of excellence researched and assimilated until it yielded him its gift: the sense of a coherent world, the substance from which to make a language. You cannot gain a *sprezzatura* of style until you have absorbed the culture which created the concept.[104] You cannot imagine that Coole's fall might affect "the *world*" ("Upon a House . . .") unless you know Jonson thoroughly. Yeats took risks which Browning, similarly fascinated by Renaissance exuberance, never dared: the evocation of an historical period as if it were a personal recollection. His achievement in "The People" (1915) is his vision of Castiglione's Italy, seen through the lens of a private understanding:

> I might have lived,
> And you know well how great the longing has been,
> Where every day my footfall should have lit
> In the green shadow of Ferrara wall;
> Or climbed among the images of the past—
> The unperturbed and courtly images—
> Evening and morning, the steep street of Urbino
> To where the Duchess and her people talked
> The stately midnight through until they stood
> In their great window looking at the dawn;
> I might have had no friend that could not mix
> Courtesy and passion into one like those
> That saw the wicks grow yellow in the dawn . . .

The realization is so intimate that the speaker's outrageous claim—"I might have lived"—seems only a hairsbreadth away from being plausible: this is no elegiac longing for an Edenic city never visited but an intense "longing" for a known—and almost available—reality.

V

In his great occasional poem, "To a Wealthy Man Who Promised a Second Subscription to the Dublin Municipal Gallery If It Were Proved

---

[104] Arnold Stein, "Yeats: A Study in Recklessness," *Sewanee Review* 57 (1949): 603–26, has given a good acount of the kind of *sprezzatura* Yeats sought in his syntax and diction.

the People Wanted Pictures" (1912), Yeats explicitly attempted to import into Ireland his Renaissance myth. Founded on "imitative energy," the poem treats a subject—aristocratic service—which his Renaissance studies had inevitably clarified. The ideal Platonic harmony between active and contemplative modes stipulated public service as the counterpart to a self-perfecting courtesy. Certainly Yeats knew Spenser's characterization of Sidney's equilibrated unity: his "wise and civill governaunce" is the logical end of "wise discourse" among "Sweete Ladie Muses" (*Mother Hubberds Tale*, 11. 782, 760–63). Living in a country whose aristocracy had repeatedly violated the public trust, Yeats must have felt the ironic pertinence of Ottaviano's admonition concerning service in *The Courtier*: if the aristocrat "brought forth no other fruit than merely being what he is, I should not deem it right for a man to devote so much study and pains to acquiring this perfection."[105] Yeats considered the aristocrat's disinterested service a mandatory reciprocation for the grant of "leisure, wealth, privilege"; he found his patterns of magnanimity in the Gregory tradition. Sir Hugh Lane, in whose defense he wrote the poem, was Lady Gregory's nephew; his will to "restore dignity to Ireland"[106] was no less than the family's. Sir William Gregory, throughout his parliamentary career, had pursued an ideal of national welfare which ran counter to Anglo-Irish self-interest: during the Famine he vehemently opposed the British government's policy that relief should come only from private enterprise; prominent in the Home Rule party, he supported land reform and the division of estates among the peasantry; at Coole, he reduced rents "when there was a good case for it."[107] Of Shawe-Taylor, Yeats wrote: "I do not think I have known another man whose motives were so entirely pure, so entirely unmixed with any personal calculation, whether of ambition, of prudence or of vanity. He caught up into his imagination the public gain as other men their private gain."[108] And Yeats knew that Lady Gregory, although inveterately shy, had toured *The Playboy* in America, endured near-riots and personal threats for the sake of a play she "never really loved"; as with the Dublin production, she knew she was engaged in a "definite fight for freedom from mob censorship."[109]

---

[105] Castiglione, *The Courtier*, trans. Opdyke, p. 246. Opdyke's translation of this passage is more comprehensible than Hoby's.

[106] Yeats, "Modern Ireland: An Address to American Audiences, 1932–1933," ed. Curtis Bradford, *Massachusetts Review* 5 (1964): 259.

[107] Lady Gregory, *Journals*, p. 41.

[108] *Essays*, p. 344.

[109] Lady Gregory, *Our Irish Theatre*, pp. 244, 115.

The questions which the poem's background raised for Yeats were these: What can be the future of a nation which does not allow its most able men to serve? What should be the judgment on an aristocracy whose representative, obliged by position to serve, refuses?

Lane, a renowned connoisseur of art, knew how corrupt Ireland's aesthetic sensibilities had become since the eighteenth century. Laboring indefatigably to enlighten a nation destitute of visual tradition, he wanted to give Dublin his significant collection of Impressionist paintings and a gallery to house it. The gallery would provide models of excellence for Irish artists; its director would know how to educate taste.[110] "The property involved," Yeats later said of Lane's pictures, "though great in monetary value, is more than property, for it means the possession of the implements of national culture."[111] Lane, seeking to engender civic pride, consciously emulated Renaissance patterns; when he proposed that the gallery be built on a bridge spanning the Liffey, he was imagining the Ponte Vecchio in Florence. Lady Gregory associated the project with the founding of the public library at Oxford during the reign of James I.[112] Lane's boldness, even the propulsive frenzy in his service, augmented the atmosphere of princely humanism. For Ricketts, Lane had a Medicean magnificence;[113] to J. B. Yeats, his flawless courtesy mirrored "the time when all men were soldiers." For Yeats himself, although he had once thought Lane supercilious, Lane's Renaissance stature crystallized during a crisis. In 1907, the year of *The Playboy* riots, Lane was asked to apply for the curatorship of the Dublin National Museum and was assured of the appointment. Immediately he "began buying precious gifts" for the museum[114] —only to be informed that Count Plunkett had been appointed instead. Lady Gregory shared Yeats's rage: "It was, in his mind, one of the worst of crimes, that neglect to use the best man, the man of genius, in place of the timid, obedient official. That use of the best had been practised in the great days of the Renaissance."[115] Lane neverthe-

---

110 Lady Gregory, *Hugh Lane's Life and Achievement* (London: Murray, 1921), pp. 50–51.

111 W. B. Yeats, *The Senate Speeches of W. B. Yeats*, ed. Donald Pearce (Bloomington: Indiana University Press, 1960), p. 119.

112 Lady Gregory, *Hugh Lane's Life*, p. 269.

113 Lady Gregory, MS to *Coole*, Book VII. Ricketts' words are given slightly differently by Joseph Hone, *W. B. Yeats*, 2nd ed. (1943; rpt. London: Macmillan, 1962), pp. 225–26. See also *Senate Speeches*, p. 123.

114 Lady Gregory, *Hugh Lane's Life*, p. 39.

115 Ibid., pp. 83, 85. Donald T. Torchiana (*W. B. Yeats and Georgian Ireland* [Evanston: Northwestern University Press, 1966], pp. 58–64) emphasizes the Anglo-

less reconfirmed his bequest on condition that a subscription be raised for a gallery. But Dublin, in the years that followed, did not reciprocate. Patrons of the arts responded with no more alacrity than when Yeats and Lady Gregory had planned a national theater. The fact that Lane's architect, Lutyens, was English stirred rancor. Murphy, Parnell's enemy, waged a newspaper campaign against the project; Lord Ardilaun, who disliked the idea and perceived no public support for it, refused to donate St. Stephen's Green as a site. When Yeats urged Lane to buy his own site,[116] Lane refused, wanting the commitment of other Anglo-Irish aristocrats before proceeding. Although he disagreed with Lane's demand, Yeats was appalled by the provincial ignorance and apathy of the Dublin Corporation; in his notes to the poem he delivered a scathing aesthetic and moral criticism of minds presumably cultivated but in fact barren, unfitted—despite "privilege"—to govern.

When Yeats composed "To a Wealthy Man . . .," he had Ardilaun in mind; nevertheless, he wrote Lane, "The 'correspondent' to whom the poem is addressed is of course an imaginary person."[117] *The Poetaster* had taught Yeats the classical lesson that satire, to retain scope, cannot dwindle into personal invective; unlike "At the Abbey Theatre" (1911), the poem harbors no concealed malice. The "wealthy man" symbolizes men of standing who fail to comprehend their function; Yeats's concern, as later in *Purgatory,* was the degeneration of the one class upon which Ireland would have to rely for its political and intellectual guidance. The poem makes its standards of criticism plain. Subsuming

---

Irish element in Lane's service, e.g. "we may look upon the public aesthetic dedication of Sir Hugh Lane as a graceful continuation of the efforts of an eighteenth-century Anglo-Irish aristocracy to beautify what became the second city of the Empire. It was his favorite Irish century" (pp. 61—62). There is a good measure of truth to this, but it is not an entirely accurate judgment on the way Lane appeared to his friends. Indeed, the lines from Lionel Johnson's elegy "A Friend," which reminded Gogarty and Yeats of Lane (Lady Gregory, *Hugh Lane's Life,* p. 211), lead directly into a classical and Elizabethan, *not* Augustan, context (cf. Torchiana, *W. B. Yeats,* p. 62). I quote the two pertinent stanzas:

> Magnificence and grace,
> Excellent courtesy:
> A brightness on the face,
> Airs of high memory:
> Whence came all these, to such as he?
> Like young Shakespearian kings,
> He won the adoring throng:
> And, as Apollo sings,
> He triumphed with a song:
> Triumphed, and sang, and passed along.

116 *Letters,* p. 574.
117 Ibid., p. 573.

the matter of patronage to larger considerations, it underscores the direct connection between individual aristocratic service and national excellence. Beyond vindicating Lane and his gallery, the poem presents, through intricate allusions to the Renaissance, an image of ideal aristocratic "manhood."

The speaker begins in jibing double-satire:

> You gave, but will not give again
> Until enough of Paudeen's pence
> By Biddy's halfpennies have lain
> To be 'some sort of evidence,'
> Before you'll put your guineas down,
> That things it were a pride to give
> Are what the blind and ignorant town
> Imagines best to make it thrive.

The brilliant caesura in the first line suddenly alters compliment to denunciation as the speaker derisively echoes the aristocrat's excuses. His evasion of responsibility, his failure to understand the national issues or the collection's worth—these signs of a fruitless aristocratic "soil" constitute but part of the speaker's charge. The wealthy man's real immorality is his self-debasement—his discourteous behavior. As the verse-structure of the first two lines shows with brutal dexterity, he has surrendered aristocratic freedom to the "contagious opinions of poorer minds," whose deluded perception of their own welfare is exacerbated by an ignorant materialism. Conjunctive rhyme—"pence"/"evidence"—compounds the satire upon an aristocrat more derelict than any other in Yeats's work.

Because satire's end is correction, the speaker turns to instruct a man who has forgotten his spiritual ancestry. His subject, the function of the historical imagination, implies that enervated Anglo-Ireland can only revive by imitating an aristocracy greater than itself—a theme Yeats had explored in chastising the eighteenth century for having ignored Celtic culture. The three Renaissance princes illustrate aristocratic behavior at its finest; given the speaker's scope of attack, they appear as men, not simply patrons. "Men will be born among us," Yeats had hoped earlier, "of whom it is possible to say, not 'What a philanthropist' . . . but, as we say of the men of the Renaissance, 'What a nature', 'How much abundant life'."[118]   All but present within the poem, Lane has found his vision through "imitative energy," studied

---

118 *Explorations*, p. 162. Cf. Salvadori (*Yeats and Castiglione*, pp. 61–64), who argues that the poem is principally concerned with patronage.

remembrance of the great humanists: the speaker's choice of images forces the wealthy man to recognize Lane's superiority by establishing its proper context. In a humiliating irony, criticism of the wealthy man intersects with compliment to Lane; the poem's toughness comes from Yeats's Popeian deftness in handling allusion. The proud, ambitious princes, questing for personal and civic perfection, all suggest Lane's character. The image of Urbino recalls Lane's courtesy and his rediscovery of Titian's portrait of Castiglione; Cosimo's life becomes an allegory of the gallery controversy. The complex interplay between past and present is ambiguously satiric: everything the speaker praises in Lane and the Renaissance princes at once censures the wealthy man's failure, goads him toward regeneration—and compliments him ahead of time (is the flattery transparently satiric?) for having won that most alluring of Renaissance virtues, Fame. One could not want a finer decorum of metaphor.

Ercole exemplifies more than the rejection of common opinion necessary to foster great art. His inspiration—like Lane's, unlike the wealthy man's—comes from a dialogue with history: classical Rome fires his imagination.[119] "What cared Duke Ercole . . .?"—the very flair of the haughty rhetorical question mirrors Ercole's aristocratic nonchalance. His commanding presence, the personal enthusiasm (*"his* Plautus"), the love of public achievement—all reflect that striving for magnificence which is so foreign to the wealthy man's mentality.

Urbino correlates the making of art with the fashioning of the self. Geography strengthens the opposition between high and low desire: "Urbino's windy hill" surmounts the shepherds' fields. The oxymoronic epithet—Guidobaldo's "grammar school of courtesies"—opens with a nonchalant understatement so seemingly inappropriate that it is exactly right: courtesy, for all its extraordinary sophistication, is elementary, absolutely fundamental. Personified wit and beauty, imperfect by nature, come to learn their aristocratic "trade"; perfected by art, they marry to engender the bodily radiance Castiglione praised. But behind Urbino's exaltation lies tragedy. Few readers of *The Courtier* would think Guidobaldo the creator of the "grammar school"; indeed, having contracted gout as a young man, he "used continuallye, by reason of his infirmytye, soone after supper to go to his rest,"[120] leaving the

---

119 Opdyke's note no. 203 to his translation of *The Courtier* (p. 363) has often been taken as Yeats's source for the imagery of the "Italian comedies." The note, however, does not provide enough material for Yeats's uses. The more likely source—and one which has a good deal to say about "th' onion-sellers"—is Edmund G. Gardner's *Dukes and Poets in Ferrara* (New York: Dutton, 1904), pp. 214–18. Yeats owned the book (Torchiana, *W. B. Yeats*, p. 99, n. 49).

120 Castiglione, *The Courtier*, trans. Hoby, p. 32.

other nobility to center round the Duchess, Elizabetta Gonzaga. Yeats knew Castiglione's admiration for his courage; Guidobaldo "lyved wyth great dignytye and estimation emonge all men: in sickenesse, as one that was sounde, and in adversitye, as one that was most fortu-nate."[121]   Yeats's willful shift of focus from the Duchess to Guido-baldo generates heroic paradox. The intent to create high civility, as with Mabel Beardsley, arises from suffering and disfigurement; the agent of transformation is art, love of beauty in all forms.

Cosimo's experience amplifies the paradox: art—whether Michel-ozzo's library or Cosimo's own aristocratic mind—springs from physical exile. The interrelation of these simultaneous creations foreshadows a major theme in the 'tower' poems, the organic evolution of a man with his building. Cosimo, in fact, did not commission the Museo di San Marco until three years *after* he had returned to Florence from his Venetian exile; but by antedating its planning to the time of estrange-ment (1433), Yeats sharply clarified the disinterested fervor of Cosimo's service. "He gave": the words reverberate against the poem's opening. Imprisoned, he conceives a library, place of the liberated mind. His architecture will alter the course of Italian history:

> He gave the hours they had set free
> To Michelozzo's latest plan
> For the San Marco Library,
> Whence turbulent Italy should draw
> Delight in Art whose end is peace,
> In logic and in natural law
> By sucking at the dugs of Greece.

Cosimo's heroic vision encapsulates the poem's historical dialogue: Renaissance Italy gained its power by imitating not simply Rome but Rome's object of imitation, the source of Western civilization. As allegory, the episode pays profound tribute to Lane's visionary design—Lane: Cosimo; Lutyens: Michelozzo; art gallery: library—and not least because Lane too endures an emotional exile. Against this panorama, the wealthy man's refusal appears criminal. The issue is not paintings, but the survival of the European imagination in an Ireland still too "turbulent" to fulfill its destiny.

That sudden broadening of scope occasions the poem's sternest

---

121 Ibid., p. 31. In "Poetry and Tradition" (*Essays*, p. 252) Yeats drew from this passage an example of the discipline of the mask, describing "Duke Guidobaldo in his sickness . . . who understood that life is not lived, if not lived for contemplation or excitement." See the portrait of Synge in "In Memory of Major Robert Gregory."

rebuke. Cosimo's public generosity was also a private, self-completing act; "Your open hand but shows our loss, / For he knew better *how to live.*" Judgment pronounced, the speaker exchanges satire for exhortation:

> Look up in the sun's eye and give
> What the exultant heart calls good
> That some new day may breed the best
> Because you gave, not what they would,
> But the right twigs for an eagle's nest!

As in Blake, the eagle is "a portion of Genius."[122] These lines call for a joyous humanism almost beyond history. Yet the heroic vision of Ireland perfected begins in memory of historical greatness; and its fruition will also occur within history. Appropriately, then, an image of natural construction within time carries the preceding images of art to their final condition: the end of art is nature, redeemed from imperfection. The image satisfies because, without violating the nest's natural integrity, it echoes the building of Cosimo's library, anticipates the building of Lane's gallery and the remaking of the nation. Prefigured by the wittily modified allusion to Romulus and Remus ("sucking at the dugs of Greece"), the naturalizing metaphors transform the wealthy man's gift into the environment necessary to "*breed* the best"; like Mary Bell, who devotes her art to making a bird's nest,[123] he becomes midwife to the creations of nature. The concluding line, with its breathtaking stress on "the *right* twigs," hints that the self-delighting joy of service will work a metamorphosis in the wealthy man himself; it provides as precise a natural analogy as possible to Guidobaldo's "grammar school of courtesies." In this final *sprezzatura*, the principal Yeatsian cycle of imperfect nature transmuted by art into highest nature is completed.

"To a Wealthy Man . . .," beyond defining aristocracy by Renaissance standards, is Yeats's sole sustained effort to cope with Dublin in constructive terms. The poem contemplates its transformation into a new Urbino or Florence and furnishes the city with an aristocratic urban lineage such as Renaissance Englishmen did when they thought of London as Troynovant. Yet between glorification and satire Yeats could find no middle ground; Henley's sentimental realism, crushing a

---

122 William Blake, "The Proverbs of Hell," No. 54, in *The Poetry and Prose of William Blake*, ed. David V. Erdman, with a commentary by Harold Bloom (Garden City, N.Y.: Doubleday, 1965), p. 37.

123 *A Vision*, pp. 44–49.

private dream of Florentine civic beauty, repelled him.[124]   The very title of "No Second Troy" (1908) implies Yeats's problem with Dublin; an ignoble chaos has "hurled the little streets upon the great," metaphorically wrecked whatever aristocratic urban design the city once possessed. Lane had offered Dublin its chance to regain heroic proportions; when Dublin failed to respond honorably, Yeats's brief myth of Renaissance men in a Renaissance city collapsed. "To a Shade" (1913) reverts to the old bitterness. With its ironic echoes of Wordsworth's "Composed upon Westminster Bridge, 1802," "the gaunt houses put on majesty" only because a shimmering dusk conceals the city's deformity; "put on" suggests fraudulence, usurpation. Dublin's ugliness mirrors its uncivil treatment of Lane; invoking Parnell's ghost, the speaker vents his outrage:

> A man
> Of your own passionate serving kind who had brought
> In his full hands what, had they only known,
> Had given their children's children loftier thought,
> Sweeter emotion, working in their veins
> Like gentle blood, has been driven from the place,
> And insult heaped upon him for his pains,
> And for his open-handedness, disgrace.

No Renaissance myth can accommodate Ireland's neurotic predilection for martyring its most heroic servants. Lane, once Cosimo's incarnation, now joins the distinguished, defeated Anglo-Irish heroes whom Yeats bitterly named in "Reprisals" (1920) "the other cheated dead." But if Dublin was intractable, Yeats's Renaissance myth was hardly extinct. There was Coole.

[124] *Autobiography*, p. 110.

Coole Transformed: Yeats's Use of the Country House Poem

I

... the dream of my early manhood, that a modern nation can return to Unity of Culture, is false; though it may be we can achieve it for some small circle of men and women, and there leave it till the moon bring round its century.[1]

Renaissance literature had profoundly altered Yeats's vision of Coole. Where he had once seen woods, he now saw a house, an ordered estate; instead of invoking shadows of Ireland's epic past, he conversed with Lady Gregory; the Renaissance art in his room delighted him. He understood that Coole offered "old forms, old situations" of nearly classical dimension, an environment he could justifiably mythologize as a world whose inhabitants, unifying personal beauty with national service and love of art, knew "how to live." Without Coole his Renaissance images would have atrophied into daydream.

The influence of Castiglione's Urbino on Yeats's perception of Coole, however, has been overestimated. Yeats indeed created an analogy between Coole and Urbino, but he was too tough and skeptical about matters of plausibility ever to employ it in his poetry. He understood the impossibility of elaborating an aristocratic court on the

[1] W. B. Yeats, *The Autobiography of William Butler Yeats* (New York: Macmillan, 1938), pp. 250–51.

Renaissance model: "Perhaps we may find in the spectacle of some
beautiful woman our Ferrara, our Urbino. Perhaps that is why we have
no longer any poetry but the poetry of love."[2] Although Yeats intuited
The Courtier's latent threat of disorder, he plainly considered Urbino
an "unperturbed" sanctuary from physical and mental violence; despite
Guidobaldo's suffering, Urbino lacked tragedy. Coole reflected the
fierceness of Yeats's contemporary world: given his awareness of Irish
history, his Renaissance myth almost necessarily entailed heroic defeat;
except for the epilogue to *Responsibilities*, all his Coole poems are
elegies or embattled defenses. Further, Urbino had no poet to praise it;
restoring that bond, Yeats at Coole meditated on Spenser and Elizabeth, Donne and the Countess of Bedford, Jonson and the Countess of
Pembroke—and Raftery. Castiglione's courtiers, moreover, were edu-
cated neo-Platonists dwelling in a city; they eschewed the peasantry,
lacked the sense of consecrated place, "contact with the soil," so
central to Yeats's vision of Coole. More various than the "grammar
school of courtesies," Coole fused in one estate three aristocratic
traditions: the ancient Irish legacy, the courtly beauty of the Renaissance—and later, the Anglo-Irish heritage.

Yeats's prose analogies between Coole and Urbino were less equations implying belief than metaphors to explore Coole's aristocratic
nature. Its Renaissance identity became clear in 1909, when Lady
Gregory's severe illness prompted Yeats's new recognition of her symbolic stature: "All Wednesday I heard Castiglione's phrase ringing in my
memory, 'Never be it spoken without tears, the Duchess, too, is dead',
and that phrase, which—coming where it did among the numbering of
his dead—often moved me till my eyes dimmed, brought before me now
all his sorrow and my own, as though one saw the worth of life fade for
ever."[3] For Yeats, Lady Gregory possessed the same unostentatious
grandeur as the Duchess: intense but quiet authority mingled with
unusual empathy, superb self-discipline. With "an ear . . . indifferent to
praise or blame," she had been "Bred to a harder thing / Than
Triumph."[4] Like the Duchess, whom Castiglione admired for creating
"a chaine that kept all lincked together in love," Lady Gregory revealed
an inexplicable capacity to forge social coherence. During his early
years at Coole, she was his "centre of peace."[5] When the circle

---

[2] W. B. Yeats, *Memoirs,* ed. Denis Donoghue (New York: Macmillan, 1973), p. 156.
[3] *Autobiography,* p. 408.
[4] Ibid., p. 323; "To a Friend Whose Work Has Come to Nothing."
[5] Baldesar Castiglione, *The Book of the Courtier,* trans. Sir Thomas Hoby (1561;
rpt. London: Nutt, 1900), p. 32; *Autobiography,* p. 388.

expanded, she gave firm but discreet guidance (" 'The only wrong act that matters is not doing one's best work' ") and fused into a single aesthetic and national movement widely divergent imaginations—"half a dozen in formation there, / That seemed to whirl upon a compass-point."[6]

Through these ideal geometries Yeats symbolized his relationship with Lady Gregory; lonely, increasingly "unmarried" as he aged, he thought her "more than kin. . . . She has been to me mother, friend, sister and brother."[7] Renaissance cosmology provided him metaphors for her "steadfast nobility."[8] "A Friend's Illness" (1909), joining Spenserian personification with tensed metaphysical conceit, plays the double theme of personal revelation and cosmic judgment: mere apocalypse cannot match the internal, refining fire which exalts Lady Gregory's soul into a type of the indestructible *anima mundi*.[9] Lady Gregory in "These Are the Clouds" (1910) is a symbol of universal order, a Renaissance monarch aureoled in the sun's sacramental light. Distilled from Horace's praise of Caesar in *The Poetaster* (V.i.44–50) and the warfare Yeats envisaged between Richard II and Henry V, the Renaissance imagery creates analogies between past and present versions of the Fall: as he adumbrates for the first time in the poetry Shakespeare's central myth of usurpation,[10] the speaker considers Lady Gregory's death the result of a violent democratic conspiracy to destroy excellence:

> The weak lay hand on what the strong has done,
> Till that be tumbled that was lifted high

---

6 *Autobiography*, p. 348; "Coole Park," III.

7 *Autobiography*, p. 407.

8 Ibid., p. 408.

9 The metaphor is a Renaissance commonplace, e.g., Donne's *The First Anniversary*, 11. 427–28. William M. Carpenter cites Donne's "A Feaver" and Herbert's "Vertue" ("The *Green Helmet* Poems and Yeats's Myth of the Renaissance," *Modern Philology* 67 [1969]: 58). Whether or not by conscious design, the poem, printed in *Estrangement* (section 29), culminates a long, eclectic rumination on poetic and aristocratic excellence.

10 W. B. Yeats, *Essays and Introductions* (New York: Macmillan, 1961), p. 107: "Shakespeare's myth, it may be, describes a wise man who was blind from very wisdom, and an empty man who thrust him from his place, and saw all that could be seen from very emptiness." Carpenter ("The *Green Helmet* Poems," p. 57) aptly comments that "These Are the Clouds" so clearly uses the "Renaissance tradition that it may be said to work largely through allusion, taking its strength from the reader's recognition of the Renaissance world order which is the basis of the poem." He finds models for the imagery in *Romeo and Juliet* (II.iii.5–8) and, of course, Ulysses' speech on degree (*Troilus and Cressida*, I.iii.89–94).

> And discord follow upon unison,
> And all things at one common level lie.

"Majesty" requires the noble endurance of defeat:

> And therefore, friend, if your great race were run
> And these things came, so much the more thereby
> Have you made greatness your companion,
> Although it be for children that you sigh.

This austere compliment is the central point at which the poem seeks—and fails—to transcend its academic Elizabethan correspondences. It fails, paradoxically, because Yeats knew what he was doing. He wanted—not a myth of the Great Archer—but a human being possessing mythic stature; without that duality, Lady Gregory's heroic power could have no living force. But Yeats's attempts to humanize her were abrupt and awkward. "Friend" sounds both pompous and inappropriately intimate. The last line, while it domesticates the Shakespearean parallel between the dissolution of the family and the destruction of the state, is tonally askew. The archaic subjunctive falls flat; syntax and rhyme scheme throw all the weight to "sigh," making Lady Gregory seem incongruously sentimental and leaving the sonorous regality of the final refrain dangling.

Despite these flaws, Yeats's general design in mythologizing Lady Gregory is clear: the unity of being these poems attribute to her remains a constant value. Strictly speaking, Yeats in *A Vision* placed Lady Gregory in Phase 24, a phase of self-sacrificial obedience to the aristocratic code, and thus denied her the creative independence he had praised in *Estrangement* and *Dramatis Personae*; "unity of being," moreover, was a term whose magical luminosity he reserved for the ancients.[11] But in questing for present images of the completed self, he sometimes disregarded his own categories. He analyzed her totality in his eulogy:

> She sought in the depths of her mind and expressed habitually in all she said and did virtue which Aristotle calls "magnificence, greatness of soul." . . . Edmund Spenser had meant to make King Arthur the symbol of this mysterious quality, and celebrate it in a book of *The Faery Queen*. . . .
> Lady Gregory was not philosophic, she seldom reflected upon her work, but one phrase she used again and again: "We do our

11 *Autobiography*, p. 247.

work to restore dignity to Ireland." She remained to the end of her
life a connoisseur in nobility in living and in thought. During this
last year she kept an unmoved face amid great pain. A woman like a
rock, as a great painter said of her years ago, at her side always
Arabia Deserta and the *New Testament* in Gaelic; she never separated the discipline of religion from the discipline of style.[12]

Culminating medieval and Renaissance epic tradition, Lady Gregory
was a paradigm of perfection who unified multiplicity. Yeats's parallel
phrasings, his yoking of antitheses reinforce that image of reconciled
opposites:

She sought   in the depths of her mind ⎫
and expressed in all she said   ⎬ virtue
                      and did   ⎭

a connoisseur   in nobility
                      in living
              and in thought

at her side always   *Arabia Deserta*
                      and the *New Testament* in Gaelic

She never separated   the discipline of religion
                      from the discipline of style.

Other harmonies of inner and outer energies sound: her passionate
nationalism, her courteous demeanor in sickness; her aristocratic consciousness of an invaluable peasant tradition. Others among Yeats's
aristocratic heroes had greater imaginations (Swift, Cuchulain, Blake);
Robert Gregory's *sprezzatura* was more impressive, Lane's passion for
service more violent; but none possessed the stabilized dignity Yeats
found in Lady Gregory.

Yeats consequently revised his conception of proper relations between poet and aristocrat in an ideal humanist society. In the broad
social spectrum of *The King's Threshold* the poet is civilization's center,
the creator of all value; when King Guaire rashly dismisses Seanchan
from court, the social structure threatens to disintegrate. Now, however, Shelley's influence had waned; Yeats, as he ruminated on "imitative energy" in *Estrangement* (section 25), revoked the poet's heroic

12 W. B. Yeats, "Modern Ireland: An Address to American Audiences, 1932–
1933," ed. Curtis Bradford, *Massachussetts Review* 5 (1964): 259–60.

centrality and acknowledged a more intricate bond between aristocrat and poet than patronage can adequately explain:

> Lady Gregory is planting trees. . . . Her grandson will be fifty years old before they can be cut. We artists, do not we also plant trees and it is only after some fifty years that we are of much value? Every day I notice some new analogy between the long-established life of the well-born and the artist's life. . . . we carry in our heads always that form of society aristocracies create now and again for some brief moment at Urbino or Versailles. We too despise the mob and suffer at its hands, and when we are happiest we have some little post in the house of Duke Frederick where we watch the proud dreamless world with humility, knowing that our knowledge is invisible and that at the first breath of ambition our dreams vanish. If we do not see daily beautiful life at which we look as old men and women do at young children, we become theorists— thinkers as it is called,—or else give ourselves to strained emotions, to some overflow of sentiment 'sighing after Jerusalem in the regions of the grave'. How can we sing without our bush of whins, our clump of heather, and does not Blake say that it takes a thousand years to create a flower?[13]

Linked in an organic interdependence, poet and aristocrat each imitate the shared ancestral vision of "an impossibly noble life"[14] initially transmitted by the peasantry. For the poet, "an uncompleted are perhaps," "Those whom it is our business to cherish and celebrate are complete arcs."[15] The aristocrat, because he embodies the poet's dreams, is poetry's fit subject; in "Fallen Majesty" (1912), as in the Maud-Helen poems of *The Green Helmet,* Yeats transformed Castiglione's courtier into a poet-historian:

> Although crowds gathered once if she but showed her face,
> And even old men's eyes grew dim, this hand alone,
> Like some last courtier at a gypsy camping-place
> Babbling of fallen majesty, records what's gone.

Yet the poet, beauty's servant and imitator, is also responsible for furnishing the aristocrat with images of perfection to imitate. The aristocrat thus owes the poet debts not only for eternizing his court's transient loveliness but for impelling him to achieve "magnificence."

[13] *Autobiography*, pp. 404–5; see also *Essays,* p. 293.

[14] *Essays,* p. 303.

[15] *Autobiography*, p. 405.

But the poet, if he is to avoid sterility, paradoxically requires the historical reality of "beautiful life" in order to transform an abstract idea into myth and image; he cannot "wander where it please him amid the splendours of ancient Courts"[16] unless he can see Lady Gregory "planting trees." Imagination tinges the poet's observation with desire: the court or country house is his tangible shadow of the New Jerusalem; its members, Edenic children—"dreamless," like Adam, because dream and reality have fused. They have redeemed their natures—both by practicing their own difficult courtesy and by assimilating the poet's vision.

That innocence of the whole person is exactly what the poet must painfully relinquish for himself in order to nurture it among the aristocracy. He remains fallen, a creator of images, not of himself; as poet he creates "the symbolic rose";[17] as man he has only his "bush of whins." He may observe, from "some little post," the great panoply of serene nobility but may not join its ceremony. The capacity to give beauty form comes from passionate desire stripped of envy; the satisfaction of desire means the closing of necessary aesthetic distance: "At the first breath of ambition our dreams vanish." Bembo, Yeats knew, understood the strange exhilaration of the poet's position: " 'Would that I were a shepherd that I might look daily down upon Urbino.' "[18] As in "The Shadowy Waters," the poet is exiled in Eden; in compensatory paradox, his Eden depends on his exile. To consecrate beauty, he must become the peripheral man in the society he loves.

This exquisite passage defines Yeats's *persona* in the Coole poems. First, the speaker never claims aristocratic nobility for himself. His critical self-portrait in "Coole Park" (II) is paradigmatic: "one that ruffled in a manly pose / For all his timid heart." The speaker celebrates what he lacks, and much of his imaginative power derives from that deprivation. Second, with the sole exception of "Upon a House . . .," he defines aristocratic excellence by ruthlessly probing his own deficiencies. The speaker of "In the Seven Woods," who desires the Great Archer's magisterial calm, prefigures Yeats's later *persona:* Lady Gregory and Robert are never merely observed emblems of beauty but intensely personal symbols of his own failure. Yet here the *persona* differs radically from the poet in *Estrangement,* who is "happiest" when he has "some little post" in an aristocratic world: he feels the agony of separation. A poet-celebrant, he constantly seeks to become a poet-aristocrat, the subject of his own celebration; after Yeats

16 *Essays,* p. 253.
17 "Meditations in Time of Civil War," II.i.
18 W. B. Yeats, *A Vision* (New York: Macmillan, 1961), p. 109.

bought Thoor Ballylee, he attempted to fuse the two roles. Third, the speaker is acutely conscious of losing his "proud, dreamless world"; he celebrates despite impending defeat, knowing, in hate and scorn of the "mob," that both Coole and his defense are anachronisms.

When Yeats left Coole's woods, a changeless realm of natural cycle, and made the house his symbol of aristocratic grandeur, he confronted history and committed his myth of Coole's Renaissance identity to experience. Only the house, a human construction, could provide social as well as individual form for the paradox of organic artifice—courtesy— he sought to elucidate; only the house could give permanent shape to the "Traditional sanctity and loveliness" he sought to praise. Yet the house, though it had come unscathed through the Land Wars, had an uncertain future. Coole—for twenty years of poetry—is about to fall. Yeats, when he localized his aristocratic values within its physical structure, gained new metaphors and took new risks.

II

Yeats's initial manipulations of the house metaphor produced brief, elaborate poems, less famous than "Coole Park" and "Coole Park and Ballylee" but important: "Upon a House Shaken by the Land Agitation" (1909), "The New Faces" (1912), and the epilogue to *Responsibilities* (1914).

"Upon a House . . . ," unlike the other two, formally defends Coole against its enemies:

> How should the world be luckier if this house,
> Where passion and precision have been one
> Time out of mind, became too ruinous
> To breed the lidless eye that loves the sun?
> And the sweet laughing eagle thoughts that grow
> Where wings have memory of wings, and all
> That comes of the best knit to the best? Although
> Mean roof-trees were the sturdier for its fall,
> How should their luck run high enough to reach
> The gifts that govern men, and after these
> To gradual Time's last gift, a written speech
> Wrought of high laughter, loveliness and ease?

Celebrating "beautiful life," the poem illustrates Yeats's sense of the poet's public responsibility. It responds directly to the Land Act of

Courtesy of Michael Yeats

COOLE HOUSE
from a pastel by W. B. Yeats

How should the world be luckier if this house,
Where passion and precision have been one
Time out of mind, became too ruinous
To breed the lidless eye that loves the sun?

1909, which compelled large landholders to sell portions of their estates
to the peasantry.[19] The speaker counters the attack on property with
his own interrogation.[20] Because his rhetorical questions, loaded with
declarative praise of Coole, describe a greatness which must be obvious,
their effect is to make the Act's proponents seem ignorant of history,
lacking scope of vision. Cannily admitting enough of their argument to

[19] For full details of the Act, see F. S. L. Lyons, *The Irish Parliamentary Party,*
1890–1910 (London: Faber, 1951), pp. 252–53. In his journal for August 7, 1909,
Yeats noted the immediate occasion which prompted the poem, the "reductions of
rents made by the courts. One feels always that where all must make their living
they will live not for life's sake but the work's, and all be the poorer. . . . This house
has enriched my soul out of measure, because here life moves without restraint
through spacious forms. Here there has been no compelled labour, no poverty-
thwarted impulse" (Yeats, *Memoirs,* p. 226).

[20] Cf. Bernard Levine, *The Dissolving Image: The Spiritual-Esthetic Development*
of W. B. Yeats (Detroit: Wayne State University Press, 1970), pp. 91–92, who

nullify its relevance ("Although / Mean roof-trees were the sturdier for its fall"), he asserts that the irrevocable loss of Coole—no mere division of another, or any, Anglo-Irish estate[21] —must reverberate beyond Ireland: with the willfully panoramic word "world," he measures Coole's importance, and thereafter seeks to justify his hyperbole.

His method, as in "To a Wealthy Man . . .," is to show that the house, while plainly an artifact, has become part of a transcendental natural pattern: an eagle's nest. Its inhabitants, quelling base rudenesses of human nature, have practiced an art of living so courteous, a quest for perfection so passionate that its creations seem spontaneous. The imagery fuses intellectual and aesthetic joy with natural process in paradoxes of generation:[22] the house (artifact) breeds (procreates naturally). But instead of breeding children (the dynastic image is too conventional), it breeds metaphors of visionary aspiration: "the lidless eye that loves the sun." How can a house . . . breed . . . an eagle's lidless eye? Unimaginable, fearsome, the metaphor dramatizes the unbelievable intensity of the Gregory creativity; the disjunction between the terms of the image demands recognition that Coole has achieved the impossible collaboration between them. "Grow" (1. 5), heightening the organic metaphor, suggests momentarily a vegetable fruition which parallels the eagle's ascent. The stressed word "Where" (1. 6) consequently designates a place which unifies earth and air: the house, a rooted tree and an eagle's nest. At Coole, not only does imagination have a concrete body ("eagle thoughts"), but the body thinks ("Where wings have memory of wings")—that spiritualized condition Yeats called unity of being. As the house harmonizes earth and air, mind and body, nature and art, it makes "passion and precision . . . one." The speaker's sense of these reconciliations permeates his defense. He extols Coole's tradition for breeding *both* "the lidless eye" *and* "the sweet

---

believes the poem addressed to Lady Gregory, a supposition not corroborated by the way in which the speaker alludes to her crafting of "Kiltartan." The closest analogue to Yeats's method of dealing with Lady Gregory here is "Coole Park and Ballylee" (IV), where he plainly does not address her directly. Levine finds something quizzical in the speaker's tone, partly because he misses the poem's public purpose, partly because he seems to misunderstand the intent of Yeats's rhetorical questions.

21 Cf. Louis MacNeice, *The Poetry of W. B. Yeats* (1941; rpt. London: Faber, 1967), p. 95, who argues that the speaker "deplores the fall of the big *houses*" [italics mine]. The text does not justify MacNeice's generalization. The poem was originally entitled "To a Certain Country House in Time of Change" (W. B. Yeats, *The Variorum Edition of the Poems of W. B. Yeats*, eds. Peter Allt and Russell K. Alspach [New York: Macmillan, 1966], p. 264).

22 T. R. Henn thinks the images "simple and self-sufficient" (*The Lonely Tower* [1950; rpt. London: Methuen, 1965], p. 120).

laughing eagle thoughts." When he details Coole's most recent achieve-
ments, he thinks of a pair which marries active and contemplative
modes: Sir William Gregory's political service and—what he prefers—
Lady Gregory's "Kiltartan" dialect. The dialect itself fuses "high laughter, loveliness and ease" into a work of art which, while "wrought" into
form, seems natural. Coole's excellences, like its generations, are "knit"
together.

The astonishing amount of word repetition, even more than the
persistent linking of disparate qualities into unity, dogmatically emphasizes Coole's dominant characteristics. "And all / That comes of the
best knit to the best" assumes the known identity of "the best."
"Where wings have memory of wings" assumes Coole's transcendent
nature. As "the lidless eye that loves the sun" modulates into "loveliness," passionate aspiration merges with universal serenity. Most important, the repetitions intensify the historical context of Coole's creativity and give substance to the disaster at hand. "How should the
world be luckier . . .?" "How should their luck run high enough . . .?"
The modern world, prepared to ruin the last model of established
greatness, can only rely on mere luck, and even "high" luck cannot
reach the "high" Gregory laughter which derives from an intricate sense
of history, long nurture of precise art. "Luck," accident, is something
other than art; "gifts" (what Yeats once called "luckless luck"),[23]
something in addition to art which only art, *sprezzatura*, can elicit.

Yet the speaker's knowledge of Coole's imminent doom tinges with
poignant helplessness his insistence upon Coole's virtues. "Gradual
Time's last gift": the rich oxymoron focusses the poem's central tension. Although Time's unequalled gift is the literary capacity to give
human experience permanent form, Time ironically bestows it precisely
when Coole's own permanence becomes most transitory. And if the gift
is "last," Coole's intimate collaboration with history has broken.
"Last" also implies apocalypse: Coole's demise ends all significant
history; nothing which follows can matter.[24] Both the mythical origin
of Coole's greatness in a "Time out of mind" and its imperceptible
evolution in a specific place make its "fall" (1. 8) a catastrophe, the fall
of the Renaissance into the modern world. Thoroughly reversing
Spenser's tentatively optimistic conclusion to the "Epithalamion"
("Song . . . Be unto her a goodly ornament, / And for short time an
endlesse moniment"), the speaker sees "gradual Time" abruptly trun-

23 *Autobiography*, p. 77.

24 Thomas R. Whitaker believes that the poem transcends the "temporal agitation"
of the conclusion (*Swan and Shadow: Yeats's Dialogue with History* [Chapel Hill:
North Carolina University Press, 1964], p. 151).

cated. The deep refulgence of his phrasing barely conceals the darkness of his mind.

The public character of "Upon a House . . ." accounts for its strengths and weaknesses. Although a superbly patterned exposition of Coole's perfection, the poem fails to validate its initial claim that the "world" will suffer if Coole falls—hardly because Coole appears inglorious, but because the speaker lacks complexity of vision. He is a spokesman uttering preexistent beliefs, not a dramatic figure whose beliefs evolve through considered testing. The poem thus clarifies a problem Yeats perpetually tackled in portraying his ideal world. Because Coole, unlike Eden, is never subject to internal corruption, because Yeats's speakers never doubt its excellence, Yeats needed techniques of tension, impurities, to make its virtues credible. The Renaissance myth of Coole's impending destruction was poetically indispensable, and not least because the conflict dramatically magnified an aspect of Coole's heritage always hard to render—its lofty serenity. But if you happen to be rooting for the wrong side in this Armageddon, Yeats's reiterations of doom will not move you. Yeats saw the difficulty and consequently sought additional techniques. "Upon a House . . ." makes greatness vivid by complicating it: the elaborate metaphors and intricate repetitions are attempts to vivify a bundle of abstractions—"passion," "precision," "thoughts." Yet the complication tends to remain merely ingenious. The poem shows that neither the sense of danger nor the complication can work adequately unless the speaker has internalized them in personal drama; it shows, too, that alluring abstraction and brilliant metonymy cannot substitute for qualities of mind embodied in human shape. The house itself is the poem's central character; its inhabitants are ideas, not people.

In "The New Faces," Yeats wisely reverted to his earlier methods of self-portraiture:

> If you, that have grown old, were the first dead,
> Neither catalpa-tree nor scented lime
> Should hear my living feet, nor would I tread
> Where we wrought that shall break the teeth of Time.
> Let the new faces play what tricks they will
> In the old rooms; night can outbalance day,
> Our shadows rove the garden gravel still,
> The living seem more shadowy than they.

The poem handles the themes of "Upon a House . . ."—death and usurpation, the relation between time and art—with such personally dramatic fluency that "Upon a House . . ." seems but a preliminary study. For the first time in Yeats's poetry, Coole's true inhabitants step forth, walking quietly in the garden. Lady Gregory's illness emerges from the speaker's immediate experience (compare "These Are the Clouds"); his concern for the Abbey Theatre reflects his friendship with Lady Gregory. History, both public and private, is internally felt, a mixture of memory and desire.

Most important, the poem is a private conversation in Browning's manner. The speaker's tone implies antecedent discussion; and, like the pause between the second and third stanzas of Donne's "The Flea," his break in thought between quatrains is sufficiently obvious to "allow" Lady Gregory to comment. But she modestly refrains from joining in the speaker's self-congratulatory praise of the Abbey. Her silence, a crucial index of their relationship, suggests the measured calm which Yeats in "Upon a House . . ." could state but not portray, the constancy he symbolized in "These Are the Clouds" but here evoked wholly through dramatic illusion. By comparison, the speaker is initially troubled by memories of a disaster which did not occur, perturbed by Lady Gregory's future death: "If you, that have grown old, were the first dead" encompasses both anxieties. He makes no effort to conceal his feeling that she possesses the greater self-sufficiency; his opening statement intensifies his dependence and enhances her stature.

Brilliant syntax and a discreetly realized landscape mesh these anxieties into a seamless psychological totality. As the speaker contemplates his hypothetical losses he affirms his actual gains. The first hypothesis is densely ambiguous: "Neither catalpa-tree nor scented lime / Should hear my living feet"—if Lady Gregory had died, he would have been exiled from the garden, or, in extreme symbiosis, he himself would have died; yet, with her, he still enjoys the garden's sensuality, and the escape from disaster immeasurably heightens his pleasure. The second hypothesis—"Nor would I tread / Where we wrought that [which] shall break the teeth of Time"—contains four time-levels whose dazzlingly swift juxtaposition gives the speaker's resurgent power the force of a sudden revelation. As he *now* walks, he envisages the premature end of the Abbey project which *would have come* had Lady Gregory died; yet their collaborative effort, still intact—begun in the past ("Where we *wrought*")—"*shall break*" Time's dominance. The jubilant affirmation is a war-cry: Time, no longer a giver of gifts, has threatened Lady Gregory with death, but her survival ensures his defeat. Asserting continuities by treading "*Where* we wrought," the speaker recognizes that Coole is a consecrated spot of time, an emblem which permanently conjoins the Abbey's founding with his unbroken friendship. His dramatic, possessive relation to land contrasts sharply with the detached appreciation of place in "Upon a House. . . ." All

external challenges now become trifles; Coole's invasion by a new mob
seems ludicrous. With cavalier satiric joy he exposes the vaudevillian
facial distortions which signify their hypocrisy and moral degeneracy;
like Face in *The Alchemist,* this ill-bred breed is all face. Their theater,
realistic, commercial, is not "wrought"; they play "tricks," not plays.
So ebullient is the speaker that he can transform his initial fears of
dissolution into the materials of triumph. Even, he says to Lady
Gregory, let this rabble displace us from your ancestral home and our
traditional theater; even let us suffer exile to the garden, death. Yet

> Our shadows rove the garden gravel still,
> The living seem more shadowy than they.

Becoming spirits of the place like the "immortal, mild, proud shadows"
of "The Shadowy Waters," he and Lady Gregory cannot be removed;
through life-in-death, Coole is once again permanently theirs.

These joyous claims manifest an unperturbed serenity in con-
templating Coole's invasion which is unique in Yeats's poems. "Upon a
House . . ." attempts to forestall destruction; in "Coole Park," the
knowledge of desecration fills the speaker with heart-gnawing hollowness. The exhilaration of "The New Faces" is all the more remarkable
because the usurpation is concrete, immediate: he imagines the de-
stroyers of excellence already playing gleefully in "the old rooms";
there is no buffer zone between Dublin and Coole such as the one in
"In the Seven Woods." Compare this encroachment with the friendly
visits of peasantry and royalty in Jonson's country house poems: Yeats
did everything possible to heighten the heroic intensity of his speaker's
triumphant scorn. That he and Lady Gregory walk in the garden, hardly
a neutral dramatic situation, connotes superb ironies. Dispossessed from
the "old rooms," he still possesses what he needs, Lady Gregory's
friendship. The "new faces," in gaining possession of the "old rooms,"
have only appropriated a satiric mirror which reflects their own un-
tempered folly. Amidst signs of aristocratic courtesy and passion, they
are more "displaced" than those they have ousted.

"The New Faces" deviates radically from the conventions of the
country house poem. From Jonson through Pope the house gives
architectural form to its inhabitants' courtesy and taste; here, the
pointed discrepancy between the house and its new possessors brutally
dramatizes their corruption. The corollary of Yeats's brilliant inver-
sion[25] is equally significant: a poem such as "Upon a House . . ."

---

[25] Yeats may have been remotely inspired by *The Alchemist:* during Lovewit's
absence, Subtle and his ingenious crew make a shambles of the house. But there is
nothing like this in the genre of the country house poem.

depends metaphorically on the traditional belief that aristocratic values coexist with the house which shelters them; but in "The New Faces," these values are carried wholly in the mind and cannot be damaged by loss of the physical structure. Yeats, when he learned of Lady Gregory's illness, wrote with apocalyptic desperation, "All the day the thought of losing her is like a conflagration in the rafters. Friendship is all the house I have."[26] These images spiritualize Coole: the house, a metaphor of emotional and psychological coherence, is not composed of brick and mortar, Arundel prints, fine bindings. What "The New Faces" victoriously asserts is freedom from the material world: all is brought within the mind, the one landscape that cannot be violated.

Yeats plainly altered Coole's symbolic value to accord with his speaker's needs. In the *English Review* (January 1914), George Moore had accused Lady Gregory of mediocrity and plagiarism, denigrated Yeats's aristocratic manner, slurred his relations with Maud, and claimed his poetical career finished. Smarting from these insinuations, Yeats craved not only retaliation but escape. The witty haven of shadows in "The New Faces" was hardly satisfactory; Coole in the epilogue to *Responsibilities* is a physical sanctuary from injustice and pain:

> While I, from that reed-throated whisperer
> Who comes at need, although not now as once
> A clear articulation in the air,
> But inwardly, surmise companions
> Beyond the fling of the dull ass's hoof
> —Ben Jonson's phrase—and find when June is come
> At Kyle-na-no under that ancient roof
> A sterner conscience and a friendlier home,
> I can forgive even that wrong of wrongs,
> Those undreamt accidents that have made me
> —Seeing that Fame has perished this long while,
> Being but a part of ancient ceremony—
> Notorious, till all my priceless things
> Are but a post the passing dogs defile.

Coole appears warm, luminous, precisely because the speaker is exiled from its safety; trapped in the city, he cannot get free of backbiting and harassment. His intolerable physical separation from Coole is the poem's axis: neither his anguished frustration nor the pain of his moral dilemma (what does "I can forgive" mean?) makes sense unless that separation is understood. As in "In the Seven Woods" and "The New

---

[26] *Autobiography*, p. 408.

Faces," Yeats constructed his psychological and dramatic situation on principles of implied physical movement from one place to another; the Browningesque technique culminates in "Meditations in Time of Civil War." What gives the epilogue to *Responsibilities* such tension is that the implied movement remains only a thwarted possibility.

Although Henn, Mr. Torchiana, and Mr. McAlindon assume that the speaker has gotten to Coole,[27] his vision of Coole is not an observation but a despondent "surmise." The time-references in the octave show his wintry isolation even more vividly. They drastically qualify the pivotal statement, "I can forgive," turning it from actual charity to a possibility both desired and loathed. The conditions under which the speaker *could* forgive, moreover, are desperately hypothetical. Although Coole's friendship, as in "The New Faces," can render all threats insignificant and thus provide the strength to forgive, the speaker's image of Coole is blurred: "While" (1. 1) connotes precariously brief periods of time, and the imagination's reed-throated whisperer has lost its voice. The second condition—"and [while I] find when June is come"—depends on a future protection. But the speaker lacks, now, the example of Lady Gregory's rigorous moral discipline. Finally, the conjunction "and" (1. 6)—not "or"—stipulates that the two conditions must be satisfied simultaneously, clearly an impossibility since present and future time are not the same. Mr. McAlindon has written of the poem's "firm purpose of insulting while formally forgiving";[28] but instead of such hypocrisy the octave shows only the agonized craving for moral integrity. The speaker suffers a hideous self-division, imaged in the polarized landscape, between the demands of conscience to act honorably and the instinct to vent satiric hatred upon his calumniators. He knows retaliation discourteous yet cannot check his fury. The helplessly bitter excremental imagery of the conclusion,[29] recurrent throughout *Responsibilities,* is characteristically Jonsonian: the mere sterile lust to destroy entails the bestialization of the destroyer; his enemies are lovers of infamy, wanton malice. What keeps the attack from degenerating into self-pitying invective is that the

---

[27] Henn, *The Lonely Tower,* p. 97; Donald T. Torchiana, *W. B. Yeats and Georgian Ireland* (Evanston: Northwestern University Press, 1966), p. 291; T. McAlindon, "Yeats and the English Renaissance," *PMLA* 82 (1967): 166. Whitaker (*Swan and Shadow,* p. 158) recognizes a correlation between the speaker's physical placement and the "precarious nature of his moral equilibrium," but his interpretation of the speaker's character is too mild.

[28] McAlindon, "Yeats and the English Renaissance," p. 167.

[29] Yeats claimed to have adapted the image from Erasmus (W. B. Yeats, *Explorations* [New York: Macmillan, 1962], p. 330), but no one has located its source. It seems more likely that Yeats was actually remembering Rabelais's *Gargantua,* Book II, Chapter 22. I am indebted to Craig R. Thompson, of the English Department at the University of Pennsylvania, for this suggestion.

speaker, while he plainly invokes Coole's virtues to rebuke his enemies, also judges himself by the same high standards of aristocratic magnanimity. The crucial element of self-criticism validates his outrage by defining him as a man who seeks the accurate discrimination of value. "All my priceless things" is a phrase of such utter devastation that the reader, unable to judge the worth of unnamed "things," must rely on the speaker's word. If the reader had no reason to accept the speaker's judgment, the poem—its ostensible motivation, the speaker's responses—would collapse.

More specifically than "Upon a House . . .," the epilogue to *Responsibilities* accomplishes what Yeats in "To a Wealthy Man . . ." had hoped for Dublin: the creation of a Renaissance culture in Ireland. The swift aside, "Ben Jonson's phrase," joins with "that ancient roof" to make Coole—like Penshurst "an ancient pile" (1. 5)—an Elizabethan country house. Its distinctively humanist achievement is the quality of its moral intelligence, neither zealous nor legalistic. The very balance in "A sterner conscience and a friendlier home" points to Lady Gregory's Horatian intermixture of instruction with pleasure. Erasmus's colloquy *The Godly Feast* and Jonson's "Inviting a Friend to Supper" (Epigram CI), as well as *The Courtier,* provide models for Coole's ambience of courteous moral discourse. Coole houses—for the first time— "companions," that aristocratically "small circle of men and women" who will, the speaker knows, assert his innocence of the scurrilous charges laid against him—not because they are his friends, but because they understand true merit. But his defiant self-justification is subsumed to a dark vision of the degeneration of civilized history Victimized by time, the speaker has become "notorious"; Fame—what Jonson called "legitimate fame" (Epigram XVII), the honest publication of a person's nature and acts—has been subverted by her malicious and illegitimate half-sister Rumor. Mixing satiric scorn with his grief, the speaker mimics the callow indifference of those who dismiss the concept of just reputation as old-fashioned. The pessimism is bleak: if Fame remains a "part" of the "ancient ceremony" Coole's "ancient roof" still shelters, it survives there and nowhere else.

Ultimately the speaker appeals to Jonson himself to vindicate the nobility of his life. "Beyond the fling of the dull ass's hoof" is cited from the Apologeticall Dialogue which concludes *The Poetaster.* Craving the pure austerity of tragedy, sickened like Yeats by false art and false honor, Jonson leaves "the Comic *Muse*"—but not before issuing a last satiric thrust:

> I, that spend halfe my nights, and all my dayes,
>   Here in a cell, to get a darke, pale face,
> To come forth worth the ivy, or the bayes,

And in this age can hope no other grace—
Leave me. There's something come into my thought,
That must, and shall be sung, high, and aloofe,
Safe from the wolves black jaw, and the dull asses hoofe.

[11. 233–39]

With his allusion Yeats invoked the entire Stage Quarrel between
Jonson, Marston, Dekker, others; he had studied it in 1906.[30] Jonson,
thinking himself ridiculed by Ignorance's fustian invective in Marston's
Histriomastix, had retaliated with the character of Clove in *Every Man
Out of His Humour.* After labyrinthine squabblings, Jonson sought a
coup de grâce and produced *The Poetaster,* in which he portrayed
himself as Horace, and Marston and Dekker as the envious, in-
competent, immoral Crispinus and Demetrius. At the court of Augustus
he vindicated both himself and true poetry, stressed as Yeats did the
connection between good art and good government. By quoting Jonson, Yeats's speaker assumes Jonson's nature as his mask, as Jonson had
become Horace; and Moore becomes a composite version of Marston
and Dekker, Crispinus and Demetrius. The allegorical logic is inexorable: Moore's motives in aspersing Yeats are jealousy and envy; his
artistic ability, that of a hack; his character, sinister. Yeats's speaker is a
man of integrity unjustly maligned by a fool. The attack on Moore,
however, remains tactfully muted; like Jonson, Yeats was more concerned with satire than personal vendetta, and he used Jonson's allegory
principally to gain objectivity and stature for his speaker. Joining the
authoritative tradition of public moralists which extends back to
Horace, the speaker denounces folly and praises excellence in terms
made seemingly absolute by virtue of the classical tradition to which he
appeals. He takes strength from Jonson's relentless wit, his tough
refusal to relinquish the poet's role of discerning true value. Yet he
cannot match Jonson, who self-confidently *intends* to get "Beyond the
fling of the dull ass's hoof." He wishes he could, but cannot; "Ben
Jonson's phrase" seethes with ferocity precisely because he has only
verbal analogies to use in self-defense. Coole, its bust of Maecenas in the
garden, remains excruciatingly distant; and the poem thus becomes, in
this respect, the most unusual country house poem in the genre: its
speaker must sing Coole's praises from afar.

---

30 W. B. Yeats, *The Letters of W. B. Yeats,* ed. Allan Wade (London: Hart-Davis,
1954), pp. 478–79. A brief account of the quarrel may be found in Ben Jonson,
The Works of Ben Jonson, eds. C. H. Herford and Percy Simpson (Oxford:
Clarendon, 1925), I: 24–31. All subsequent references to Jonson are to this edition,
11 vols. (Oxford: Clarendon, 1925–52).

III

> Nay, sometimes it is the reward of a mans study,
> the praise of quoting an other man fitly.
>
> —Jonson, *Discoveries*[31]

Yeats's allusion to Jonson, one of his most intricate maskings, shows his immersion in Jonson's thought. His prose and letters give ample evidence that he knew the *Conversations* with Drummond of Hawthornden, *Discoveries,* most of the plays and masques. There is no external evidence, however, that he knew the nondramatic poetry—in particular the two country house poems, "To Penshurst" and "To Sir Robert Wroth," from which he crafted his own version of the genre. As Mr. McAlindon has said, one *hears* extensive "resemblances" between Yeats and Jonson; these include a shared aristocratic ideology, "syntax and epigram-theme,"[32] vocabulary and rhythm. Mr. Davie has argued that Jonson "presides" over "A Prayer for My Daughter."[33] But proof of Yeats's actual debt to Jonson's verse has been elusive. The following list is therefore as specific as possible.

I have already mentioned Coole's "ancient roof" and the "ancient pile" of "To Penshurst." Jonson's praise of Sir Robert Wroth,

> Nor throng'st (when masquing is) to have a sight
> Of the short braverie of the night;
> To view the jewels, stuffes, the paines, the wit
> There wasted, some not paid for yet!
> ["To Sir Robert Wroth," 11.9—12]

may have prompted Yeats's barb in "To a Shade":

> If you have revisited the town, thin Shade,
> Whether to look upon your monument
> (I wonder if the builder has been paid) . . .

Lady Mary Wroth was born a Sidney; in Epigram CIII Jonson used her father's name to symbolize her greatness. Mr. McAlindon thinks[34] that

---

31 Jonson, *Works*, VIII: 616—17.

32 McAlindon, "Yeats and the English Renaissance," p. 167.

33 Donald Davie, *"Michael Robartes and the Dancer,"* in *An Honoured Guest: New Essays on W. B. Yeats*, eds. Denis Donoghue and J. R. Mulryne (London: Edward Arnold, 1965), pp. 82—84.

34 McAlindon, "Yeats and the English Renaissance," p. 168.

Yeats's technique of turning the surname into a symbol—"Our Sidney
and our perfect man"—derives from "To the Immortall Memorie, and
Friendship of that Noble Paire, Sir Lucius Cary, and Sir H. Morison":

> You liv'd to be the great surnames,
> And titles, by which all made claimes
> Unto the Vertue. Nothing perfect done,
> But as a Cary, or a Morison.
>   [11. 113–16]

"And all he did done perfectly" ("In Memory of Major Robert Gregory," X) lends the suggestion credence; but the technique, typically
Jonsonian, appears elsewhere, as in the epigram "On Lucy Countesse of
Bedford" (LXXVI), a woman whose relationship with Donne fascinated
Yeats.[35] Given Yeats's interest in Sidney, it seems unlikely that he
would have missed the "Ode. To Sir William Sydney, on his Birth-day";
his colloquial opening to the Gregory elegy,

> Now that we're almost settled in our house
> I'll name the friends that cannot sup with us
> Beside a fire of turf in th' ancient tower,

ironically recalls Jonson's joyous, ceremonial beginning ("Now that the
harth is crown'd with smiling fire"). Yeats's self-deprecation later in the
elegy, "Some burn damp faggots" (XI), probably derives from "An
Execration upon Vulcan": "Or in small Fagots have him blaze about /
Vile Tavernes, and the Drunkards pisse him out" (11. 185–86). When
Yeats wrote, in "In Memory of Eva Gore-Booth and Con Markiewicz,"

> Arise and bid me strike a match
> And strike another till time catch,

he remembered more of Jonson's incendiary fury in the "Execration":

> Meddle with your match,
> And the strong lines, that so the time doe catch,
> Or Captaine Pamphlets horse, and foot . . . .
>   [11. 77–9]

Yeats's phrase, "break the teeth of Time" ("The New Faces") varies
Jonson's image—"stryke the eare of tyme"—in "Yff Men, and tymes

35 *Letters*, p. 571.

were nowe" (1. 32). Another ode, "Come leave the loathed Stage," influenced not only the general conception of "The Fascination of What's Difficult" but its quality of exasperation. Yeats's imitation of rough Jonsonian rhythm is particularly noticeable: compare "Runne on, and rage, sweat, censure, and condemn" (Jonson) with "Shiver under the lash, strain, sweat and jolt" (Yeats). In "The Gyres," Yeats's enigmatic "Rocky Face" echoes Jonson's sardonic self-portrait in "My Picture Left in Scotland": "My mountaine belly, and my rockie face." Finally, there is a strong connection between Jonson's "Eupheme" (I) and Yeats's "A Prayer for My Son" (II): in each case the poet blesses the child's cradle, knowing that Envy of a laurel crown (Jonson) or "hatred of the bays" (Yeats) will seek to destroy the child's predestined greatness.

Yeats's relationship with Jonson was personal as well as literary; his essay on Jonson, projected but not written,[36] would have differed vastly from Eliot's, which impersonally conceals Jonson behind his work. Yeats, impelled to discover the temperament which generated the art, would have explored Jonson's life, the glittering intellectual and social milieu he enjoyed, the crotchety gloom of his later years; naturally approving Jonson's scorn for an encroaching democracy which was destroying the old Anglo-French nation, he would have praised Jonson above his contemporaries for being the most perspicuous if not impartial analyst of that cultural crisis. And he would have extolled Jonson's unassuageable Platonic vision of a perfect and just society. Jonson was Yeats's most natural kin among Renaissance writers; he expressed both what Yeats was and what Yeats sought to become: duellist,[37] scholar, poet, and implicitly "a true epitome of the whole mass, a Herrick and Dr. Johnson in the same body"[38] Unlike Shakespeare, Jonson was vivid to Yeats. Hot-tempered, he quarreled violently—yet praised Lady Aubigny's impervious calm; seeking companionship, he "dominated" the Mermaid Tavern, yet privately served with "cold implacability" Nature's invisible order.[39] Did Yeats think Jonson had reconciled these tensions? Was Jonson's satiric rancor the "loam of his Eden," as Yeats once remarked of Donne's obscenity;[40] or was it more like Swift's "blood-sodden breast" dragging him helplessly down into a humankind forever practicing an evil he could not

---

[36] Ibid., pp. 478–79.

[37] *A Vision*, p. 153.

[38] *Autobiography*, pp. 251–52. By contrast, Shakespeare's actual personality seemed "faint and passionless" to Yeats (*A Vision*, p. 153).

[39] *A Vision*, p. 153; *Explorations*, p. 445.

[40] *Letters*, p. 570.

control? Yeats, when he created emblems of aristocratic perfection, frequently enhanced their greatness by self-deprecation. Did he learn this method from Jonson, who used his epistles—to Lady Aubigny, Elizabeth Countess of Rutland, John Selden—to explore his own limitations and furnish himself images to imitate?[41] Did Yeats see in the poetry Jonson's painful struggle for humility and moderation, a self-perfection beyond his discipline, his "acute social insecurity clothing itself in the mantle of achieved status"?[42] Yeats and Jonson were both poet-celebrants seeking to become poet-aristocrats: would Jonson have appeared in Yeats's essay as an incipient Keats, the "coarse-bred son" of a bricklayer who made "Luxuriant song" from an aristocratic world to which he did not quite belong? If Yeats chose to create analogies between himself and Jonson, the material was ample.

Yeats, as he sought a passionate but natural style to toughen his outward image, was undeniably drawn to Jonson's public manner. "*Language* most shewes a man: speake that I may see thee."[43] Unlike Spenser, Jonson spoke in his own voice, a sinewy self-dramatizing speech whose infinite modulations, contrapuntal rhythms, complicated syntax all revealed the mind in action. Simultaneously, and without becoming a poetry "of the surface,"[44] it retained the "high breeding" Yeats respected, the manly dignity of a "plaine and customary" language sanctioned by "the consent of the Learned."[45] Jonson enacted his public role with superb invention and grace, distinguishing true from false aristocracy, lambasting the morally disfigured. Proudly antidemocratic, "at fewd / With sinne and vice,"[46] Jonson tutored Yeats in satire, showed him that outspokenness on contemporary issues need not sacrifice poetry to propaganda. He proved to Yeats that the insistent praise of existing aristocratic excellence was no less a subject-matter than the ineffectual celebration of lost heroic glory.

Jonson sharpened Yeats's Spenserian sense of ceremony; almost

---

[41] McAlindon ("Yeats and the English Renaissance," p. 167) remarks on *The Forrest* and *The Under-Wood* that "Jonson's noble friends, as well as a select group of poets and scholars," constitute "a kind of mythology of ideal types."

[42] Jonas A. Barish, *Ben Jonson and the Language of Prose Comedy* (Cambridge: Harvard University Press, 1967), p. 89.

[43] Jonson, *Works*, VIII: 625.

[44] T. S. Eliot, *Selected Essays, 1917–1932* (New York: Harcourt, Brace, 1932), p. 128. In emphasizing the depth in Jonson's style, Yeats anticipated current tendencies in Jonson criticism, as he had also heralded the recent understanding that Shakespeare's attitude towards Henry V was less than complimentary (*Essays*, pp. 103–8).

[45] *Essays*, p. 253; Jonson, *Works*, VIII: 620, 622.

[46] Jonson, "Epistle. To Katherine, Lady Aubigny," ll. 9–10.

certainly his essay would have discussed "the ideal of life that flitted before the imagination of Jonson and the others when they thought of the Court."[47] Jonson's ideal society, in the masques, reflected the absolute order of the Divine Mind; with all evils exorcised, all threats of usurpation ritually banished, it was a "small circle of men and women" whose masks revealed rather than concealed their true natures. That mystical concord between internal and external forms, a part of Jonson's assiduous attention to the moral aspects of courtesy, touched Yeats profoundly—so much so that, years later, Stockholm's eighteenth-century pageantry merged with his memories of Jonson's address to Elizabeth's court:

> Thou art a beautiful and brave spring and waterest all the noble plants of this Island. In thee the whole Kingdom dresseth itself and is ambitious to use thee as her glass. Beware then thou render men's figures truly and teach them no less to hate their deformities, than to love their forms.[48]

As "Upon a House . . ." and the epilogue to *Responsibilities* demonstrate, Yeats readily assimilated Jonson's conviction that the nobility were the nation's model of imitation. He was struck, too, by Jonson's tone, the decorous and self-respecting pride in his conclusion: "Thy servant but not slave, Ben Jonson." The phrase, reinforcing Yeats's ideal of reciprocity between poet and aristocrat, showed Jonson's ethics: blood and rank mattered far less than the virtues they could nevertheless symbolize. As "To a Wealthy Man . . ." and "To a Friend . . ." make plain, Yeats admired Jonson's complete integrity in advising the aristocracy upon whom he depended both for financial support and imaginative stimulus. Jonson knew that the ideal court of his masques was a fiction; but he at least moved, Yeats believed, in a society sufficiently beautiful to validate its mythology. As "master of ceremony," he stirred Yeats's envy. Writing a court poetry was obviously impossible for Yeats,[49] and he had no taste for glorifying the Anglo-Irish as a class. But as the Coole poems discussed above indicate, a country house poetry was still feasible; and Yeats appropriated Jonson's form with extraordinary resourcefulness.

---

[47] *Letters*, pp. 478–79.

[48] *Autobiography*, p. 463. See the Epistle Dedicatory to Jonson's *Cynthia's Revels*.

[49] Yeats tried to write a masque (*Letters*, p. 411) but must have known that the genre could not flourish in such adverse soil as the modern world; he would have understood why Auden, in *The Age of Anxiety*, could use the masque only for parodistic purposes. In the Berg Collection of the New York Public Library there is

Wyatt's conclusion to "Of the Courtier's Life, written to John Poins" conveniently anticipates some central features of the country house poem: "But I am here in Kent and Christendom, / Among the Muses, where I read and rhyme." Wyatt consciously demarcates the national, religious, and aesthetic spirituality of his soil. Jonson makes a similar demarcation when he states: "Thou art not, Penshurst, built to envious show." So too, as he invokes the *beatus ille* tradition: "How blest art thou, canst love the countrey, Wroth." So also Yeats, not only in "A Prayer on Going into My House" but when, in "Upon a House . . .," he immediately opposes "the world" and Coole. The genre deals with a consecrated place set apart from the corruption of city and court alike, a place of peace where art and nature collaborate. The estate is a microcosm of God's kingdom. "Their lords have built, but thy lord dwells," Jonson concludes "To Penshurst": beyond the contrast between tradition and new money, his praise implies that Penshurst's true lord is God, Whose own vicegerent King James finds the estate no less hospitable. In Marvell's "Upon Appleton House," the *"Architect"*—of the house, the poem, and its speaker—is, finally, God. In Yeats the religious elements of Elizabethan hierarchy are far less conspicuous, and nature is often hostile. But the hierarchic ideal prevails: in "Upon a House . . .," Coole is the aristocratic source of good government; in "Coole Park and Ballylee," the house remains a place "Where none has *reigned* that lacked a name and fame." The model of perfect human society, the estate is also the ground of imaginative freedom, whether that freedom derives from Christianity or the magical presence of swans. A paradigm of civilized excellence, it seems transcendent. Yet the whole point of a country house poem, far from being restricted to the praise of a friend or patron, is that such a world actually exists. Edenic or utopian dream coincides with reality: Jonson gourmandizes at Pembroke's table; Yeats walks near the catalpa tree with Lady Gregory.

The visible emblem of this special world, its permanence and continuity, is the house. Because Jonson created the genre and Yeats adopted it in periods of extensive social upheaval, permanence has a specific meaning. To Jonson, the inflation of honors under James I had eroded Tudor aristocratic power; since new titles could be bought, the identification of rank with excellence was nullified; the purchase of property invalidated the traditional symbol of aristocratic virtue—

---

a plot-outline for a masque entitled "Opening Ceremony for Masquers." It is signed "WBY" in Lady Gregory's hand, and undated; but Hone states that Yeats belonged to a group called The Masquers which functioned sporadically during the spring and summer of 1903 (*W. B. Yeats* [1943; rpt. London: Macmillan, 1965], p. 192).

land;[50] money had depersonalized human relationships; the decline of
the extended family, together with the disappearance of the "great
hall" in country house architecture, hastened the end of "hospitality."[51] Yeats's fear was the complete elimination of aristocratic
culture: land reform and the rise of "new" middle-class "faces," peasant emigrations, nationalist enmity toward Anglo-Irish tradition—all
portended Coole's dissolution. Throughout the genre the country house
is a conservative structure; geographically, morally, politically, it is the
center of traditional society, unity of culture.

Feudal organization alone, however, cannot account for Jonson's
and Yeats's unique emphasis on the presence of the peasantry. They
seek to show that the amplitude of aristocratic hospitality at Penshurst,
Durrants, and Coole integrates all social groups. Yeats, moreover, because his peasantry embody an imaginative ideal, considers their presence a sign of the self-perfecting aristocratic sensibility which constantly seeks innocence through imitation. In "To Penshurst" and "To
Sir Robert Wroth," the peasantry flock into the houses, impelled not
by grievances ("To Penshurst," 1. 50; "To Sir Robert Wroth," 11.
61—62) but by the joyous desire to express a love no less abundant than
the produce they bring as gifts. Although Jonson's society hardly lacks
economic distinctions, aristocratic "Freedome doth with degree dis-
pense" ("To Sir Robert Wroth," 1. 58).[52] Courtesy and Christian
liberty create an egalitarian spirit resembling that of "soft" pastoral:
"As if in Saturnes raigne it were" ("To Sir Robert Wroth," 1. 50). In
Yeats's "Shepherd and Goatherd," a pastoral elegy deeply indebted to
the country house poem, Gregory's death brings the peasantry to
Coole: the Shepherd, having been in the house earlier that day, knows
of Lady Gregory's fortitude; both he and the Goatherd, ceremoniously
observing decorum, plan to leave their elegies at Coole's door. Although
Coole's ancient roof more typically shelters "traveller, scholar, poet"
("Coole Park," IV), a coterie explicitly dedicated to Ireland's cultural

---

[50] See Charles Molesworth, "Property and Virtue: The Genre of the Country-
House Poem in the Seventeenth Century," *Genre* I (1968): 146. Lawrence Stone's
The Crisis of the Aristocracy, 1558—1641 (London: Oxford University Press, 1965)
is extraordinarily useful for understanding the social context in which Jonson wrote
his poems.

[51] For a concise discussion of the effects of architectural change upon the genre of
the country house poem, see G. R. Hibbard, "The Country House Poem in the
Seventeenth Century," in *Essential Articles for the Study of Alexander Pope*, ed.
Maynard Mack (Hamden, Conn.: Archon, 1964), pp. 403—5.

[52] Hibbard's comment is to the point: "It is precisely because there is general
acceptance of the idea of degree, with all that it entails, that degree can be
dispensed with" ("The Country House Poem," p. 415).

welfare, "Coole Park and Ballylee" (VI) acknowledges debts of con-
siderable magnitude to the "book of the people." In both these poems
Yeats treats hospitality more narrowly than Jonson, but the richness
ascribed to communal activity—"A dance-like glory that those walls
begot" ("Coole Park," I)—is much the same.

The central concern with preserving traditional culture focusses on
family lineage. Coole, once imaging Tara revived, stands upon "A spot
whereon the founders lived and died" ("Coole Park and Ballylee," V);
its "ancestral trees," like Penshurst's copse "nam'd of Gamage" (1. 19),
link familial continuity with nature's permanence. The reiterated pun
on "breeding," as in "Upon a House . . .," fuses organic creation with
the personal excellence which results from intelligent nurture. Jonson's
penultimate glorification of Penshurst—"Thy lady's noble, fruitfull,
chaste withall" (1. 90)—is more than conventional compliment: the
Countess' chaste fertility mirrors the moral element in the natural order
and illustrates the proper use of God's abundance; as such, it fittingly
climaxes a poem whose every detail reveals humankind's complete,
self-regulated harmony with the environment. In Yeats, family continuity remains a symbol of social and natural order: "Shepherd and
Goatherd" establishes careful correspondences between Gregory's family and the Shepherd's flock. Gregory's death, however, compelled
Yeats to alter his adumbration of the dynastic theme. He transferred his
concern with living tradition from Coole to Thoor Ballylee—"God grant
a blessing on this tower and cottage / And on my heirs" ("A Prayer on
Going into My House"). The theme recurs in "A Prayer for My
Daughter" and, more fiercely, in "Meditations in Time of Civil War" (I,
IV), where the threat of family dissolution has catastrophic personal
and historical ramifications.

The distinguishing characteristic of Jonson's and Yeats's country
house poems, and the highest excellence of the houses they praise, is
that Penshurst and Coole generate heirs *and* poets. The conjunction has
a clear historical dimension: a "written speech," like the building and
its children, perpetuates values considered indispensable to civilization.
Jonson's "On my First Sonne" presents the connection between making children and making poems in quintessential form:

> Rest in soft peace, and, ask'd, say here doth lye
> Ben. Jonson his best piece of poetrie.
>
> [Epigram XLV]

In the "Epistle to Elizabeth Countess of Rutland," Elizabeth carries not
only Sidney's blood but, potentially, his poetic greatness:

> For what a sinne 'gainst your great fathers spirit,
> Were it to thinke, that you should not inherit
> His love unto the Muses, when his skill
> Almost you have, or may have, when you will?
>
> [11. 31–34]

Jonson follows this anticipatory praise with its complement: "My best of wishes, may you beare a sonne" (1. 100). As with Yeats's balancing of passion and courtesy, aristocratic excellence equilibrates marital fertility with the fertility of the imagination. In "To Penshurst," as Jonson gracefully commends not the potential existence but the reality of a consummate tradition for which the house itself is the final symbol, child and poet—Sidney—are born simultaneously; the "taller tree" commemorating his "great birth" becomes an organic symbol of his personal and imaginative growth (11. 13–14). Yeats, skipping over Carew, Herrick, Marvell, and Pope, picks up the same configuration. "Upon a House . . .," an early and baroque example, shows why the cluster attracted him: it harmonizes the antinomies of body and soul, nature and art within a single architecture located upon a consecrated "spot." In "Shepherd and Goatherd," Gregory is both poet-musician and heir; to Coole he wills the Elizabethan tokens of his immortality, his children, and "half a score" of "lofty pipe tunes." But Yeats's manipulation of this configuration, because it evoked intense torments about his sexual adequacy, self-completion, self-perpetuation, is usually more drastic than Jonson's. "Pardon, Old Fathers" is its most frightening manifestation: the poet can produce only poems, not children. Both "A Prayer for My Son" and particularly "A Prayer for My Daughter" answer its desperation: child, heir, incipient poet seem the same. The transformation scene in "A Prayer for My Daughter" (VI) epitomizes the luminous fusion of aesthetic and natural creation; by the poem's end, the speaker can envisage Anne, both a poet and the mother of innocence and beauty, dwelling in "a house / Where all's accustomed, ceremonious."

The basis of the genre is the correspondence between the aristocrat and his architecture. Unlike Spenser's houses, whose external appearance often belies the life inside,[53] Jonson's and Yeats's houses accurately reflect the spiritual and aesthetic values its inhabitants hold. Not simply because they represent an ideal life inside but because they represent without distortion, these houses are perfect artifacts, the realization of an Edenic art in which the symbol and the values

---

53 The Hous of Holiness, of course, is the notable exception (*Faerie Queene*, I.x).

symbolized are identical. When Yeats deviates from the principle of correspondence, as in "The New Faces," he does so in order to validate it. So also in "Meditations . . ." (I.iii):

> But when the master's buried mice can play,
> And maybe the great-grandson of that house,
> For all its bronze and marble, 's but a mouse.

The house contains the tradition established by a "haughtier age" (I.v); the discrepancy between the present inhabitant and his dwelling shows his betrayal. In the ideal world of the country house in its pristine state, such discrepancies between mind and physical environment do not exist.

In applying the principle of correspondence to Penshurst and Coole, Jonson and Yeats studiously avoid describing their exteriors.[54] The outside is but the body, not the soul; spiritual beauty, not material possession, is the proper result of "leisure, wealth, privilege." As Marvell writes of Appleton House, "*Humility* alone designs / Those short but admirable Lines" (11. 41–42). Jonson's "description" of Penshurst brilliantly describes nothing physical:

> Thou art not, Penshurst, built to envious show,
> Of touch, or marble; nor canst boast a row
> Of polish'd pillars, or a roofe of gold:
> Thou hast no lantherne, whereof tales are told;
> Or stayre, or courts; but stand'st an ancient pile,
> And these grudg'd at, art reverenc'd the while.
>
> [11. 1–6]

To demonstrate that proud ostentation has no part in Penshurst's life, he makes the house invisible; the literary trick works. Invisibility suggests moderation, spirituality, and—paradoxically—solidity. As Jonson implicitly describes houses built by the newly rich, the reader's

---

54 The argument that Coole, "plain and box-like" (*Autobiography*, p. 334), offered Yeats little material to work with is irrelevant; the salient point is that Yeats's description of Coole comes in the prose, not the poetry. Cf. Marjorie Perloff, "*'Another* Emblem There': Theme and Convention in Yeats's 'Coole Park and Ballylee, 1931,'" *Journal of English and Germanic Philology* 69 (1970): 235–36. Perloff argues that because Coole and Fairfax's Nunappleton House were "relatively modest houses," it was "natural, therefore, for Marvell and Yeats to celebrate the moderation, the proper use of riches of their patrons, and to contemplate the landscape rather than to characterize banquet halls and galleries." The argument from nature obscures the ethical intent behind Marvell's and Yeats's suppression of external description.

visual imagination is uncomfortably buffeted from detail to detail—until Jonson concludes his praise of Penshurst with a nonvisual clause which stresses unitary wholeness: "but stand'st an ancient pile." Self-aggrandizing indulgence in architectural show is morally and aesthetically corrupt.[55] The truest art is the most natural; and Penshurst, a *locus amoenus,* is "faire" because it enjoys (i.e., has) and *takes joy in* "better markes, of soyle, of ayre, / Of wood, of water" (11. 7—8). In creating Penshurst's interior, Jonson makes the presence of physical details as significant as their earlier omission. Its most remarkable feature is spaciousness; structural elements—floors (1. 70), rooms (1. 87)—are not barriers. Free and open space corresponds to the hospitality and sense of Christian liberty which characterizes Penshurst's communal life.[56] Objects, emblems of ethical demeanor, provide a physical focus for social experience and make celebration tangible. In the central hall is Pembroke's "liberall boord" (1. 59), loaded with abundance. Beacons of warm welcome, the "fires / Shine bright on every harth" (11. 77—78). The linen and plate (1. 86), however costly, are valuable because they are *ready,* even for unexpected visits from royalty; they are the outward signs of "high huswifery" (1. 85). Property has a moral use.

Yeats's handling of Coole's interior changes as the series evolves. Although alterations in style and theme, as well as vacillations in the speaker's attitude, affect the mode of presentation, generalizations are still possible. Yeats, like Jonson, makes highly selective use of symbolic detail; as a comparison of "Upon a House . . . " with "Coole Park and Ballylee" indicates, the speaker's consciousness of Coole's architecture and its interior becomes gradually more concrete; yet, unlike Jonson, he is not interested in distinct objects. His most thoroughly Jonsonian passage is atypical:

> She goes about her house erect and calm
> Between the pantry and the linen-chest.
> ["Shepherd and Goatherd"]

These details have simplicity, clarity. But while the classical plainness wholly suits Lady Gregory's stoic belief that daily rhythms must continue unbroken, it lacks the impressionism characteristic of Yeats's method. The books mentioned in "Coole Park and Ballylee" (IV)

---

[55] See Jonson's condemnation of Inigo Jones for thinking "Painting and Carpentry . . . the Soule of Masque!" ("An Expostulacion with Inigo Jones," 1. 50).

[56] Spenser attributes a similar meaning to open spaces—known through the free, unimpeded movement of bodies—in delineating the Hous of Holinesse (*Faerie Queene,* I.x); compare the claustrophobia of the Hous of Pryde (I.iv).

almost disappear in a welter of significant associations: the Gregorys'
love of literature (a love now dying with Lady Gregory's approaching
death), the speaker's love for those books, famous binders from unknown countries who had not lost "the old nonchalance of the hand."
The detailed descriptions of Coole's interior in *Dramatis Personae* are
no gloss on Coole the poetic symbol. You cannot explain "old pictures
everywhere" ("Coole Park and Ballylee," IV) by reference to the
"mezzotints and engravings of the masters and friends of the old
Gregorys that hung round the small downstairs breakfast room, Pitt,
Fox, Lord Wellesley . . . ."[57] Beyond evoking the love of art intrinsic
to the Gregory tradition, the real point of the phrase lies in its
indeterminacy, a vague plethora calculated to produce an impression of
indefinable visual richness.

   Yeats masses units of space similarly. In the prose, Coole has a
drawing-room, a breakfast room, and so forth. But the poems speak of
"old rooms," "all those rooms and passages," "Great rooms." These
phrases all but refuse to perform their function of defining spaces;
instead, they generate a sense of multiplicity, an intricate vastness
which corresponds to the varied resonances of the Gregory tradition. At
his best Yeats conveys that vastness not through rhetoric but, paradoxically, through the empirical observation of spatial relations:

> Sound of a stick upon the floor, a sound
> From somebody that toils from chair to chair;
> Beloved books that famous hands have bound,
> Old marble heads, old pictures everywhere;
> Great rooms . . .

                    ["Coole Park and Ballylee," IV]

Lady Gregory takes small steps; the distance "from chair to chair" is
relatively short, but for a sick person much greater. Here Yeats shifts
from horizontal to vertical and centrifugal movements: floor, stick,
books and hands (waist-level), marble heads, pictures on the walls.
Through the arrangement of objects, he has led the reader's eye out to
the library's furthest reaches. Through carefully calibrated increases in
dimension, he has made the size of the "Great" rooms self-evident. His
speaker's awareness of Coole's "great" tradition follows as a matter of
course; ingeniously, precise measurement validates an emotion of inexplicable magnitude. Yeats's interior details have just enough definition to ensure that their real indefiniteness matters. The ultimate

[57] *Autobiography*, pp. 333–34.

correlative of this indefiniteness is mystery; and that, finally, is what Coole possesses and Penshurst lacks.

"Jonson has provided no creative stimulus for a very long time," Eliot wrote before Yeats had produced his major poems about Coole and Thoor Ballylee; "consequently we must look back as far as Dryden—precisely, a poetic practitioner who learned from Jonson— before we find a living criticism of Jonson's work."[58] Yeats's poems offer such a criticism: they clarify the nature of Jonson's work; so also, Jonson's poems put Yeats's in perspective. Yeats's premises in modifying Jonson's genre emerge most strikingly in the "tower" poems. These, founded no less than the Coole poems on the correspondence between mind and house, manifest that correspondence in ways Jonson did not conceive. The unassailable difference between Penshurst and Thoor Ballylee is not architectural. It is, rather, that the tower is a kinetic, not a static, symbol; it alters shape and character according to the speaker's emotional condition, both from poem to poem and within a single poem:

> And what if my descendants lose the flower
> Through natural declension of the soul,
> Through too much business with the passing hour,
> Through too much play, or marriage with a fool?
> May this laborious stair and this stark tower
> Become a roofless ruin that the owl
> May build in the cracked masonry and cry
> Her desolation to the desolate sky.
>
> ["Meditations . . .," IV.ii]

By imagining his building's transformation, the speaker thinks about the tower in a completely un-Jonsonian manner. The point is not that Jonson, writing a poem of compliment, cannot think about destructive change, but that he does not consider change at all: Penshurst is not organic. Ownership of the tower of course makes a difference: the soul is not only inside the tower; it permeates its structure. But the spirit's capacity to enter stone is part of Yeats's conception of Coole also: "When she died the great house died too."[59] That statement of causality implies Yeats's further deviation from Jonson. In Jonson, although mind and house correspond, they share no interplay; in Yeats,

---

58 Eliot, *Selected Essays*, p. 127.

59 *Letters*, p. 796. See "Coole Park" (I): "A dance-like glory that those walls *begot*."

the interplay is rich, and the mind acts as if it dominates material reality.

Principally Romantic, Yeats's criticism of Jonson entails matters of history and self-dramatization. What motivates "Upon a House . . ." is not the poet's desire to praise his patrons' hospitality, but a land-reform bill which threatens the estate. The public theme of "The New Faces," dispossession, emerges through the speaker's private turmoil. Personal crisis generates the epilogue to *Responsibilities*. These poems, like those which follow, are far more "occasional" than Jonson's. They belong to temporal process; Clio is their muse. Jonson's worlds exist in "Saturnes raigne," an eternal cycle untouched by generation and decay, much less any thought of "gradual Time's last gift."

> In spring, oft roused for thy masters sport,
>   Who, for it, makes thy house his court;
> Or with thy friends; the heart of all the yeere,
>   Divid'st, upon the lesser Deere;
> In autumne, at the Partrich makes a flight,
>   And giv'st thy gladder guests the sight;
> And, in the winter, hunt'st the flying hare,
>   More for thy exercise, then fare.
>   ["To Sir Robert Wroth," 11. 23–30]

This catalogue, like calendar miniatures from some Book of Hours, so stylizes time that change all but vanishes from consciousness. In both this poem and "To Penshurst," Jonson—omniscient—uses an "eternal" present tense; he thus eliminates all possibility of future threat. Even the past disappears. King James's visit is a "past" event ("To Penshurst," 11. 76–88), but what can "past" mean in a world eternally present? Jonson denies linear time; he praises in no season. Compare Yeats, who uses particular times not only to create symbolic tensions but to validate his vision, his presence in a scene: "The New Faces" occurs *before* nightfall and *after* Lady Gregory's illness; the epilogue to *Responsibilities,* in winter—*after* summer has passed. The result of Jonson's omniscience, in "To Penshurst," is that he is not actually present in the landscape he evokes with such confident familiarity; it is, consequently, a shock to find him dining at Pembroke's table. But Jonson the omniscient observer is, again, not dramatically present: he visualizes himself eating a meal which is not an actual event prior to 1616 but a symbol of continuous hospitality. Penshurst is an ideal world Jonson has made, but never experienced; desiring to *find* an uncorrupted portion of the fallen world, he purifies a great deal.[60] The

---

60 Cf. Hibbard ("The Country House Poem," p. 403), who remarks that the world of Penshurst is "slightly idealized, perhaps."

poem's magnificence is its sleight-of-hand, its illusion that Penshurst obeys the same principles of reality as "our" world. But Nature's world, as Sidney said, "is brazen, the poets only deliver a golden."[61] That atemporal condition is one which Yeats's Coole never enjoys.

Jonson is a voice, not an actor. His discursive presentation, the factuality of his seemingly dramatic observation, is meant to assert that his world has an objective existence. But his observation is logical, not natural: his eyes never blink. "To Penshurst" progresses according to preordained designs of order; Jonson himself does not "appear" until the poem has moved sufficiently far up the Great Chain of Being for humankind—especially poets—to be present. Spatializing the hierarchical design, the poem's centripetal organization stresses family unity: after the introduction, it moves from outlying grounds to the house; inside, it focusses first on the circle of society and finally on the nuclear family. Within this structure, from which Yeats learned immensely (see, e.g., "Meditations . . .," I–II), Jonson's transitions are brilliant, but they do not reflect a fallible human mind. They show, instead, the infallible order of the universe. Look how he gets from the grounds to the house, from nature to humankind:

> The blushing apricot, and woolly peach
> Hang on thy walls, that every child may reach.
>
> [11. 43–44]

The Great Chain continues unbroken; the teleology of the universe is plain, for the peach and apricot exist *so that* children may reach; accidents do not occur (King James's "accidental" arrival is included to illustrate that courtesy easily absorbs accidents into normal pattern). Compare Yeats:

> I meditate upon a swallow's flight,
> Upon an aged woman and her house,
> A sycamore and lime-tree lost in night
> Although that western cloud is luminous,
> Great works constructed there in nature's spite
> For scholars and for poets after us,
> Thoughts long knitted into a single thought,
> A dance-like glory that those walls begot.
>
> ["Coole Park," I]

This, admittedly, is Yeats's most random stanza. Unlike Penshurst's systematized wholeness, Coole's order is not self-evident. The speaker

---

61 *Defense of Poesy*, ed. Dorothy M. Macardle (London: Macmillan, 1963), p. 7.

seeks meaning from apparently inscrutable images; he knows there must be a principle of organization, but not until the last line does he discover a unifying image which closes the fantastic gaps in his associations. The unity he recognizes, typically, is not a rational order but an emotional consciousness of unity which emerges because he has found an adequate language: self-discovery and discovery of Coole occur simultaneously. Such a drama is not Jonsonian. Yeats's speakers, freed from omniscience, act in concrete historical situations, undergo sudden transformations. What they see is sometimes wholly unexpected: "Another emblem there!" ("Coole Park and Ballylee," III). The sequence of images seemingly emanates from an invisible flow of the exploring mind, not from rationalized observation. The objects, the landscapes have some kind of external existence; but they are so permeated by the speaker's consciousness that you cannot discern whether emotion follows perception or causes it. This is Yeats's radical subjectivity, and the chief means by which he creates wonder.

Not Yeats's mind only, but his "body thinks." Physical action, a second language, incorporates thought and emotion. In "The Wild Swans at Coole" (III), the difference in the muscular pressure of a footstep embodies the psychological discrepancy between past and present experiences. Physical movement may be actual: "I pace upon the battlements" ("The Tower," II.i). An imagined future action may imply the speaker's present behavior: "Here, traveller, scholar, poet, take your stand" ("Coole Park," IV). Movement may involve its opposite, immobility—as in Self's refusal to stand and do Soul's bidding ("A Dialogue of Self and Soul," I.ii) and the thwarted escape to Coole in the epilogue to *Responsibilities*. So entirely does movement reflect emotion that any change in its verbal definition signifies an altered consciousness. If Yeats had written, "I *walk* upon the battlements," he would have quelled his speaker's defiant restlessness. Yeats's habit of defining his speaker's dramatic presence by showing his physical action derives largely from Browning—and Marvell, who revolutionized English poetry when, in "Upon Appleton House," he turned the Jonsonian country house poem into a topographical poem through whose landscape the speaker actually walks, creating reality as he observes it. Thus, in "The New Faces," "catalpa-tree and scented lime" appear because the speaker roves "the garden gravel"; in "Meditations . . ." (II.i–ii), the speaker's world comes into existence as he walks from the "ancient bridge" to his study, designating details of landscape and architecture as he passes. Bodily movement simultaneously creates space and transforms it into an extension of consciousness: the speaker will "Climb up the *narrow*" stairs because he feels trapped ("In Memory of Major Robert Gregory," I). Present movement in space can also validate a visionary reality, as Chaucer knew in "The Parliament of Fowls," when his speaker dreams of Nature's assembly on a "hil of floures": "unethe was there space / For me to stonde, so ful was al the place" (11. 314–15). That intimately felt claustrophobia makes the dream entirely tangible. When in "Meditations . . ." (VII.v) Yeats's speaker turns away and shuts the door, he creates a physical barrier between himself and a nightmare of future desolation which his very action has rendered physically present. Similarly, the bodily movement from tower to country house in "Coole Park and Ballylee" concretizes his symbolic vision of Irish history: as he passes through seven centuries, he also walks on solid earth.

For Yeats, no mode other than the dramatic present would suffice. He understood, as Marvell had before him, that Jonson's disembodied voice militated against Jonson's own claim that his Edenic world could actually be visited. Yet the world of Penshurst, although Jonson is not an actor, abounds in movement: King James arrives while the Countess is away; "all come in, the farmer, and the clowne" (1. 48); the servants can go "below." These movements give spatial reality to a realm which lacks a significant temporal dimension. The consequence of that reality ought to be that anyone can enter the territory. But Jonson's laws of space are metaphysical and moral, not existential: the corrupt external world cannot impinge. An inviolable boundary immunizes Penshurst from modernity. The real action behind the poem—the movement of history, socioeconomic change in Jacobean England—is never seriously considered. Jonson is uncomfortably aware of this outer world, and the virtues he celebrates gain power and beauty from that consciousness; but the tension, characteristic of the genre, between these opposed systems of value remains intellectual, static. Mr. Hart's comment that the celebration of Penshurst "is carried out under the aspect of a potentially tragic danger"[62] applies far more accurately to Yeats than to Jonson. No protective boundaries surround Coole or Thoor Ballylee, as poems like "The New Faces" and "Meditations . . ." (V–VI) demonstrate. The threatening movement of time, symbolized by spatial incursion, is everywhere felt.

Yeats's unrelenting emphasis on dynamic energy, on movement in the mind and body of his speaker, constitutes his major modification of Jonson's form. He accepted what Jonson sought but chiefly evaded, the historical reality of the country house. Yeats's country house poems are consequently "about" something quite different from Jonson's: the complex interaction between an individual personality and an ideal, actual world almost lost. More important than the elegiac glorification

[62] Jeffrey Hart, "Ben Jonson's Good Society," *Modern Age* 7 (1963): 61.

and the subjective discovery of value is the interaction itself. In adapting Jonson's form, Yeats was making not only a *speculum perfectionis* but a reflector both of his own emotions and of historical pressures, past and present, creative and destructive alike. What he found in Jonson was a literary map of an agrarian, aristocratic world with which, in the West of Ireland, he was already familiar. The map's value was that it linked important themes—communal coherence, familial and poetic continuities at war with an encroaching modernity—in a single geography whose roads all converged at Coole. It gave him principles of correspondence and modes of organization. In Yeats's hands, such a map was a concrete metaphor of experience, an outline, quite literally, of "old forms, old situations," a large-scale dramatic world in which to move.

The Shadow of
the Tower

Yeats, after he had written his first country house poems, possessed a literary form in whose landscape he was nevertheless an outsider. The speaker of "The New Faces" is present at Coole only by virtue of Lady Gregory's survival; and Yeats sometimes feared to strain the limits of her hospitality.[1] Jonson could not give Yeats what he most craved, a place to live in, a portion of the West of Ireland to which he could lay private claim. "I constantly see people, as a portrait painter, posing them in the mind's eye before such and such a background":[2] the problem with Coole was that it was not *his* background.

Yeats's lack of a house symptomatized his restless anxiety during the years before he purchased Thoor Ballylee. As he wrote *Reveries over Childhood and Youth* (1914), a work dominated by houses, furnishings, interiors, he recognized how much continuity he had lost through frequent changes of place.[3] "The struggle of the fly in marma-

[1] E.g., Yeats wrote to Lady Gregory (December, 1912): "I wish I had stayed on at Coole—when I got your note saying that you wished I had [,] I half made up my mind to start off to you but I might have arrived at the same moment as Robert and Margaret, and you would not have wanted me then." Donald T. Torchiana and Glenn O'Malley, eds., "Some New Letters from W. B. Yeats to Lady Gregory," *Review of English Literature* 4 (1963): 11. Yeats's relations with Robert Gregory and his wife were not always smooth.

[2] W. B. Yeats, *The Autobiography of William Butler Yeats* (New York: Macmillan, 1938), p. 74.

[3] Torchiana and O'Malley, "Some New Letters...," pp. 45–46. Yeats's rooms at Woburn Buildings, London, temporary lodgings which had somehow become permanent, never entirely satisfied him. He wrote to Lady Gregory, just after his marriage: "I wish you could see Woburn Buildings now—nothing changed in plan but little touches here and there, and my own bedroom (the old bathroom) with furniture of unpainted unpolished wood such as for years I have wished for" (*The Letters of W. B. Yeats*, ed. Allan Wade [London: Hart-Davis, 1954], p. 634).

lade" had frayed his nerves: the *Playboy* crisis, the Lane controversy, Moore's attack. His Jonsonian "tavern comrades" from the Rhymers' Club had died, leaving him "in no good repute / With the loud host before the sea";[4] he pondered their chaos and dissipation as if he had but narrowly escaped their mental doom. Synge, "the best labourer," had died in 1909, leaving "all the sheaves to bind" and Yeats in dread of the "monstrous crying of wind."[5] His father had emigrated to America; his uncle George Pollexfen's death in 1910 severed his last major connection with Sligo.[6] He became increasingly introverted and self-critical: "I fear strangers, I fear the representatives of the collective opinion and so rage stupidly & rudely, exaggerating what I feel & think"[7]—and hating his discourtesy. With his collected works published in 1908, he doubted if he could generate enough passion for his poetic vision to survive middle age. "The Magi" (1913) opens with a compensatory affirmation: "Now as at all times I can see in the mind's eye. . . ." In "Lines Written in Dejection" (1915), he was more desperately honest:

> When have I last looked on
> The round green eyes and the long wavering bodies
> Of the dark leopards of the moon?

Reveries, although it summarizes Yeats's past, implies his fear of future blankness. Its structure, having the primary form of a completed life, details an expulsion from the Garden, exile from Ireland and Sligo, known family and places. It opens with images of Creation, Yeats's embarrassed mythification of his origin; the narrative concludes (section xxxii) with the deaths of his Pollexfen grandparents and the destructive pilfering of their house—symbolic events which displace what Yeats might have written of himself. Between these poles, Milton's invocation to *Paradise Lost* (quoted in section xxxi) encapsulates the guilt felt throughout. Closing in a present tense which parallels its beginning, the book is a mental journey whose myth of dispossession remains an aspect of Yeats's present consciousness. Although Mr. Fletcher has argued that the writing of *Reveries* liberated Yeats from

[4] "The Grey Rock."

[5] "To a Child Dancing in the Wind."

[6] B. L. Reid, "The House of Yeats," *Hudson Review* 18 (1965), p. 338, has also noted this point of division in Yeats's life. See also Ian Fletcher, "Rhythm and Pattern in 'Autobiographies,'" in *An Honoured Guest,* eds. Denis Donoghue and J. R. Mulryne (London: Edward Arnold, 1965), p. 166.

[7] Quoted from Yeats's 1908 diary; printed by Richard Ellmann, *Yeats: The Man and the Masks* (1948; rpt. New York: Dutton, n. d.), p. 190.

"guilt, self-pity, historical necessity,"[8] its mythological structure shows an ominous entrance into vacancy, a freedom without meaning. As in *Per Amica Silentia Lunae* (1917), a deep uncertainty hovers over the final section (xxxiii). Gnawed by self-recrimination, defensively disclaiming his poetic ambitions, Yeats had somehow reached a point of transition with no Miltonic "place of rest" in sight:

> For some months now I have lived with my own youth and childhood, ... and I am sorrowful and disturbed. It is not that I have accomplished too few of my plans, for I am not ambitious; but when I think of all the books I have read, and of the wise words I have heard spoken, and of the anxiety I have given to parents and grandparents, and of the hopes that I have had, all life weighed in the scales of my own life seems to me a preparation for something that never happens.[9]

Typically, defeat is not disaster. *Reveries* represents Yeats's necessary attempt, at this crucial juncture, to counterbalance his present rootlessness by merging his lonely "tradition of myself"[10] with the tradition of his family. Its purpose echoes that of "Swedenborg, Mediums, and the Desolate Places" (1914), in which Yeats postulated a network of psychic communication between the living and the dead through which he could expand the operative field of his inner self. Yeats's attention to family, his logical internalization of Jonson and the Renaissance, gave him vivid contact with a personal history reaching back to Tudor times. While critics have ridiculed his affection for the "beautiful silver cup that had belonged to my great-great-grandfather," bearing the Butler crest and dated 1534, Yeats considered such objects "hints of earlier and other creation."[11] His attempt to retain continuities, if it was artificial, reflected the poverty of modernity: "We have the General's portrait," he wrote of an ancestor who had fought with Marlborough, "and he looks very fine in his armour and his long curly wig, and underneath it, after his name, are many honours that have left no tradition among us. *Were we country people, we could have summarised his life in a legend*" [italics mine].[12] Having long distrusted Anglo-Ireland, he was now pleased to think that his family represented, of course with exceptions, its best aspects: civility, professionalism, and respect for scholarship; nimble and fiercely independent

---

8 Fletcher, "Rhythm and Pattern," p. 174.

9 *Autobiography*, p. 94.

10 Ibid., p. 395.

11 Ibid., p. 20; T. S. Eliot, "The Dry Salvages," I, in *Four Quartets*.

12 *Autobiography*, pp. 20–21.

minds; romantic bravery, physical prowess. His friendship with Lady Gregory had brought him far: "I am delighted with all that joins my life to those who had power in Ireland or with those anywhere that were good servants and poor bargainers."[13]

Yeats explored his past less to glorify it than to discover ways of using the intricate strands of tradition which had produced him. Yet his verbal assertion of continuities did not function as he had expected: instead of satisfying his need for security, it brought his life into question. His ancestors were images of imitation; throughout *Reveries* he relentlessly judged himself against them and invariably found himself diminished. As he examined an eighteenth-century miniature of his great-great-grandfather, he saw a courtesy and gentleness, a "half-feminine charm" which showed him "a something clumsy and heavy" in himself.[14] As a child at school he had been "ashamed of my lack of courage; for I wanted to be like my grandfather who thought so little of danger that he had jumped overboard in the Bay of Biscay after an old hat."[15] He remembered that, in Sligo, his father had been "indignant and threatening because he did not think I rode well. 'You must do everything well,' he said, 'that the Pollexfens respect, though you must do other things also'."[16] Yeats's stress on bodily inadequacy is part of the larger sexual anxiety, felt throughout *Reveries,* which later spawned the compensatory masks of swordsman and sexual profligate. In middle age, still frustrated by Maud's desire for a "spiritual marriage" only, he remembered with burning clarity the sexual traumas of his youth: a description of "the mechanism of sex" which "made me miserable for weeks," his father's insistence on his "moral degradation," the alleged homosexuality of his Greek master.[17] He had no family of his own: was the tradition he now felt so keenly responsible for perpetuating to reach a dead halt with himself?

Reveries holds these problems at arms' length by means of a carefully gauged aesthetic distance. But in "Pardon, Old Fathers" (December 1913), they erupt with shattering vengeance. With good reason this "violent and terrible epistle dedicatory" to *Responsibilities* moved Eliot;[18] its theme, the same which runs from "The Love Song of J. Alfred Prufrock" through "Ash Wednesday," is the seemingly

---

[13] Ibid., p. 21.

[14] Ibid., p. 22.

[15] Ibid., p. 34.

[16] Ibid., p. 48.

[17] Ibid., pp. 25–26, 30, 38–39.

[18] T. S. Eliot, "The Poetry of W. B. Yeats," in *The Permanence of Yeats,* James Hall and Martin Steinmann, eds. (1950; rpt. New York: Collier, 1961), p. 300.

irremediable conflict between sexuality and imaginative vision. If the country house culture as Yeats construed it had reconciled these antinomies, Yeats himself had not. Far more than "Words" (1909) or "A Woman Homer Sung" (1910), the poem is Yeats's most brutal attack against his art prior to "Nineteen Hundred and Nineteen." No redemption from unendurable remorse alleviates the self-condemnation:

> Pardon that for a barren passion's sake,
> Although I have come close on forty-nine,
> I have no child, I have nothing but a book,
> Nothing but that to prove your blood and mine.

Art is not its own end, but either the sublimation of thwarted sexual and emotional desire, or the speaker's contemptibly tenuous and insufficient link to his heritage. The legal connotations of "to prove" (validate) point to a hopelessly demented logic: because he cannot produce an heir to the tradition, he must consider himself almost illegitimate.[19] In its very wastage his "barren" passion ironically perverts the abundant energy extolled in William Pollexfen's Blakean adage, " 'Only the wasteful virtues earn the sun.' " And, unlike that "silent and fierce old man," unlike O'Leary in his Roman stoicism, the speaker must cry in public.

Although Mr. Bloom has called it "tendentious,"[20] this agonized confession attains a perfect correspondence with its literary form. Quite properly, considering the heroic stature the speaker grants his ancestors, the poem is epic invocation; familial, Sligo muses have supplanted the "high invisible ones" of "The Shadowy Waters." Ironically, he requests forgiveness, not literary inspiration. For the poem's concept of epic and the epic poet rails against the irrelevance of art. The speaker's ancestors themselves constitute a live epic world. Even the speaker belongs to that panorama: with crushing self-derision, he is "the story's end," a

---

[19] Henn's remark ("*The Green Helmet* and *Responsibilities*," in *An Honoured Guest*, p. 39), "Yeats depicts himself as 'propp'd by ancestry,' " misinterprets the poet-speaker's relation to his family and fails to indicate that Yeats is, in effect, undone by recognition of ancestral greatness. Cf. also John Unterecker, *A Reader's Guide to William Butler Yeats* (New York: Farrar, Strauss, 1959), pp. 114–15, who argues that the speaker thinks his "progeny of words" sufficient to "prove a kinship" with his ancestors; the interpretation disregards the speaker's act of apology. Even Whitaker's judgment on this poem (*Swan and Shadow*, p. 170) seems more generous to Yeats than Yeats was to himself: "In the restraint, irony, and well-grounded pride of his apology, as in the breadth of his admirations, the speaker himself thus incarnates the inheritance that he addresses."

[20] Harold Bloom, *Yeats* (New York: Oxford, 1970), p. 171.

mock-hero who cannot act. If life itself is epic, then what is the point of literature? Further, his ancestors are not only in the epic; they are its court audience, seeking to know how their heir has matched their exploits. Yet as the mere bard "recites" his part in the epic—not the poem, but his life—what happens?

> Pardon, old fathers, if you still remain
> Somewhere in ear-shot for the story's end.

The implied dramatic situation spatializes the speaker's sense of separation and failure. His ancestors are walking out, for "the story's end" is not epic but bathos. The invocation, no conventional catalogue of heroic deeds, is an increasingly desperate crying out for the vanishing ancestors to return. The swelling invocation finally crashes, leaving the speaker nakedly aware that he has nothing to compare with their ancestral greatness, least of all a child. But not until you reach the word "nothing" do you understand that his enumeration of their imaginative and physical virtues has also defined, invisibly, his own deficiencies: each image of praise involves an inaudible self-judgment. Indeed, the first "Pardon" seems almost a throw-away word—precisely because the speaker does not yet completely realize the magnitude of the guilt he feels, the forgiveness he must ask. The concluding request for "Pardon," producing as incisive a circular structure as any in Yeats, is filled with astonishing helplessness. The poem, showing the speaker's sudden revelation, achieves Yeats's constant goal: the illusion of the mind's imperceptible operations beneath the surface of the language. What distinguishes this poem from much of Yeats's other mature work is that the attainment of revelation through profound personal suffering does not confer a redemptive tragic joy. There is only knowledge without catharsis, and that is not enough.

"Pardon, Old Fathers" is a self-command for productive sexual action, imaginative action which displays itself in the fullness of being, not in poems. In 1914 Robert Gregory suggested to Yeats that he might want to purchase Thoor Ballylee, which had been part of the Gregory estate since 1783. The Congested Districts Board had recently acquired it for redistribution among the peasantry, but only Yeats wanted it. When, in the spring of 1917, he took title to the islanded tower and its adjoining cottages, he began the actual and symbolic reconstruction of his life. His motives were necessarily complex, tinged by sympathetic magic. In moving to the West of Ireland he was not simply strengthening his ties with Lady Gregory. He was repossessing an earth which "had still its sheltering sacredness," the spiritualized soil which had inspired his youth with joy. Becoming a participant in that vital epic world, he sought to end the exclusion confronted in "Pardon, Old Fathers" and to "prove" his blood-relationship with his family. Yet "cold Clare rock and Galway rock and thorn"[21] were not Sligo's landscape, and Yeats knew it. In "Under Saturn" (1918), he detailed in a piercingly oblique self-judgment the remorse induced by his long separation from the Sligo community: "I am thinking of a child's vow sworn in vain / Never to leave that valley his fathers called their home." In "In Memory of Alfred Pollexfen" (1916), a poem in which Yeats tried to transform family history into local legend, he was equally disturbed by having traveled "Far from the customary skies"; George Pollexfen "had ended where his breath began"—an Elizabethan son-neteer's circular image of stability. Although farewells to Sligo, both poems return vicariously to a neglected source of personal coherence. Yeats's new sense of "my people" ("Under Saturn"), gained only after a protracted struggle against them for his own identity, was clannish without being class-oriented; and he brought it with him to the tower when he made George Pollexfen a spiritual inhabitant of Thoor Bally-lee.[22]

The Easter Rising unquestionably influenced Yeats's move. "I am very despondent about the future," he wrote to Lady Gregory. "At the moment I feel that all the work of years has been overturned, all the bringing together of classes, all the freeing of Irish literature and criticism from politics."[23] Unlike Joyce, he could not remain aloof from the turbulence. Yet although he expected to "return to Dublin to live, to begin building again," he dreaded "the temptation to contro-versy one finds in Dublin."[24] Yeats's uneasiness, the tension between acknowledged responsibilities and personal needs, was justified; he knew his limitations. He would later write to Lady Gregory that he had come to live at the tower in order to avoid the loss of creative power attendant upon public life; Thoor Ballylee insured the brooding isola-tion he now needed to generate poetic intensity.[25] Yeats's purchase of the tower was a compromise maneuver: if Thoor Ballylee was an escape from Dublin, it also represented a very strong emotional involvement, at the least, in Ireland's future. As "Easter 1916" makes plain, Yeats immediately understood that his own reconstruction and the emergence of a new national consciousness were connected. The equally significant result of the Rising was Yeats's marriage. Despite his attraction to "The

21 "In Memory of Major Robert Gregory," IX.

22 Ibid., V.

23 *Letters*, p. 613.

24 Ibid., p. 614.

25 Lady Gregory, Unpublished Journals, Book XII, March 22, 1921.

lonely light that Samuel Palmer engraved,"[26] the prospect of living isolated in the tower can hardly have cheered him. When MacBride's execution left Maud free to remarry, Yeats again proposed and was rejected; practicing metonymy, he turned to Iseult, Maud's daughter, and was affectionately staved off. In confused anxiety, his mind "unhinged by strain,"[27] he married Bertha Georgiana Hyde-Lees, whose stepfather was the brother of another lost love, Olivia Shakespear. The marriage, in October 1917, seemed symbolical, alchemical, fraught with mystical sexuality. His Dante had found his Beatrice; his Solomon, Sheba:

> All those abstractions that you fancied were
> From the great Treatise of Parmenides;
> All, all those gyres and cubes and midnight things
> Are but a new expression of her body
> Drunk with the bitter sweetness of her youth.
>   ["The Gift of Harun Al-Rashid"]

The marriage was also quite real; as well as "wisdom," Mrs. Yeats brought "comfort," "glad kindness," and "a girl's love."[28] A family had begun; Yeats would rebut his ancestors. And Thoor Ballylee, although no Jonsonian country house, would become, as Yeats wished, an enduring physical structure sheltering poetry and the poet's heirs.

II

Yeats's tower dwarfs all critical structures. No compilation of the visual and literary sources which filtered through his imagination as he made his greatest poetry—the "topless towers of Ilium," the towers of Maeterlinck, Villiers de L'Isle-Adam, and the Tarot pack—can explain the wholeness of Thoor Ballylee. This is because the tower is not an adopted symbol but an ancient image built anew in Yeats's mind; the allusions, the history contained within it belong in the most intimate way to Yeats himself. What is most radical about the tower is how far Yeats managed, poetically, to transmute the *prima materia* of its stone into a spiritual presence without denying the physical solidity of his place. The degree of congruence between self and stone is awesome;

---

26 "The Phases of the Moon."

27 *Letters*, p. 633.

28 "Under Saturn"; "A Prayer for My Daughter," V; "Meditations in Time of Civil War," IV.iii.

precisely because the tower's changing shape follows the contours of Yeats's myriad-minded nature, it remains mysterious. You may walk around the tower, and in it; but when you come out, you cannot tell whether you have been in a building or an imagination. "It is only by ancient symbols," Yeats wrote of Shelley's towers, "by symbols that have numberless meanings besides the one or two the writer lays an emphasis upon, or the half-score he knows of, that any highly subjective art can escape from the barrenness and shallowness of a too conscious arrangement, into the abundance and depth of Nature."[29]

It is a mistake to forget that Yeats considered the tower his symbol *and* his home; the elegant Georgian town-house he later rented on Merrion Square never summoned that double response. The felt correlation between house and imagination made his refurbishing of the dilapidated tower not simply a matter of tasteful decoration but a self-renewal and a self-projection; by reconstructing it, he gained the intimacy necessary for a poetry in which the outward environment could become a syntax for his emotions. He had chosen his "soil"—"all the matter in which the soul works, the walls of our houses, the serving-up of our meals, and the chairs and tables of our rooms, and the instincts of our bodies."[30] In Adamic fashion he changed the tower's name from Ballylee Castle to Thoor Ballylee. "Thoor is Irish for tower," he wrote Olivia Shakespear, "and it will keep people from suspecting us of modern gothic and a deer park."[31] As he wittily rejected West Britonism and the imputations of a leisured magnificence,[32] he asserted his Irishness. Possessing a fourteenth-century Norman tower, he thought himself back to the epic beginnings of Irish history. "My idea is to keep the contrast between the mediaeval castle and the peasant's cottage":[33] his territory, visualizing his theory of imaginative reciprocity between aristocrat and peasant, was a microcosm of feudal "equality of culture." Yeats's deliberate medievalism—all the more striking because he now considered Coole a Renaissance house—was the historical correlative of beginning a new life.

Yeats furnished the tower with Morris's early medieval style in mind: "No table or chair or stool not simple enough / For shepherd lads in Galilee" ("A Prayer on Going into My House"). Embedded in the religious pastoral was Yeats's desire to have his own mask—

29 W. B. Yeats, *Essays and Introductions* (New York: Macmillan, 1961), p. 87.

30 W. B. Yeats, *Explorations* (New York: Macmillan, 1962), p. 273.

31 *Letters*, p. 680.

32 See W. B. Yeats, *Mythologies* (New York: Macmillan, 1959), p. 22, n. 1.

33 *Letters*, p. 625.

"simplification through intensity,"[34]   the aim of complex aristocratic artifice—actualized in objects. Expanding Jonson's conception of the static relation between house and person, Yeats regarded his surroundings as dynamic properties capable of generating psychological change. Thus, he commissioned the drunken genius Scott to design heavy, plain elm furniture: three-legged chairs in the Norman manner, plank-and-trestle tables, a massive bed with side-tables attached. The great vaulted ceiling of the ground-floor dining area was whitewashed; the window frames Yeats painted a bright red, the only color, he thought, that complemented the weathered stones.[35] Mrs. Yeats painted the bedroom ceiling "in blue and black and gold,"[36] like the "Heavens" of an Elizabethan stage-canopy; the stairwell, ascending to an inviolable study and then to the unfinished Stranger's Room, was also blue. The stark, primary color, together with curtains and tapestries, compensated for limestone walls too damp for pictures. Yeats could not even hang the great treasure the Linnells had given him years earlier—Blake's illustrations to Dante, the tower's first ancestral ghost. Two large brass Persian candlesticks, reminding him of "All Asiatic vague immensities,"[37]   flanked the great-hearthed fireplace, above which he intended to place the Butler crest.

As in the Gregory tradition, planting was an act of faith, a metaphoric linking of organic and poetic fertility: "We artists, do not we also plant trees and it is only after some fifty years that we are of much value?"[38]   In the small garden enclosed by the newly thatched cottages, the spiritual and the mundane grew side by side, "the symbolic rose" and some vegetables. Yeats intended to plant apple trees "because it will make me popular with the little boys who will eat my apples in the early mornings."[39]   Dante had hungered, in "Ego Dominus Tuus," for "the apple on the bough / Most out of reach"; Yeats's garden, approximating Penshurst's earthly paradise instead of Dante's impossible Eden, would not tantalize. In all, he reflected to Quinn: "It is a great pleasure

---

[34] W. B. Yeats, *A Vision* (New York: Macmillan, 1961), p. 140.

[35] Lady Gregory, Unpublished Journals, Book XX, September 9, 1922.

[36] *Letters*, p. 682.

[37] "The Statues," II.

[38] *Autobiography*, p. 404.

[39] *Letters*, p. 615. Conscious of a small flaw in an ancestor's behavior, Yeats was reversing an episode he had narrated in *Reveries*: his uncle Mat Yeats "had once waited up every night for a week to catch some boys who stole his apples and when he caught them had given them six-pence and told them not to do it again" (*Autobiography*, p. 22).

to live in a place where George makes at every moment a fourteenth century picture. And out of doors, with the hawthorn all in blossom all along the river banks, everything is so beautiful that to go elsewhere is to leave beauty behind."[40]

In the midst of restoration, Yeats dedicated the tower. "To Be Carved on a Stone at Thoor Ballylee" (1918) defines the tower's place in the West of Ireland, gives Mrs. Yeats the tower as a wedding present, and, in merging physical with imaginative creation, designates the reconstruction a self-unifying act. Yet he hesitated about the attitude toward experience—time, human achievement, joy—which his tower should signify:

> [early version] [41]
> I, the poet, William Yeats,
> With common sedge and broken slates
> And smithy work from the Gort forge,
> Restored this tower for my wife George;
> And on my heirs I lay a curse
> If they should alter for the worse,
> From fashion or an empty mind,
> What Raftery built and Scott designed.

> [final version]
> I, the poet William Yeats,
> With old mill boards and sea-green slates,
> And smithy work from the Gort forge,
> Restored this tower for my wife George;
> And may these characters remain
> When all is ruin once again.

Even in changing the building materials (1. 2), Yeats experimented with his spiritual environment. Heroic paradoxes essential to his conception of the tower—creation of the miraculous from the commonplace, construction out of ruin—give way to a less secure awareness of an impersonal temporal power the speaker cannot control: the sea, whose winds will pummel the tower in "A Prayer for My Daughter." These minute changes accord with the altered conclusion. The first dedication, ending in fierce patriarchal affirmations, lacks tragic perspective. Reflecting Yeats's readings in Jonson as well as Morris, Thoor Ballylee embodies the most extended of claims against future time: the potential existence of a family tradition. Betrayal—the same sin of which he had found

---

[40] *Letters*, p. 683.
[41] Ibid., p. 651.

himself so guilty in "Pardon, Old Fathers"—is possible, but not inevitable. The disaster, "If" (1. 6) it occurs, is limited; he can already predict its causes; and alteration "for the worse" is hardly "ruin." Above all, he believes that language can control future history; his curse is prophylactic. In the revision Yeats confronted his dread of loss and forced himself to recognize the barest of elements which might "remain" to him; the minimalism of "Meditations . . ." and "The Black Tower" surfaces early in the series. The tragic historical knowledge that the cycle of generation must also bring dissolution severely tempers his speaker's self-deceiving optimism. The speaker now knows language inadequate; despite literary convention (Yeats may well have remembered Spenser's 75th sonnet in the *Amoretti*), poetry cannot eternize. Assured only of "ruin" and not knowing its cause, he humbly prays that the mere memory of his symbol (contained in "these characters") survive.[42] A sense of panoramic doom concludes the poem with epigrammatic sharpness. Yet he has married, knowing death; restored his tower, knowing its collapse; made his poem, knowing it may vanish though carved in' stone. What the poem finally celebrates is neither established relationships nor created monuments, but the act of creating. It leads directly into "Lapis Lazuli": "All things fall and are built again, / And those that build them again are gay." And this is what the tower symbolizes: the perpetual and all-humbling urge, amidst all risk, to reconstruct.

Yeats's mind, however, contained another tower, an ideal image combining the religious, alchemical, psychological, and poetic traditions of Europe. The visionary Robartes implicitly refers to it when, gesturing toward the actual tower, he says: "that shadow is the tower" ("The Phases of the Moon"). This mysterious clause does more than distinguish shades of moonlit darkness: Thoor Ballylee *is* only the earthly "shadow" of its Platonic archetype. The ideal tower, Edenic like Yeats's Byzantium, cannot fall. A macrocosmic symbol of harmony, it reconciles all antinomies, answers the cry of the poet in his actual tower—"O may the moon and sunlight seem / One inextricable beam" ("The Tower," II.v). This spiritual tower, because it denies the "tragic war" out of which poetry is made, seldom appears in Yeats's work; a transcendent emblem, it can be hypostatized only in dream or momentary vision.

"Under the Round Tower" (1918), written shortly after Yeats's wedding, deals explicitly with the twin themes of cosmic marriage and the soul's perfection. Emphatically, the tower envisaged is not Thoor

---

[42] Cf. Unterecker (*A Reader's Guide*, p. 168), who underestimates the element of prayer in "And *may* these characters remain."

Ballylee; Yeats, knowing that poems alter reality, could not give his own tower an unnatural identity. In a poem as ebullient as any Yeats wrote, the down-and-out Billy Byrne stretches his bones in cruciform position "On great-grandfather's battered tomb" and dreams ancestral memories

> Of sun and moon that a good hour
> Bellowed and pranced in the round tower;
>
> Of golden king and silver lady,
> Bellowing up and bellowing round,
> Till toes mastered a sweet measure,
> Mouth mastered a sweet sound,
> Prancing round and prancing up
> Until they pranced upon the top.

As these planetary bodies ascend the tower, the outward boundary of the universe, they enact what Yeats had asserted many years before: "the highest life unites, as in one fire, the greatest passion and the greatest courtesy."[43] With perfect discipline in their "toes," their bodies think; that formal precision gives passion its all but bursting power. Sun and moon consummate their marriage in a self-celebrating whirl so swift that they generate their own environment, transform the cosmos into pure Imagination:

> Hands gripped in hands, toes close together,
> Hair spread on the wind they made;
> That lady and that golden king
> Could like a brace of blackbirds sing.

Yet Yeats's dreamer, in a high comic irony, is an indifferent visionary. He rejects his dream—not because it is impossible but because it is too noisy. If a cosmic rumpus is going to break his rest, he'll move. This is Yeats playing delightedly with his own new-found wisdom, but it is also Yeats recognizing that "human kind / Cannot bear very much reality."[44]

"A Tower on the Apennines" (1907) presents the same mystical totality in more complicated form. In this extraordinary essay written ten years before Yeats purchased Thoor Ballylee,[45] the ideal tower is the dwelling-place of perfect humanity: the poet, married to his

---

[43] *Explorations*, p. 162.
[44] T. S. Eliot, "Burnt Norton," I, in *Four Quartets*.
[45] *Essays*, pp. 290–91.

"buried self" in an apotheosis unrivaled in Yeats's work. The essay begins with deceptive simplicity: "The other day I was walking towards Urbino, where I was to spend the night, having crossed the Apennines from San Sepolcro, and had come to a level place on the mountain-top near the journey's end." But immediately the landscape becomes symbolic of spiritual ascent, anticipating the spiral staircase in "Under the Round Tower" and the gyres of *A Vision:* "My friends were in a carriage somewhere behind, on a road which was still ascending in great loops, and I was alone amid a visionary, fantastic, impossible scenery." Although Yeats *walks,* he outstrips Lady Gregory and Robert, who *ride.* The paradox of motion, his symbolic location, and the movement toward Urbino, the Renaissance citadel of the self's completion—these are metaphors of the imagination's intensity at the point of visionary stasis. Natural portents enhance his awareness of imminent vision, among them the apocalyptic lightning traditionally associated with the Crucifixion.

> Away south upon another mountain a mediaeval tower, with no building near nor any sign of life, rose into the clouds. I saw suddenly in the mind's eye an old man, erect and a little gaunt, standing in the door of the tower, while about him broke a windy light. He was the poet who had at last, because he had done so much for the word's sake, come to share in the dignity of the saint.

This is Yeats's anti-self upon a corresponding mountain, a projection not of Yeats as he is but of the poet he would become; Yeats clothes that sacramental image in a synaesthetic mandala of "windy light." The poet, standing in a tower which joins earth to heaven, has resolved Yeats's most haunting problem—the choice between "Perfection of the life, or of the work"[46] —by showing that the artist's necessary self-sacrifice can lead to self-completion. There is nothing self-vaunting in Yeats's vision of the poet's magical wholeness, for it arises from his own incompletion, unfulfillment.

The poet has his mask also: Blake's "human form divine," Christ, who inspires him to recreate totality. In Yeats's imagination the poet has imitated his mask so completely that he has virtually become Christ's mask—the reward of all his discipline. As early as the *Rosa Alchemica* and *The Tables of the Law* Yeats had pondered God's desire for incarnation.[47] Here, Christ needs the poet as an emblem of His perpetual presence and sacrifice. This intricate marriage between Christ

---

[46] "The Choice."

[47] See also *Autobiography,* p. 321, where Yeats narrates a vision he had after walking near Inchy Wood at Coole (ca. 1897–98): "The next morning I awoke near

and the poet is mediated; the poet "has in his ears well-instructed voices," Christ's emanations, which "come to him among his memories which are of women's faces." The women are Sheba, Laura, Beatrice, perhaps even Maud, transformed from objects of sexual desire into *theotokoi,* those who point the way toward heavenly love.[48] As in "Under the Round Tower," the conjunction of male and female symbolizes cosmic unity and psychic wholeness. Christ, as Eliot knew in "The Wasteland" (V), is an hermaphrodite; in countless Aramaic, Byzantine, and medieval visualizations of the Crucifixion, His extended arms join sun and moon in "One inextricable beam." That unity has become the poet's. The radical poetic consequence is that his language becomes identical with the Logos. The poet is "not, as we say of many a one, speaking in metaphor, but as [if] this were Delphi or Eleusis." His tower is the world's omphalos.

"A Tower on the Apennines" prefigures the motion of Yeats's mind at Thoor Ballylee: by the time of *The Tower* (1929) and *The Winding Stair* (1933), he had made his tower the historical center of the West of Ireland. Yet only once, in "A Dialogue of Self and Soul," was he tempted to superimpose the ideal tower upon his own shadowy home. It is indicative of Yeats's prevailing attitude that Soul, battling for Self's heart, seeking to aetherealize Thoor Ballylee, fails before he begins. The reasons are plain: the visionary condition also entails blankness, shapelessness, the personality's complete diffusion into imagination. As a permanent state, it excludes the momentary visionary ecstasy in which laborious contemplation catches fire. Yeats valued these moments deeply, and was prepared to forego complete transcendence in order to keep them. "I shall find the dark grow luminous, the void fruitful when I understand I have nothing, that the ringers in the tower have appointed for the hymen of the soul a *passing* bell" [italics mine].[49] That transient marriage could emerge only through deprivation, perpetual confrontation with new bitterness. As Yeats rejected the heavenly peace of the sainted poet, he dismissed both classical retirement and peaceful acquiescence to the world. Of himself, the ageing poet tempted by tranquillity, he wrote in indirect admonition:

Surely, he may think, now that I have found vision and mask I need not suffer any longer. He will buy perhaps some small old

---

dawn, to hear a voice saying, 'The love of God is infinite for every human soul because every human soul is unique, no other can satisfy the same need in God.' "

48 Cf. Daniel Albright, *The Myth Against Myth: A Study of Yeats's Imagination in Old Age* (London: Oxford University Press, 1972), pp. 51–52, who finds "faint traces of Hanrahan's motivating lechery" in the poet's vision of "women's faces."

49 *Mythologies,* p. 332. See Bloom, *Yeats,* pp. 22, 181.

house, where, like Ariosto, he can dig his garden, and think that in the return of birds and leaves, or moon and sun, and in the evening flight of the rooks he may discover rhythm and pattern like those in sleep and so never awake out of vision. Then he will remember Wordsworth withering into eighty years, honoured and empty-witted, and climb to some waste room and find, forgotten there by youth, some bitter crust.[50]

Yeats's architecture made claims upon him which he could not evade: rooted in history, the tower demanded quest for an earthly sanctity, the difficult transubstantiation of a "bitter crust"—not into Christ's symbolic body but into an experiential sweetness which could redeem, in time, the devastating cycles of history.

Yeats began his quest by consecrating his ground as a place of revelation. This is the common concern of the 'tower' poems grouped together in *The Wild Swans at Coole:* "Ego Dominus Tuus" (1915), "A Prayer on Going into My House" (1918), and "The Phases of the Moon" (1918). That Yeats chose Thoor Ballylee as the dramatic setting for his discourses on the anti-self and the Great Wheel of history indicates the crucial function these poems had at the time of writing: [51] they rooted a mythology in the earth. At Thoor Ballylee Yeats confronted the problem he had faced in "In the Seven Woods": his territory was no Delphi or Eleusis sanctified by traditional experience. Yet convinced from his earliest years that revelation was inseparably bound to particular location, he set about creating a *genius* of place, establishing the emotional and spiritual character of his home. The tower's inhabitants in these poems are extraordinarily conscious of subtle gradations between profane and sacred territory; they passionately seek and expect epiphany to occur on their "spot" of ground; their belief that the place can generate redemptive knowledge makes it numinous. In "Ego . . ." Ille prophesies the embodied coming of his anti-self. The speaker of "A Prayer on Going into My House" hopes, more tentatively, that Sinbad (like the anti-self) will bring a redemptive dream. "Yeats" in the tower of "Phases . . ." must learn by "toil" the "mysterious wisdom" which the earlier speakers seek from annunciation. Although the poems take an increasingly pessimistic view of human capability, the belief in the possibility of earthly sanctity remains constant.

[50] *Mythologies*, p. 342.

[51] Yeats himself later called "Ego Dominus Tuus" and "The Phases of the Moon" merely a "text for exposition" (W. B. Yeats, *The Variorum Edition of the Poems of W. B. Yeats*, eds. Peter Allt and Russell K. Alspach [New York: Macmillan, 1966], p. 821); commentators, following Yeats, have largely confined themselves to discussing the manifest doctrinal content of these poems.

This is Yeats's concern, too, but from a different angle. When he grouped the poems together, he presented them as multiple perspectives on the single theme of revelation; through this Browningesque method he examined himself and his relation to Thoor Ballylee. Ille, although Yeats's disguise, is an independent dramatic character; the speaker of "A Prayer on Going into My House" typifies the Yeatsian speaker of "In Memory of Major Robert Gregory" and after; the "Yeats" in "Phases . . ." is the historical Yeats who, in the nineties, had written of Robartes "in that extravagant style / He had learnt from Pater." Each of these figures understands differently his territory's potential sacredness, its possible profanation, its relation to previous history. Most important, the quest which appears so significant at one point may seem mere folly at another; Robartes scorns "Yeats's" venture as absurd masochism; and his withering satire obviously qualifies the earlier claims to vision. These multiple perspectives offer a complex evocation of revelation as experience, impenetrable precisely because its myriad ramifications, even its limits, have been shown. Grouped, the poems discuss Thoor Ballylee's sacredness as a question and thus make Yeats's point through nondogmatic means.

As Ille traces "Magical shapes" on his "grey sand," he deliberately transforms his soil into a subject of meditation: what he draws may well be the Great Wheel. "Enthralled by the unconquerable delusion," he performs this consecration to conjure his buried anti-self—who will come forth, seemingly, from that very "spot." The landscape will then reflect Ille's psychic wholeness: "grey sand" and "shallow stream" will become "wet sands," an elemental marriage like the one shown in Sturge Moore's cover design for *The Tower.*[52] Ille's really crucial meditation, however, concerns Dante's ancestral presence in Thoor Ballylee:

> Being mocked by Guido for his lecherous life,
> Derided and deriding, driven out
> To climb that stair and eat that bitter bread,
> He found the unpersuadable justice, he found
> The most exalted lady loved by a man.

Dante, exiled to Ille's tower, is an earthly version of the poet-saint in "A Tower on the Apennines," a talismanic figure whose own attainment augurs the completion of Ille's quest. His suffering, the fierce, unassuageable hunger—these become, in bitter paradox, signs of encouragement. What Ille imagines, Yeats at Thoor Ballylee practiced: Dante,

52 W. B. Yeats, *W. B. Yeats and T. Sturge Moore: Their Correspondence*, ed. Ursula Bridge (London: Routledge, 1953), p. 111.

using art as an epistemological technique to discover his "image," the indispensable link between his two selves, simultaneously made a sculpture and wrought a building:

> I think he fashioned from his opposite
> An image that might have been a stony face
> Staring upon a Bedouin's horse-hair roof
> From doored and windowed cliff . . .

Long before Yeats, in "Blood and the Moon," attributed the tower's construction to the Anglo-Normans, he made Dante its first mythological architect. Despite the hint of an Arabian geography, this "doored and windowed cliff" is Yeats's tower in its primordial form, before the "old wind-beaten tower" had been eroded into its present shape; the "image" of a "stony face" is Thoor Ballylee's most distinctive feature, the grim visage carved high upon its west side. Dante, beginning from scratch, "set his chisel to the hardest stone." The superb paradox of the "doored and windowed cliff"—natural and impermeable, yet a habitable human artifact—is the result of his art. He reconciled humankind and nature, humankind and that undifferentiated unconscious mind which contains the eternal archetypes of the "age-long memoried self." The tower is nature brought to the verge of humanization, yet with such craft that (as in "Lapis Lazuli") nature's integrity is not violated. Viewed in reverse, the "stony face" represents humankind returning as far as possible—without losing identity—to pure nature, humankind defying transience by paradoxically becoming part of a temporal evolution so gradual that it spans eons of geological change. Unassailable as the cliff, that face stares upon the nomadic, transient world of "common dream"—not with the transcendent nostalgia of Yeats's golden bird in "Sailing to Byzantium," but with a hard contempt for anything less than the quest to achieve complete humanity without sacrificing "bodily form." Dante's architecture, in short, sets forth a visible paradigm not only of the quest but of the quest's end.

What Yeats achieved through Ille's consecrations, he characteristically mocked in "The Phases of the Moon." He viewed Ille's heroic intentions, hierophantic flamboyance with skepticism, saw that Ille's self-absorption had damaged his sense of proportion. Between the two poems Mrs. Yeats's automatic writing had given Yeats the system of psychology and history which Robartes propounds; and Yeats quite plainly understood that influx of knowledge to have come from beyond himself, though he had explored its constituent elements for years. Thus, while "Phases . . ." celebrates that revelation by debunking the limitations of "Yeats" in his tower, the self-irony is not wholly trium-

Courtesy of Robert Ross

THOOR BALLYLEE
the carving on the west façade
I think he fashioned from his opposite
An image that might have been a stony face . . .

phant. More darkly, it shows Yeats's knowledge that the unaided human intellect was entirely insufficient. Read as an autobiographical fragment, not a tract, "Phases . . ." is a chastening self-judgment. The creature Yeats placed in the tower is a drudge; the tower, no longer a place of liberation, is a prison. What Ille had considered an exalted architecture urging his perseverance now serves only to deride "Yeats's" failure to gain knowledge. Aherne calls it "a place set out for wisdom / That he will never find." And at the poem's closure "Yeats," exhausted by study, snuffs out his candle and falls asleep[53] —a most undignified end to the Romantic visionary tradition. Robartes has earlier satirized "Yeats's" Romantic pretensions, reeling off his putative ancestry—his literary poses—in a series of epithets whose meaning is "Yeats's" emptiness:

> He has found, after the manner of his kind,
> Mere images; chosen this place to live in
> Because, it may be, of the candle-light
> From the far tower where Milton's Platonist
> Sat late, or Shelley's visionary prince:
> The lonely light that Samuel Palmer engraved,
> An image of mysterious wisdom won by toil . . .

Ille, who had paid Dante long obeisance, would have abhorred Robartes's irreverence. Ille had seen himself heroically bucking contemporary intellectual history, but Robartes understands that "Yeats's" very methods of rejecting modernity are modern. "Yeats," thinking himself a hero, is a fraud.

Robartes' satire is not simply the result of his grudge. "Half out of life," he differs in kind from "Yeats." Like Chaucer's Troilus translated, gazing upon "This litel spot of erthe, that with the se / Embraced is,"[54] he possesses a scope of vision which mortality lacks. Observing the tower as an outsider (the only such instance in Yeats's poetry), he demonstrates its minimal importance. "Yeats" doesn't even know enough to know how much he is deluded in his quest; for the "Mere images" he has discovered—so vaunted by Ille—constitute but part of the total system. In the crowning, brutal irony, Robartes announces the entire cosmology *out of "Yeats's" earshot*. Thus, revelation *does* occur at Thoor Ballylee, but hardly as Ille had intended; the poem's philosophical bitterness runs deep. The revelation comes not from "Yeats's"

[53] Cf. Balachandra Rajan, *W. B. Yeats: A Critical Introduction* (London: Hutchinson, 1965), p. 114.

[54] *Troilus and Criseyde*, V.1815–16.

willed summoning but by accident; and, far from being a redemptive knowledge, it exposes his abysmal ignorance. Yeats's selfless capacity to manipulate his most central hopes and fears into poetry, to augment his mythology by parodying his worst dilemma, constantly astounds.

These two poems display Yeats's polarities at Thoor Ballylee. The structural importance of "A Prayer on Going into My House" in the series is that it renders, in a single self-dramatizing vision, the complex intersection of these antinomies. The claims to self-liberation in "Ego . . ." have become prayers; wisdom is not impossible, as in "Phases . . .," but difficult to achieve. The territory, neither an inviolable sanctuary nor a plot of sterile ground, may be consecrated by intense effort. The tower, a paradigm neither of the completed quest nor the mind's delusion, is a home where, in a properly designed environment, visionary dream may occur. The poem occupies the middle ground of Yeats's 'tower' poetry in general—the ground of conflict, potentiality, setback, pride and self-criticism. Here, absolutes are foreign. The human symbol of this ground is the speaker's position: he stands at the threshold of his tower, neither outside ("Ego . . .") nor within ("Phases . . .").

Like Herbert's "The Church-Porch" or Fairfax's poem on Nunappleton House,[55] this poem is a ceremony of purification prior to entrance. In setting forth the requirements of his ideal life, the speaker simultaneously separates Thoor Ballylee from the realm of ordinary experience and begins his own reformation. That process involves the entire environment, physical, aesthetic, psychic. Ille's tracing of "Magical shapes" is not enough: the necessary precondition of desired vision is "beautiful life." The poet, so long restricted to the fringes of aristocratic society, now undertakes to establish his own. No other of Yeats's 'tower' poems attends so explicitly to the artistry of daily behavior; Yeats was attempting to reconcile the tragic conflict between "Perfection of the life, or of the work" which permeates the 'tower' series as a whole. Thus, having renovated the tower, the speaker submits his environment to the Divine aesthetic judgment and asks His blessing:

---

[55] Quoted by G. R. Hibbard, "The Country House Poem in the Seventeenth Century," in *Essential Articles for the Study of Alexander Pope*, ed. Maynard Mack (Hamden, Conn.: Archon, 1964), p. 425. Hibbard cites C. R. Markham, *A Life of the Great Lord Fairfax* (London, 1870), pp. 365–66:

> Think not, O man! that dwells herein,
> This house's a stay, but as an inn
> Which for convenience fitly stands
> In way to one not made with hands;
> But if a time here thou take rest,
> Yet think eternity the best.

> God grant a blessing on this tower and cottage
> And on my heirs, if all remain unspoiled,
> No table or chair or stool not simple enough
> For shepherd lads in Galilee . . .

For the moment, his fear of contamination is subsumed to resonant joy: he has recreated a pastoral environment sufficiently authentic to satisfy the rigorous aesthetic demands of shepherds who believed in Christ's birth. Their transcendental folly—like the innocence of the Celtic peasantry—has been his first model. If the tower is not a "grammar school of courtesies," he has nevertheless used *sprezzatura* to make its every detail foster his recovery of natural innocence. Like Dante, he has transformed his architecture into an emblem of meditation.

Yet he must learn the techniques of simplification. He turns from the peasantry to the aristocracy:

> and grant
> That I myself for portions of the year
> May handle nothing and set eyes on nothing
> But what the great and passionate have used
> Throughout so many varying centuries
> We take it for the norm . . .

The gravity is intimately modest: unlike Ille, he does not demand his anti-self; he knows his release from common life is temporary. Following Jonson and Marvell in defining by negation the values he prizes ("handle *nothing*"), he requests aristocratic self-completion. "Imitative energy" remains the chief principle of self-reformation: he takes his models of behavior and mental form from the organic medieval culture symbolized by his own architecture, "tower and cottage," "the hut and the castle." In his own person he will recreate the unified society envisaged in "The Galway Plains" and "Poetry and Tradition." Significantly, his hope for renewed imaginative power ("yet should I dream . . .") *follows* his stated intention to imitate the shepherds' natural innocence, the artificial discipline of innocence practiced by "the great and passionate." Psychologically and historically, he must recapitulate their development before his own poetry can flourish—as Ille, through Dante, had reenacted the tower's creation.

Visionary knowledge is thus the logical culmination of "beautiful life," and not a separate category of experience:

> yet should I dream
> Sinbad the sailor's brought a painted chest,

Or image, from beyond the Loadstone Mountain,
That dream is a norm . . .

The "norm," ironically, is nothing less than archetypal completion of
the quest; all else, as with ugly furnishings, will be rejected.[56] Like
Dante, Sinbad is a talismanic figure auguring discovery of the anti-self, a
sailor who has found revelation—inland. He brings the object of the
quest itself, the "image" which unifies humankind's divided nature.
And it is part of the speaker's elated wit that Sinbad contributes—what
else?—a piece of furniture to the tower's beautification. Yet despite the
fierce gaiety, the fallen world impinges: the speaker imagines Sinbad in
a dream, undeniably potent but nevertheless a fiction.

Precisely because annunciatory dream depends on such a delicate
balance in his psychic ecology, the speaker must defend his corruptible
approximation of an Edenic world:

and should some limb of the Devil
Destroy the view by cutting down an ash
That shades the road, or setting up a cottage
Planned in a government office, shorten his life,
Manacle his soul upon the Red Sea bottom.

Vision and physical "view" are interdependent; any disruption of the
naturally proportioned landscape will damage inspiration. (So also, the
political hopes of a revivified Tara depended on Coole's rooted trees.)
The contrast between the ill-conceived cottages and the ancient tower
follows the characteristically Jonsonian method of comparing antithetical houses; Yeats used the technique often, most notably in "Meditations . . ." and "Coole Park and Ballylee." Yet Penshurst's enemies
build elsewhere; Yeats's speaker, in a typical deviation from Jonson,
fears direct incursion. Even Ille is oblivious to such a threat: "the birds"
may carry his sacred knowledge "*away* to blasphemous men," but he
cannot imagine that "blasphemous men" may invade his property.
Thus, the speaker calls down upon his foes the wrath of the Divine
Artificer. The curse is witty, flamboyant—and self-mocking: the speaker
knows that no histrionic fiction of Mosaic fury can make his territory

56 Yeats's placing of Sinbad in a 'tower' poem had special significance. In *Reveries*
he had written of the strange, always wonderful excitement he had felt playing on
the coast between Sligo and Rosses' Point: "I have walked on Sinbad's yellow shore
and never shall another's hit my fancy" (*Autobiography*, p. 48). Transferring
Sinbad from Sligo to Thoor Ballylee was a symbolic means of recovering the lost
geography of his youth. See T. R. Henn, *The Lonely Tower* (1950; rpt. London:
Methuen, 1965), pp. 263–64.

inviolable. But it is also serious: in the battle between traditional beauty and modern ugliness, insight and torpor, his territory *is* a holy land.

Thoor Ballylee becomes a recovered Eden such as Yeats had sought in Coole's woods. Like the allusions to Jonson and Cosimo (epilogue to *Responsibilities;* "To a Wealthy Man . . ."), the climactic image of the Red Sea sparks a transforming allegory. The Cloone River, bounding the tower on three sides, is the Red Sea. The speaker's territory, associated with Galilee and the fulfillment of prophecy in Christ, is the Promised Land. Abstraction, ugliness, inept bureaucracy are the Egyptian armies, drowned "upon the Red Sea bottom."[57] The allegory of the Exodus concludes what is, despite a rearrangement of motifs, the sequence of the three primary religious dispensations in Western history; the third, represented by Sinbad's archetypal quest, is the structure of belief Yeats derived from folklore and unofficial religious tradition. All three dispensations signify the spirit's liberation from exile. Instead of stressing the irreconcilable tension between religious epochs (as in *The Resurrection* and *A Vision*), the speaker understands the essential concordance of all revelations, superimposes them all within his land. The tower—at least until the ironies of "The Phases of the Moon" have been completed—is the center of a new annunciation and a new prophecy.

"Ego Dominus Tuus," "A Prayer on Going into My House," and "The Phases of the Moon" constitute a stage in the 'tower' series which Yeats rejected. First, they are preoccupied with future events; the present is only a preparation for the future; characters are defined largely through their expectations. Exactly this postponement of the moment of greatest dramatic intensity Yeats found poetically inadequate, as he had also the mere exposition of Coole's virtues in "Upon a House . . . ." The later poems enact present experience, begin in immediate crises, personal or historical; revelation occurs within the process of the poem. Even "A Prayer for My Daughter," for all its future-orientation, treats the future as a compensation for the speaker's present anxieties.

Second, these poems recapitulate the past in a manner suggesting that Yeats, before proceeding any further, needed to traverse in abbreviated form his own development and that of Western culture as well in order to retain continuities: in addition to table and chair, he was installing his mental furniture at Thoor Ballylee; his self-consciousness in this process of retention seems less completely meshed with his speakers' characters than in the later work. "A Prayer on Going into My

---

[57] Yeats's sources for the last line are doubtless Blake's "Mock on Mock on Voltaire Rousseau" and "London."

House" summarily incorporates all aristocratic tradition, all Western religious thought into the tower. With Robartes and Aherne, Yeats reached back twenty years to resuscitate the mythological representatives of his earlier selves, used them to insist that his territory—as he had earlier claimed of Coole—was haunted by immortal shadows. Once Yeats had shown himself that he could transplant a private mythology from one epoch of his life to another, he had no need to do it again. [58] Robartes and Aherne later assumed significant roles in *A Vision*, but in the poetry Yeats turned to the more public ghosts of history. He shrewdly understood that to declare "That Goldsmith and the Dean, Berkeley and Burke have travelled there" ("Blood and the Moon," II.ii) could far more dramatically jolt an audience immunized against ghosts than any assertion concerning unidentified, or unfamiliar, evanescent spirits.

Third, as Yeats had denied Coole's Anglo-Irish heritage in order to make the estate Irish, he now ignored the tower's Irishness to make it an international symbol. These poems are far less Irish than the later work, which gathers in not only Yeats's literary compatriots but Raftery and Mary Hynes, the Gregorys and Maud, Grattan and Kevin O'Higgins. The "shepherd lads in Galilee" are not the local peasantry from whom Yeats had collected folktales. Although Robartes and Aherne are dressed in "Connemara cloth worn out of shape," they hardly image an Irish peasant community; compare Yeats's peasantry in "Shepherd and Goatherd," "Reprisals," and "The Tower." The past these poems explore is that of the Judeo-Christian tradition, English romanticism, the English decadence, pre-Renaissance Florence. Dante is the tower's medieval founder, not the deBurgos who actually built it. Through this superimposition of foreign materials Yeats mastered his home. At the same time, however, these multiple identities signify his uncertainty, his lack of an established personal relationship with his architecture. He grew into Thoor Ballylee's real past bit by bit.

In Yeats's subsequent work, the tower became a physical memory of Irish history. Yeats brilliantly recognized that the tower, by virtue of the epochal changes it had survived, spatialized time. What the tower had seen, Yeats adopting its "stony face" as his mask could see also. It is consequently a mistake to think the tower *only* an Anglo-Norman structure. Thoor Ballylee was metaphorically the foundation upon which Anglo-Irish Coole had been built: the two houses, joined by the

---

58 It is true that Hanrahan, a quest-figure whom Yeats also created in the nineties, appears in "The Tower"; but the treatment of Hanrahan within the poem, as well as Yeats's motive in reviving him, differs so radically from his handling of Robartes and Aherne that the exception proves the rule. See Chapter VI.

Cloone River (the "generated soul" of time),[59] spatialized the temporal continuity of the Irish aristocratic tradition. Still coexisting, tower and country house were the last fruition of the medieval-Renaissance feudal community before its fall—or, when Yeats's conception of Irish history altered in the twenties, eighteenth-century Anglo-Ireland's final achievement. Legitimately, Yeats could enter the tower's temporal spectrum at any point he chose, populate its environment with the entire procession of Ireland's proud, desperate past: not only its "bloody, arrogant" origins, but Swift's dark madness, Burke and Grattan's disinterested magnanimity, the romantic wildness of its nineteenth-century heyday. In the end, the tower's actual history in the West of Ireland became indistinguishable from the imaginative and mythical history with which its Irish creator endowed it. From the Irish experience, Yeats reached out by analogy to Western culture: through Raftery, he touched Homer and Helen; through Gregory, Sidney; through his own tower, Milton's and Shelley's, and those of Alexandria and Babylon; finding Sato's sword upon his table, he reached the East.

As a meditative symbol, the tower allowed Yeats immediate access to "ancestral memory," "that age-long memoried self, that shapes the elaborate shell of the mollusc and the child in the womb, that teaches the birds to make their nest."[60] The seemingly infinite ramifications of this convergence of personal identity with the self-transcending collective unconcious conclude, perhaps, with Yeats's knowledge that his tower was the dramatized form of *A Vision's* Great Wheel. Wherever he positioned himself, he could see backward and forward. When he remembered "Goldsmith and the Dean, Berkeley and Burke," he simultaneously thought himself back into that past, revivified it in the present, and connected both with the tower's earlier founding and the future death of the West. When he prayed for Anne's twentieth-century happiness in "a house / Where all's accustomed, ceremonious," he was simultaneously hoping that his own crude, aristocratic tradition might flourish in an earlier soil and symbolizing in Anne's projected movement from tower to country house the aristocracy's historical evolution from the fourteenth century to the Renaissance and after. The dramatic effect of these simultaneities is that anything which happens to the tower or its speaker both comments on the present and interprets the past—the past which, as Eliot reiterated, is never dead because present knowledge and experience constantly alter it.

These correspondent occurrences, while they indicate that the mind which conceived *A Vision* also made the poems, hardly suggest the rigid design of history which *A Vision* represents; indeed, *A Vision* is

---

[59] "Coole Park and Ballylee," I.

[60] *Autobiography*, p. 233.

generally, if not always, useless in dealing with the poems. The correspondences reflect, instead, Yeats's perpetual self-examination. He was aware not only of his relation to historical tradition but of crucial similarities and differences between himself and those who had populated his territory:

> Two men have founded here. A man-at-arms
> Gathered a score of horse and spent his days
> In this tumultuous spot,
> Where through long wars and sudden night alarms
> His dwindling score and he seemed castaways
> Forgetting and forgot;
> And I, that after me
> My bodily heirs may find,
> To exalt a lonely mind,
> Befitting emblems of adversity.
>
> ["Meditations . . ., II.iii]

The profound issue raised in this passage, and one which absorbs the matter of self-judgment, is the question which dominates *A Vision*, the place of freedom in a deterministic pattern: does the violent heritage of his "tumultuous spot" commit him, the unwilling victim of its psychic influence, to relinquish his poetry and become a swordsman? What repeatedly concerned Yeats in the poetry, however, was not the answer but the enactment of the problem.[61] The conflict is central. It is the virtue of Yeats's speakers that they humbly know less, are less accommodated than the philosopher of history. They need to discover correspondences in order to know, in that very primitive way which belongs to epic sensibility, where they have come from and where they are going; they need to know "how to live"; and they need from historical complexities the simplifying, momentary joy of understanding which redeems their brute struggle on blood-sodden ground.

---

61 See Bloom, *Yeats*, pp. 470–71: "The desperate freedom Yeats imported into *A Vision* as the Thirteenth Sphere is born of a Swiftian passion absolutely central to the poet in his final days, but it does not alter the irony that *A Vision* remains only another example of what Buber called 'the dogma of gradual process,' by which the quasi-historical thought of our time has worked 'to establish a more tenacious and oppressive belief in fate than has ever before existed.' . . . Against *A Vision*, and the poems written out of it, the voice that is great within us rises up, and asks a freedom that Yeats did not allow." The criticism is just; yet Bloom himself often portrays Yeats as more the servant of his system than he actually was (e.g., in his superimposition of the incipient system upon "In Memory of Major Robert Gregory," pp. 194–95). What needs to be studied in detail is the conflict *within* the poems between what Yeats once called his "public philosophy" (*Letters*, p. 916)— that is, *A Vision*—and the relentless insistence upon individual freedom and responsibility.

CHAPTER

FIVE

The Death of Gregory

On January 23, 1918, Major Robert Gregory was shot down over Italy. Yeats, grieved, was nevertheless conscious of many ironies. Gregory's death intersected unexpectedly with his own marriage. He had bought Thoor Ballylee to be near Lady Gregory; now, the sale of Coole became inevitable; after "Shepherd and Goatherd," he could invoke Coole only in elegy. While he was still seeking a unified image of the Galway territory, to which he had returned because it retained the lineaments of epic Ireland, Gregory's death signaled the fall of that feudal community; he would watch, with bitter fascination, its more violent disruption during the years to come. Yet paradoxically, Gregory's death enabled Yeats to contrive an image of the West of Ireland more intricately realized than any which had preceded. Through Gregory's death he made the territory his own. Read in proper sequence, Yeats's poems on Gregory—"Shepherd and Goatherd" (March 1918), "In Memory of Major Robert Gregory" (June 1918), "An Irish Airman Foresees His Death" (1918), and "Reprisals" (late 1920)[1]—constitute his most comprehensive poetic treatment of his recurrent myth, the collapse of cultural unity.

The common geography of these poems renders the West of Ireland an ideal nation—which modern Ireland, spiritually barren, has forgotten. Gregory bluntly states the limits of his national allegiances:

> My country is Kiltartan Cross,
> My countrymen Kiltartan's poor.
> ["An Irish Airman . . ."]

[1] A near-final draft of this poem, dated November 23, 1920, is in the Berg Collection of the New York Public Library; Yeats did not include the poem in his

The geography of "Shepherd and Goatherd" is Coole itself. Yeats had earlier dealt with either its woods, a natural realm of epic, or the house, the constructed symbol of "passion and precision" unified; here, following Jonson, he merged grounds and architecture to create, in a single poem, a complete emblem of the integrated human community. "In Memory of Major Robert Gregory" imaginatively includes Mayo, Clare, Galway, and the Aran Islands. The Kiltartan landscape in "Reprisals," terrorized by the Black and Tans, is both itself and the whole of Ireland. Yeats populated these poems with the vestigial pastoral society which had prevailed until the "counting-house" wedged its way between "the hut and the castle." It includes the peasantry, aristocrats of rank and mind, scholars, visionaries, poets. The "reasoners and mechanists" have been banished.

This panoramic dramatic context through which Yeats chose to explore Gregory's death suggests that no critical interpretation can suffice which disregards Gregory's central heroic role in his community. Mr. Kermode has put forth such an interpretation, one which for all its brilliance evades the poems. Arguing from Yeats's obituary on Gregory, he states that Yeats identified himself with Gregory as the artist tragically isolated from life: Gregory's death is "the artist's escape" from the self-estranging dream of an impossible, subjective beauty.[2] Mr. Kermode assumes that Yeats's personally revelatory analysis of the artist's dilemma in the obituary represents the theme Yeats also sought to render in the poems. He then minimizes the relevance of all the poems except "In Memory of Major Robert Gregory" because they "appear largely to ignore" that theme.[3] In discussing this great elegy he dismisses the stanza on Gregory's "foolhardy horsemanship" (VIII) because Yeats added it at Mrs. Gregory's request; he can thus claim that Yeats saw Gregory as an artist who had escaped into the action of war,

collected works for fear of offending Lady Gregory. It is printed in W. B. Yeats, *The Variorum Edition of the Poems of W. B. Yeats*, eds. Peter Allt and Russell K. Alspach (New York: Macmillan, 1966), p. 791.

2 Frank Kermode, *Romantic Image* (1957; rpt. New York: Random House, 1964), p. 40. See Marjorie Perloff, "The Consolation Theme in Yeats's 'In Memory of Major Robert Gregory,'" *Modern Language Quarterly* 27 (1966): 306–22. Perloff has given an astute criticism of Kermode's reading (especially pp. 308–9, 311, 313, 317–18), as well as that of Marion Witt, "The Making of an Elegy: Yeats's 'In Memory of Major Robert Gregory,'" *Modern Philology* 48 (1950): 112–21. Perloff rightly observes that Yeats's obituary for Gregory (in *The Observer*, February 19, 1918; reprinted by Kermode, *Romantic Image*, pp. 32–34) was a public piece of writing, not to be taken as representative of his actual thinking (p. 311). All subsequent references to Perloff in this chapter pertain to her essay on the Gregory elegy.

3 Kermode, *Romantic Image*, p. 35.

"a delighted escape from a typical cruel dilemma imposed by the nature of the artist and exacerbated by modern decadence."[4] Yet, inconsistently, Mr. Kermode needs stanza VIII to illustrate the theme of action-as-escape; he knows that the epithet "Soldier" (IX, X, XI) cannot alone prove his point. What he does not ask is this: if action-as-escape was really the theme Yeats strove to delineate, why did he omit all reference to Gregory's physical skills in the "original" version?

The final poem transcends these genetic difficulties: Gregory has reconciled the opposed modes of action and contemplation. But "Even so," Mr. Kermode continues, "it was only at the cost of immediate extinction that Gregory achieved [Unity of Being], . . . ending the oscillation of the poet devoted to the Image by ending the process of exile and giving himself to death."[5] Certainly the obituary tackles these issues, but the poem shows no such "oscillation" or "exile."[6] These tragic problems touch everyone else, including the speaker—but not Gregory. Nor is his action a self-defensive behavior, as it surely was for Yeats, but a natural instinct bred from the same source as his art: "A lonely impulse of delight" ("An Irish Airman . . ."). Gregory's transcendent excellence makes all art action, and action art. This resolution of the tension common to others as if it were no tension at all is Gregory's uniqueness, and Yeats celebrated the genius of that passionate equilibrium throughout. Were it not for Mr. Kermode's conviction that Yeats's "preoccupation with Sidney and the Renaissance elegy . . . was forced on the poet [by whom?], and . . . impeded his full exploration of the significance of Gregory's death as the artist's escape,"[7] it would be unnecessary to insist again that it is precisely the Renaissance capacity for total accomplishment and interior balance which Gregory embodies. In Gregory, Yeats realized the individual manifestation of his Renaissance myth most fully. More than a visionary artist, Gregory is his principal symbol of the "self-delighting, / Self-appeasing, self-affrighting" soul which has recovered "radical inno-

---

[4] Ibid., p. 38. Kermode (ibid., p. 40) follows Witt ("The Making of an Elegy," p. 117) in ignoring stanza VIII, which, Yeats commented on a draft, he added because Mrs. Gregory did not believe he had made Robert Gregory's courage sufficiently plain (Berg Collection, New York Public Library). Their procedure is no more tenable than a reading of *Comus* which excludes consideration of the 1637 revisions.

[5] Kermode, *Romantic Image*, p. 41.

[6] See D. J. Gordon et al., *W. B. Yeats: Images of a Poet* (1961; Rpt. New York: Barnes and Noble, 1970), p. 34: "Art, the poem, knows nothing of such shrinkings, such doubts." See also Perloff, "The Consolation Theme," p. 308: "the elegy itself contains no references at all to a 'basic division,' a conflict between action and contemplation in Gregory's nature."

[7] Kermode, *Romantic Image*, p. 40.

cence." The shadow of that inimitable ideal lengthens far beyond "A Prayer for My Daughter" into *The Tower* and *The Winding Stair*.

Gregory is his society's hero; his modes of behavior, as both the Shepherd and the speaker of "In Memory of Major Robert Gregory" recognize, are indispensable to its coherence. With his death, his society consequently dies: this is what the entire series implies. But Yeats hardly intended, when he wrote "Shepherd and Goatherd," to create such a radical metaphorical relation. The poem, founded on religious paradox, offers a traditional consolation: only as a result of the hero's self-sacrifice can ultimate social integration occur. It provides the series with a normative image of organic recovery. "In Memory of Major Robert Gregory," however, shows that consolation ineffectual: the hero's death becomes an irredeemable loss, symbolizing the death of the speaker's own community. Traces of the original paradox remain: for a moment—"Our Sidney and our perfect man" (VI)—the speaker understands through Gregory's death the wholeness of the aristocratic world now lost. But that coherence is the flicker of the suffering imagination, not an actuality; the speaker and his wife must enter the tower alone. In "An Irish Airman . . ." and "Reprisals," Yeats wrestled more bitterly with the psychology of the hero and emerged with the galling knowledge that Gregory himself was implicitly responsible, morally, for the wastage of his homeland. Gregory, in "An Irish Airman . . .," assumes his fate irrelevant to his Kiltartan people; but "Reprisals" fiercely demonstrates the wrongness of his assumption. As the poem stunningly demolishes the myth of communal recovery proposed in "Shepherd and Goatherd," the speaker summons Gregory's ghost to learn that

> Half-drunk or whole-mad soldiery
> Are murdering your tenants there.
> Men that revere your father yet
> Are shot at on the open plain.
> Where may new-married women sit
> And suckle children now? Armed men
> May murder them in passing by
> Nor law nor parliament take heed.

Reprisals for what? Overtly the poem denounces England's callow reward for Ireland's military service: a barbaric invasion. But the suspicion lurks that the reprisals are the consequence of Gregory's departure from Kiltartan Cross. Gregory, his society's exemplar, was also its chief defender. Should he have left? This, in its way, is Yeats playing Conchubar to Gregory's Cuchulain as the problem emerges in

On Baile's Strand. Yet the speaker possesses a terrifying understanding which Conchubar, trying to fetter Cuchulain within societal limits, lacks: the knowledge that the question is superfluous. If to Gregory "The years to come seemed waste of breath, / A waste of breath the years behind," then his suicidal exhilaration must be accepted on its own terms: the act of a hero which he cannot evade without losing heroic stature. The dark correlative follows: his society cannot have him for hero unless it is prepared to allow him full autonomy, no matter how drastic the cultural consequences. As Yeats wrote of Helen-Maud, "Was there another Troy for her to burn?" Yeats's strength in "Reprisals" is the complexity of his moral discriminations, his capacity to regard heroism from wholly antithetical perspectives without losing tonal control; the poem brings the entire heroic code into question, points out its disastrous repercussions, and still enhances Gregory's heroic stature. The biting contrast between Gregory's courageous combat and the cowardly slaughters practiced by a "Half-drunk or whole-mad soldiery" leaves no doubt that Gregory's death is the death of heroism in the modern world. And with that death, the continuity of the pastoral community breaks down forever, passes into the burning dream of the poet ageing in his tower.

II

"Shepherd and Goatherd" has not impressed Yeats's critics. Awed by the masterfully intimate yet public resonance of "In Memory of Major Robert Gregory," they have considered it only a "preliminary study"[8] and objected to Yeats's use of pastoral elegy; Mr. Ure states flatly that the "convention has swamped the perception."[9] But the poem is not a

---

[8] William M. Carpenter, "The *Green Helmet* Poems and Yeats's Myth of the Renaissance," *Modern Philology* 67 (1969): 59. Witt ("The Making of an Elegy," pp. 114–15) assumes, on the sole evidence that Yeats wrote an additional poem about Gregory, that he was dissatisfied with "Shepherd and Goatherd." She argues that Yeats had an oddly incomplete vision of Gregory in that poem: "Strangely enough, few of these concepts—the moods shared by painters and men of letters, intensity as the essential quality of all art, the division in almost every artist between dreams and action—appear in the first poem Yeats wrote" (p. 113). Witt's disappointment is the foundation of Kermode's remarks: "the basic reason for the failure [of "Shepherd and Goatherd"] is probably that Yeats's important feelings about Gregory *as an artist* were as yet unformed. The rich possibilities of the *Observer* obituary remained unrealised" (*Romantic Image*, p. 36; Kermode's italics).

[9] Peter Ure, *Towards a Mythology* (1946; rpt. New York: Russell & Russell, 1967), p. 40. Witt ("The Making of an Elegy," p. 113) claims that "Yeats fails here in what William Empson called the pastoral process, 'putting the complex into the simple.' " Cf. also Kermode, *Romantic Image*, p. 36.

work of traditional pastoral, and you cannot dismiss its special devia-
tions from convention.

Intending his elegy to have the ceremonial elegance of "literary"
pastoral, Yeats nevertheless felt the hazards of using such an artificial
form in the twentieth century. He resolved the difficulty through a
recurrent formal paradox: the pastoral is simultaneously "literary" and
actual. Conventionally pastoral shepherd and goatherd are also Gregory's tenants; their landscape is Coole Park. The pastoral is not a
disguise. Arnold, in "Thyrsis" (11. 77–100), had momentarily thought
the Cumner Hills sufficiently like Sicily for him to entice Proserpine to
Oxford, where she might then release Clough from death. But Yeats
saw the absurdity and dishonesty of transforming a rocky Irish landscape into a lush Arcadian catalogue of flowers; the stark Burren
Hills—their "scarce grass" and "barren mountain ridge" open to "winter
blasts"—were intractably local. Refusing to import foreign flora, foreign
deities, he asserted that his actual world was already mythic. And by
placing this actual world in the conventional form of pastoral dialogue,
he deliberately created strange tensions. The actual landscape is not the
expected "literary" world; but the convention insists that the territory
is something other than what it seems. Hovering between these extremities, this diaphanous world appears curiously unfamiliar, an ambiguously visitable world which fuses reality with mental landscape in such
a way that the spiritualizing element hardly seems superimposed. The
world exactly suits the mysterious stature of its dead hero.

The method of myth is historical. This strange landscape is the one
which Gregory in life loved, as Yeats noted when he ranked his
paintings in the visionary pastoral tradition of Blake, Calvert, and
Palmer.[10] Recreating that landscape in the elegy, Yeats was seeing
through Gregory's eyes; tactfully, he made a poem Gregory would have
approved, and observed a decorum no less impressive than in his choice
of Renaissance allusions to compliment Lane. He recognized, as no one
much before his time could have, that the pastoral device was a fitting
evocation of Gregory's character. You cannot imagine Milton, steeped
in a still vital convention, wondering whether he could transform
Edward King into a shepherd without loss of verisimilitude. But the
Goatherd's description of Gregory's art, although it alters his medium,
is biographical before it is conventional:

> He had often played his pipes among my hills,
> And when he played it was their loneliness,
> The exultation of their stone, that cried
> Under his fingers.

10 See the *Observer* obituary (Kermode, *Romantic Image*, p. 33).

"His paintings," Yeats wrote, "had majesty and austerity, and at the same time sweetness."[11]   Gregory remains himself; again there is no disguise. Yeats's factuality validates the humanistic implications of his form—"a pastoral, modelled on what Virgil wrote for some friend of his and on what Spenser wrote of Sidney."[12] The signs of Gregory's superiority are those of another epoch, yet one whose values still survive at Coole; simultaneously, as Gregory enacts the courtier's artistry in the present, the formal elements of Renaissance elegy pull his greatness toward the past. The historical Gregory was a dream.

Yet had Yeats really imitated Spenser's "Astrophel," he would have produced a rhetorically futile exercise and destroyed an illusion which has all its force from being an allusion, and nothing else. Yeats was consciously acting as Spenser had acted on a similar occasion; as he had adopted Jonson's mask to praise Coole, he once again performed the cermonial role of a Renaissance poet. Here the analogy between "Astrophel" and "Shepherd and Goatherd" stops; the verbal and structural resemblances are nil. Although Astrophel and Gregory are both independent men who die foreign deaths, Astrophel leaves his pastoral community because, having "vanquisht all" (1. 78), he needs new realms to conquer. His "proud desire of praise" (1. 86) is the tragic flaw of *hubris,* and a dark strain of moral criticism informs Spenser's compassion for the dilemmas of greatness: "What need perill to be sought abroad, / Since round about us it doth make abroad?" (11. 89–90). This couplet may be the germ of Yeats's thinking in "An Irish Airman . . ." and "Reprisals," but nothing like it appears in "Shepherd and Goatherd." Gregory is innocent of his fate; "No settled man," seemingly without motive, he "had thrown the crook away / And died in the great war beyond the sea." The omission of further explanation favors mystery. You cannot even surmise (what seems evident from the later poems) that Gregory sought in his life as in his art an experience of heroic confrontation unsullied by ambition.

As this divergence from Spenser indicates, Yeats's concern was not Gregory's psychology but his symbolic nature. Gregory's physical abilities signify interior qualities equally great; in the Shepherd's balanced summation, the penultimate emphasis falls on his creation of social harmony:

---

11 W. B. Yeats, *The Letters of W. B. Yeats,* ed. Allan Wade (London: Hart-Davis, 1954), p. 646.

12 Ibid., pp. 647–48. Yet Yeats's word "modelled" has misled his critics into false expectations: Ure, *Towards a Mythology,* p. 40; Witt, "The Making of an Elegy," pp. 113–14; Perloff, "The Consolation Theme," p. 306; Carpenter, "The *Green Helmet* Poems," p. 59.

> He that was best in every country sport
> And every country craft, and of us all
> Most courteous to slow age and hasty youth,
> Is dead.

Courtesy—the private discipline which fosters "equality of culture"—is Gregory's dominant characteristic and the trait which the poem, no less than "In Memory of Major Robert Gregory," most seeks to illuminate. His art, more intimate and more deeply communal than in the later elegy, extends his courtesy. As he sings the "loneliness" and "exultation" of stone, earth's chthonic power yields to a human sensibility too empathetic to falsify. Gregory, the aristocrat-poet who has achieved his own "simplification through intensity," wins through *sprezzatura* what Shepherd and Goatherd, naturally simple, find impossible: the sound of a transcendent joy. His self-sacrifice to a seemingly alien land, as Dante knew when he "set his chisel to the hardest stone," is the precondition of greatest imaginative exaltation. Because he reveals civilization's tragic root and confirms the invisible reciprocity between earth and humankind, he becomes his society's mythologer—Orpheus, Odysseus, "No settled man," wresting from underworld darkness the secrets of the universe. His art creates communal cohesion: "Have not all races had their first unity from a mythology, that marries them to rock and hill?" It is appropriate that Gregory, partly an underground-man in "Shepherd and Goatherd" and a man of middle earth in the later elegy, should ascend to the "tumult in the clouds" in "An Irish Airman . . . ."

Chiefly, however, Yeats delineated Gregory as a unifying emblem by arranging a complex interaction between Shepherd and Goatherd. If they are Gregory's tenants meeting to mourn common loss, they are also antithetical types who understand his nature in wholly different ways; only between them can they comprehend his fullness. Both as poets and as allegorical representations of Gregory's multifaceted being, they strive for his self-completion; in uniting physically they reenact the cultural cohesion his life had vouchsafed. Incarnating stages in Yeats's life, they symbolize the traumatic self-division which Gregory's death caused. Plainly, although Yeats numbered Virgil's Fifth Eclogue among his models, he ransacked the classical convention of paired elegies held in a larger pastoral framework for every dramatic and symbolic possibility. The man who had just written "Ego Dominus Tuus" could not have been satisfied with a conception of dialogue based on the singing-match.

The Goatherd, too old to be shocked by the Shepherd's presence, bluntly underscores the separateness of their terrains, lives, poetic modes:

> But what has brought you here?
> Never until this moment have we met
> Where my goats browse on the scarce grass or leap
> From stone to stone.

A "hasty youth" by his own self-conscious admission, the Shepherd is shy and uncertain, seeking self-possession. In casually mentioning the cuckoo's cry, he masks his emotion of loss; he is thinking of the symbolic "speckled bird" in the elegy he will later have barely the courage to recite. "I wished before it [the cuckoo] ceased," he adds, hinting at his turbulence and showing himself, in the Goatherd's eyes, an immature optimist. The Goatherd, although bitter about "slow age," is a fatalist; gruff but not unfriendly, he twists the Shepherd's words to conform with his own dark vision, knowing that there are beasts below man, as well as birds above. Publicly acknowledging Gregory's death, he wishes against fate that he might have substituted his own. Despite these dramatic conflicts, valley and mountain meet symbolically for the first time; the reconciliation in nature—reversing the July eclogue of Spenser's *Shepheardes Calender*—anticipates the fraternity which the herdsmen finally establish. Gregory, containing all antinomies within himself, had courteously mediated between their extremes, had understood each type of intelligence. The estate's manager, he had traversed Coole's geography: the Shepherd had seen him with a shepherd's crook; the Goatherd, possessive of solitude, had found him "among *my* hills." His presence had assured them that all latent tensions in their universe had been resolved. With that principle of unity now dissolved, the herdsmen must courteously work out their own integration. They come together for necessary companionship in crisis—not, like Virgil's Mopsus and Menalcas, for a serious diversion to which Daphnis's death is incidental. The poem, accentuating communal involvement in grief, defines Gregory's death as the tragic experience from which true cohesion emerges; its distinctive achievement is that the mourning of loss and the enactment of a new cultural synthesis occur simultaneously.

The herdsmen's elegies, although "composed" earlier, are integral parts of the evolving drama. Unlike those of Mopsus and Menalcas, they are subjective utterances which offer, inevitably, opposed interpretations of Gregory's nature. The Shepherd, who has spoken previously of his gregarious magnanimity and physical excellence, elegizes his passing in similar terms; he marvels at Gregory's poised, self-controlled independence less because it is intrinsically valuable than because it has momentarily graced the community with beauty. "You sing as always of the natural life," the Goatherd comments; the Shepherd's perception gives an outward view, earth-oriented, social. The Goatherd, however, sharing Gregory's brooding, visionary isolation, sings of his eternal imagination. Almost a vicarious participant, he envisages Gregory's future "victories of the mind," his recovery of innocence, his abounding interior joy. Regarded separately, neither elegy renders the complex unity of Gregory's symbolic person; the insufficiency of each song functions as praise: he cannot be comprehended by any single mind. Combined, however, these elegies offer an adequate statement of Gregory's central position in the universe. Because they are so interdependent, it is wrong to think the Goatherd's rapt vision the consolation which the poem extends. If that vision incorporates Yeats's own theory of the afterlife, the Goatherd's dramatic utterance nevertheless makes no claim to a "prescriptive reality."[13] Yeats had no interest in comforting Lady Gregory with esoteric doctrine, nor did he follow Virgil in affirming order restored by apotheosis. Here as throughout his elegies (although not in *A Vision*), Yeats maintained that consolation is not contingent upon the soul's progress after death; it involves, rather, a recognition of who the person *was*. It is the Shepherd, at the end, who speaks Yeats's convictions. Acknowledging the interdependence of the elegies, he knows that private acts of mourning must become ceremony; the songs of "the mountain and the valley," the communal emblems of new understanding, must be brought to Coole.

Like their poems and landscapes, Shepherd and Goatherd represent the halves of that inexplicable unity through which Gregory transcended the artist's doom, the fragmentation of personality so passionately explored in "Ego Dominus Tuus." They see in each other and in each other's song rejected or unrecognized aspects of self without which they cannot be entire. Their meeting, although it ritually imitates his reconciliation of opposites, is no substitute for personal equilibrium; brilliantly, Yeats's dialogue dramatizes the very problem which the poem claims Gregory to have solved. With melancholic wit the Shepherd states the difficulty:

> I thought of rhyme alone,
> For rhyme can beat a measure out of trouble

---

13 B. L. Reid, *William Butler Yeats: The Lyric of Tragedy* (Norman, Oklahoma: University of Oklahoma Press, 1961), p. 118. Cf. Witt, "The Making of an Elegy," p. 114; Unterecker, *A Reader's Guide*, pp. 138–39; Perloff, "The Consolation Theme," pp. 306–7; George Mills Harper, "Yeats's Quest for Eden," in *The Dolmen Press Yeats Centenary Papers*, ed. Liam Miller (Dublin: Dolmen Press, 1968), pp. 322–23.

> And make the daylight sweet once more; but when
> I had driven every rhyme into its place
> The sheep had gone from theirs.

Less capable than Gregory, the Shepherd finds the creation of imaginative order and the creation of actual order mutually exclusive endeavors:

>   I worked all day,
> And when 'twas done so little had I done
> That maybe 'I am sorry' in plain prose
> Had sounded better to your mountain fancy.

The statement conceals many hesitations. If the poetry is bad, what can justify the poet's sacrifice of his life to his art? The unobtrusive pun on "plain" asks whether the sacrifice must be total. Must he ascend the summit to gain imaginative insight? Must he renounce human fellowship? Why is the organized emotion of formal elegy (implicitly referring to "Shepherd and Goatherd" as a whole) more consolatory than common condolence, daily speech (blank verse)? For the Shepherd, Gregory's death is a critical rite of passage.

It is not true, in this poem, that poetry makes nothing happen; as Gregory knew, poetry is the most potent form of action. At the end, the Shepherd discovers that his "strayed sheep" have somehow returned. The restoration of order results directly from art and the sense of community which art engenders; elegy, transcending particularities, prompts the regrouping of "strayed" selves. Note the Goatherd's unexpectedly frank response to the Shepherd's song:

> You sing as always of the natural life,
> And I that made like music in my youth
> Hearing it now have sighed for that young man
> And certain lost companions of my own.

The Shepherd has "done" more than lament Gregory's death. He has restored to the Goatherd elements of character long forgotten: his youth, the pleasures of human society and natural loveliness. The Goatherd momentarily approximates Gregory's equilibrium; his song, reflecting his renovation in the course of the dialogue, manifests an ebullience hardly apparent in the ironical, solemn Goatherd the Shepherd first encounters. Reciprocally, the Goatherd's song makes the Shepherd revise his attitudes toward art and time. Although the Shepherd mentions Gregory's son (Lady Gregory's "grandson"), he does not regard him as Gregory's symbolic continuation in time, a sign of permanence despite apparent loss. Initially, he grieves that "There's nothing of him left but half a score / Of sorrowful, austere, sweet, lofty pipe tunes." Yet at the end, he understands that organic regeneration: "our rhymes on strips of new-torn bark" may console "wife and mother, / And children when they spring up shoulder-high." His altered perspective derives from the Goatherd's supernatural image of Gregory's afterlife:

> ['] . . . clambering at the cradle-side,
> He dreams himself his mother's pride,
> All knowledge lost in trance
> Of sweeter ignorance.'

Naturalizing the Goatherd's vision, the Shepherd easily associates his memories of actual childhood with Gregory's children. He had forgotten youth because he is "hasty," anxious to show maturity. Especially in his song, he has simulated what he assumes to be the typical attitude of old age mourning life's transience and has thus rejected his own experience, which should naturally have induced an optimistic sense of organic continuity. In imagining "children when they spring up shoulder-high," he drops the false mask of age and matures. For Shepherd and Goatherd alike, the entire dialogue involves a self-discovery through the recognition of Gregory and of each other. As age and youth begin harmoniously to converge, Gregory's courteous mediation bears new fruit.

Amidst the concluding images of restored order ("this old ram" is the fertile patriarch of a natural family), the most telling emblem of regeneration is the proposed movement toward Coole, the source of communal allegiances and the Jonsonian shelter for art and the artist's heirs, the imaginative and natural symbols of Gregory's perpetuation in time. Not simply a tactful expression of sorrow, the movement virtually metamorphoses "Shepherd and Goatherd" into a country house poem. Yeats's extraordinary deviation from poems like "To Penshurst" and "To Sir Robert Wroth"—a deviation which shows how well he understood the genre—is that the house is seen not from the poet's perspective but through the eyes of the peasantry. In an action which imitates Gregory's symbolic joining of all terrains, the herdsmen pass through the entire estate, from mountainous wildness to temperate valley to rustic sheepfold to aristocratic country house. Like the logical progression up the Great Chain of Being in "To Penshurst," but with a naturalness less arranged, the movement implies that Coole is the culmination of aesthetic and social evolution. Even more than Yeats's intricate reworkings of the pastoral dialogue, the form gives physical shape to the Renaissance world Gregory exemplified.

The political intent of Yeats's alteration is transparent: the poem is a full defense of the aristocratic order. If the poet-speaker of a country house poem may be thought biased because he stands to benefit from patronage, no such motive can be imputed to the peasantry—who, because they have "nothing to lose and so do not fear"[14] —are free from self-interest. But politics was not Yeats's main focus. By taking peasant masks and thus eliminating himself from the country house poem, he saw a way to sympathize publicly with Lady Gregory without risking a potentially bad poem whose direct condolence, with its inevitable temptations to sentiment, might wreck his purpose. This elegy attempts what no other even considers doing: consoling the bereaved *within* the poem. Yeats humbly recognized that others had lost more than he. Despite a long tradition of poets mourning their dead poetic kinsmen, and in a way which suggests that the surviving poet is the only one who suffers, Yeats broke with convention to honor Lady Gregory's courage. Thus, the Shepherd describes her heroic capacity to absorb the shock of loss without submitting to hysteria; the dignity of the plain style reflects her poise:

> She goes about her house erect and calm
> Between the pantry and the linen-chest,
> Or else at meadow or at grazing overlooks
> Her labouring men, as though her darling lived,
> But for her grandson now; there is no change
> But such as I have seen upon her face
> Watching our shepherd sports at harvest-time
> When her son's turn was over.

There is no break in her order of perception; her son's death is part of natural process, "harvest-time." Determined to preserve continuity, she possesses an understanding which Shepherd and Goatherd reach only by the end of the poem. Her quiet strength is the source of Coole's regenerative power. The wellspring of Gregory's excellence, Coole remains his distinguished survivor, the living center of community.

III

Yeats's sense of Coole's resilience was brief. Despite his affection for Lady Gregory, he knew that Gregory's death curtailed Coole's utility as

---

[14] W. B. Yeats, *Essays and Introductions* (New York: Macmillan, 1961), p. 251.

a viable symbol of aristocracy. If his myth of that luminous beauty was to survive, he needed another historical emblem, another architecture to embody it. "In Memory of Major Robert Gregory," although a chronicle of fragmentation, shifts the center of Yeats's unitary society from Coole to Thoor Ballylee and implicitly names the tower's inhabitant heir to the aristocratic legacy. Yeats could not escape the terrible burden that transference imposed. In this first full statement of selfhood to emerge from the tower, the pervasive mood of inadequacy, of overwhelming difficulty ahead, is Yeats's, not simply his speaker's.

To notice how Yeats altered motifs from "Shepherd and Goatherd" is to see that in every instance he turned positive elements negative. "The great war beyond the sea," so distant that Coole is immune from threat, becomes the "bitter . . . wind / That shakes the shutter" (XII), an immediate violence portending the tower's destruction. The Goatherd's laconic sigh for "certain lost companions of my own" becomes a brooding catalogue of the dead; Coole's warm hearth-fire, a cheerless smolder of turf. Jonsonian hospitality and courtesy are gloomily known at the tower only by their absence. Where "Shepherd and Goatherd" uses literary forms to indicate Gregory's Renaissance nature, this poem channels that metaphoric equation into a limitary epithet ("*Our* Sidney") containing just enough irony to reveal the speaker's knowledge of illusion.[15] While the Goatherd finds his visionary powers unimpaired by Gregory's death, the speaker knows that he has lost "imagination" (XII). Seen in the mirror of the earlier elegy, "In Memory of Major Robert Gregory" presents a universe as chilled and dark as the "*narrow winding stairs*" (I) themselves. This is Yeats's self-brutalizing compliment to Coole: the world from which Gregory came cannot be imitated.

Yeats exalted Gregory with cunning. The title misleads you into thinking that you are reading a classical elegy whose speaker, although he does not mention Gregory until stanza VI, nevertheless intends from the outset to devote the second half of his monologue to the dead hero. These assumptions are invalid, as Yeats's indispensable explanation (XII) of his dramatic structure makes plain.[16] First, the speaker begins

---

[15] Perloff ("The Consolation Theme," p. 317) also notes how carefully Yeats qualified his allusion to Sidney; it is characteristic of Yeats's strong feeling for linguistic decorum—as well as that imposed by historical change—that he refrained from offending credibility. Many critics have observed that Yeats adapted his stanza form from Cowley's "Ode on the Death of Mr. William Harvey," but the imitation of Cowley's form is really too subtle to constitute, rhetorically, an allusion to the Renaissance. T. McAlindon, "Yeats and the English Renaissance," *PMLA* 82 (1967): 168–69, indicates resemblances between Yeats's elegy and Jonson's "To the Immortall Memorie, and Friendship of that Noble Paire, Sir Lucius Cary, and Sir H. Morison"; but these are thematic and (in some cases) verbal, not formal.

[16] See Graham Martin, "*The Wild Swans at Coole,*" in *An Honoured Guest,* eds.

with a ceremony to welcome Mrs. Yeats, not an elegy; however disheartened his introduction, he intends—in lieu of "fitter welcome"—to offer an "appropriate commentary" on his dead friends. Second, through stanzas I–V, the thought of Gregory's death hardly dominates; he initially expects to depict Gregory as briefly as Johnson, Synge, and Pollexfen: neither Gregory nor his death, in short, seems unusual. Third, like most people, the speaker cannot predict the swerves of his mind. Thus, the monologue encompasses a revelation more poetically complex than any Yeats had previously attempted. The revelation—coming in stanza VI with the crowning epithet for Gregory—is so powerful that the speaker must break his normative pattern (one stanza for each friend), must turn his ceremony into private elegy. In the process of the poem the speaker awakes to Gregory's uniqueness and fathoms the unrecognized depths of his own loss. The image of Gregory, appearing with an unanticipated magnitude, immediately orders into clarity the previously unfocussed themes of courtesy, self-completion, and estrangement. The most stunning quality of the earlier commentaries is not that Yeats integrated them so fully with his portrait of Gregory. It is, instead, that he created the illusion that their progression toward the revelation is, in terms of the speaker's psychology, both inevitable and unconscious. The climax in new vision is the core of the poem's greatness. No other first-person elegy in English withholds its major figure for so long and gains so much by that restraint. No other elegy risks so much and succeeds so well in its feint that its true hero is not intended as the main subject, but only as part of a procession of men equalized by death. To read this poem properly after understanding Yeats's design requires a deliberate naiveté, a submission to the gradual unfolding of his speaker's mind.

The speaker's interior explosion transforms his perspective. Ms. Perloff argues that "The first two stanzas contain the invocation to the Muse in the person of the speaker himself as source of poetic inspiration,"[17] but there *is no muse* until Gregory appears as a joyous presence in stanza VI; in Yeats's fine conceit, Gregory is the informing spirit of his own celebration. Like Lamb in Coleridge's "This Lime-tree Bower My Prison," Gregory endows the speaker with the imaginative empathy to conceive beauty and unity despite personal grief; seeing

Denis Donoghue and J. R. Mulryne (London: Edward Arnold, 1965), p. 71. Although stressing the importance of stanza XII, Martin does not explicate the poem's design.

[17] Perloff, "The Consolation Theme," pp. 321–22. Perloff also contends that Johnson, Synge, and Pollexfen represent the traditional "procession of mourners" (pp. 315, 322)—an ingenious suggestion which fails to convince because it assumes the speaker's conscious intention of designing an elegy.

through Gregory's eyes, the speaker beholds an old world made lovely. The structural consequence of this metamorphosis is bafflingly simple. The monologue does not simply go on; it goes *back*. The second section (VII–XII) revises the first in the new light of Gregory's ideal nature. The speaker begins, appropriately, with a fresh comprehension of his tower's austere majesty: stanza VII reorders stanza I (as does stanza X). Stanza VIII reworks stanza V; stanza IX alters stanzas III and IV. These correspondences, created through deliberate reconsideration, help explain the economical clarity the poem achieves despite its complex materials: not the themes and types of image, but the attitude and tone of voice change. The revision underscores the speaker's awareness: Gregory is unique because, living in the same world as others, he masters the difficulties they find insurmountable, gains a complete interior harmony from the same "complexities of mire or blood" they find engulfing and chaotic.

The poem opens in joylessness. What Yeats gained from delaying Gregory's appearance is the normalcy of his speaker's morbid agitation; you cannot think it the consequence of new tragedy. Disruptions, ironies of expected fulfillment somehow thwarted abound:

> Now that we're almost settled in our house
> I'll name the friends that cannot sup with us
> Beside a fire of turf in th' ancient tower.

The brave joviality of "Now" betrays insecurity; having so long anticipated domestic pleasure, he finds himself only "almost" settled. The tower is a tomb, mocking in massive permanence the dead who already crowd his memories; imprisoned, he must ironically rely upon its strength to protect him from the howling wind.[18] These unvoiced emotions belie his superficial calm; yet not until stanza XII can he confess that the underlying purpose of his monologue is to drown out the storm:

> I had thought, *seeing* how bitter is that wind
> That shakes the shutter, to have brought to mind
> All those that manhood tried . . .

---

18 Cf. Perloff, ibid., p. 314; influenced by Yeats's actual joy in marriage, she sees the entire stanza in a very positive light. She finds the sexual consummation of his marriage implied in the word "bed," an over-reading which I believe the text does not warrant; part of her argument is based on the common assumption that "the winding stair is always an emblem of spiritual ascent in Yeats's poetry" (ibid.). Richard Ellmann (*Yeats: The Man and the Masks* [1948; rpt. New York: Dutton, n.d.] p. 239) was the first to introduce this idea; but it is invalidated, at least as a generalization, by "Meditations . . ." (VII) and "Blood and the Moon" (I, II, IV).

The primordial terror is a fear of death-in-life. His brutally ironic wit—"I'll name the friends that cannot sup with us"—touches social and personal incoherence. The communal dinner in "To Penshurst" and Jonson's festive toast to Sir William Sidney in the birthday "Ode," as well as Yeats's "To a Young Beauty" (1918), are analogues for the meal which the speaker's guests may now attend only as ghosts. The ceremonial meal, celebrating marriage and possession of the tower, would have symbolized the speaker's own selfhood. His "close companions"— "A portion of my mind and life" (VI)—would have shown him the continuity of his intellectual and aesthetic development, clarified the mutual goal of their labors: joy, vibrancy. But as at the end of *Reveries,* he knows himself caught, middle-aged and aimless, in the vacuum of a crisis.

The emphasis on ceremony in stanzas I–III, the discussion of introductions (II), the implicit idea of "appropriate commentary"— these are verbal compensations for broken continuities, surrogates for actual behavior. Through the commentaries the speaker seeks to make himself symbolically whole; simultaneously, he examines his present condition in light of past experience, searching to explain his impasse. These private needs, however, are overshadowed by the need to create a public if imaginary community through which he can make the tower seem hospitable.[19] Thus, by describing his friends, he vicariously performs the welcome they would have afforded his wife and invites her to share the past he seeks to recover. These ceremonies have neither "heart" nor the indispensable spirit of courtesy. Twice in stanza I he verges toward the later conceit (VI): death has killed courtesy, prevented both the dinner and a proper welcome. Johnson, the student of courtesy, is dead (III). As yet he does not connect the felt loss of courtesy with the death of Gregory, its greatest exemplar. He knows only that he lacks the aristocratic rhythm of "beautiful manners" needed to counteract the storm's unmeasured cacophony.

Self-division and social fragmentation press the speaker to clarify his difficulties. The contexts established by the opening stanzas are too broad to warrant limiting the problems to the tragic isolation of the modern artist: the issues, pertaining to Pollexfen as well, have epochal dimensions. Gradually the speaker discovers that his friends—unlike Dante, the tower's first inhabitant—all failed to achieve unity of being:

---

19 Perloff's reading ("The Consolation Theme," p. 314) overlooks Yeats's choice of verb tense: "Although one cannot tell at this point just who the 'we' *are,* the speaker constantly reminds both himself and his audience that he *is* a member of a larger community" [italics mine]. But the community has plainly dissolved; were it still intact, the speaker would not need to remind himself so vigorously of its existence.

either they could not reconcile conflicting aspects of self, or they could not handle the conflicting claims of imagination and outer reality.

"Lionel Johnson comes the first to mind" (III) not because Yeats followed chronology but because the speaker, seeking communion with his dead friends, is self-consciously puzzled that Johnson should have "loved his learning *better* than mankind." Loving deeply yet unable to act courteously, the speaker sees the reverse disposition in Johnson, whose courtesy, lacking love, was a ritualized mask designed to conceal alienation. Critical yet affectionate, the speaker describes Johnson's tragic self-division in language punctuated by long, questioning pauses between the run-on lines:

> much falling he
> Brooded upon sanctity
> Till all his Greek and Latin learning seemed
> A long blast upon the horn that brought
> A little nearer to his thought
> A measureless consummation that he dreamed.

Manic-depressive, solitary, Johnson could not tolerate his own sinning yet preyed upon it; prone to despair (an extension of the speaker's mood), he quested for apocalypse and, caught in that unrealizable dream, could not reconcile his foulness with its hieratic beauty.

In turning to Synge (IV), the speaker's sense of his own monologue is again pivotal: Synge, dying, "chose the living world for text"—but he himself, living, has chosen the dead. Their common impetus is the passion to link antithetical realms: Gregory, when he appears, is the unifying "image" of a living dead man. Unlike Johnson the spiritual pilgrim, Synge traveled from Paris to the Aran Islands to find a reality which fulfilled his dream of vigorous heroic life; his discovery of a congenial world matters to the speaker precisely because his own circle of friends is broken. Sharing Johnson's disillusion with the "common dream" but demanding a humanistic solution, Synge yet reached his imaginative destination too late. The repetition of "Towards nightfall" marks the speaker's knowledge of agonizingly brief accomplishment.

From the Aran Islands the speaker's memory travels up the coast to Mayo (V). If Synge was "a sick man picturing energy, a doomed man picturing gaiety,"[20] Pollexfen, healthy and active, declined into contemplative torpor, unable to maintain a balance. His early conviviality, contrasting with Johnson's aloofness, accentuates Synge's arduous

[20] W. B. Yeats, *The Autobiography of William Butler Yeats* (New York: Macmillan, 1938), p. 390.

quest for an ideal community. Like Johnson, he needed a transcendental order; yet instead of a "measureless" beatific passion, he sought to nullify passion itself: his determinism is the antithesis of the passionate freedom Synge found among the peasantry. And his sluggishness, like Johnson's melancholy, is a specter of the speaker's own crisis: will he too—almost "settled"—end in debility?

Having repossessed his friends by act of speech, the speaker has asked an unarticulated question of them all, as in "The Tower." Ironically, they cannot explain the riddles of their lives, or his: "And now their breathless faces seem to look / Out of some old picture-book" (VI). Yet his commentaries have an organizing principle. Unconsciously he has set forth, in negative terms, the disparate materials from which a unity must emerge: a fully courteous and free man whose entire life synthesizes active and contemplative modes without loss of imaginative intensity, a man in harmony with his society who unifies desire with actuality and reconciles earthly with transcendental visions. Suddenly the speaker realizes the ideal in Gregory, "Our Sidney and our perfect man." The allusion to Elizabeth's court, momentarily transforming the tower's cold spaces into a pageantry, ennobles and unifies the dispersed companions. The supremely tragic moment renders loneliness and exultation inseparable: just as the speaker's aristocratic society achieves an imagined unity of culture, the "small circle" breaks. And with Gregory's death dies its principal virtue, courtesy.

Gregory's "discourtesy of death" (VI) may be an elegant euphemism intended to lessen the speaker's bafflement. But the arch understatement, referring to dying in the language of the living, chiefly designates the ceremonial terms in which the speaker—like Lady Gregory in "Shepherd and Goatherd"—understands even the most fundamental of crises. As an awed compliment, the phrase is paradox: it is incomprehensible that Gregory, whose decorum so far outstripped Johnson's or the speaker's, should not remain in death as courteous as in life.[21] Gregory, moreover, was "our perfect man"; thus charmed with immortality, how could he have died? (Not until stanza XI can the speaker resolve the dilemma.) Finally, the phrase defines not Gregory's "discourtesy" but death's. As in "Upon a Dying Lady," death rudely

---

[21] The literary source of the paradox—which Yeats inverted—may be Browne's speculation, "I do think . . . that many mysteries ascribed to our own invention have been the courteous revelations of spirits; for those noble essences in heaven bear a friendly regard unto their fellow creatures on earth" (*Religio Medici*, Part I, Section 31). This is Yeats's slight misquotation of a passage he cited with full concurrence in "Swedenborg, Mediums, and the Desolate Places" (W. B. Yeats, *Explorations* [New York: Macmillan, 1962], p. 60).

THE DEATH OF GREGORY

destroys not only life but the very forms which make life cohere: social
discourse, forms of personal and aesthetic order. Against such barbarism the speaker affirms civility by celebrating its perfect emblem.

Yeats knew that language creates realities: his speaker must deny
his own notion that Gregory shares his friends' discourteous silence:

> For all things the delighted eye now sees
> Were loved by him . . .
>
> [VII]

"For" is a rebuttal. The speaker's new visionary delight is proof of
Gregory's continuing courtesy, unmarred by death. Moving toward the
window, he sees open spaces: the symbolic expansion of self transforms
the tower from a prison into a promontory of vision. Mr. Reid contends
that the scene is "newly poignant because now it is lost to Robert
Gregory,"[22] but the real point is that the speaker has assimilated
Gregory's courteous perception, his passionate love, and in doing so has
kept his affections alive. No longer feeling the uneasiness of being
"almost settled," he gazes upon a familiar world which, for all its
stormy roughness, translates his conflicts into aesthetic harmony.[23]
The "old storm-broken trees" have endured; violence has enhanced
their intrinsic beauty (compare stanza XII). The movement of the
water-hen disturbed by the cattle echoes the emotional displacement
caused by Gregory's death and rationalizes disruption as part of natural
process. Equally important, that scenario at the ford occurs "Nightly";
the speaker, who has earlier associated "nightfall" with irrevocable
death, now conceives the temporal rhythm of his world. Ultimately the
landscape has a visionary reality: inside the tower, he imagines it from
the outside in order to convey his sensation of stability and completed
form, and to render visually the traditional marriage of tower and
stream. His unity of aesthetic perception, Gregory's gift, has the same
function as poetry in "Shepherd and Goatherd": "For rhyme can beat
a measure out of trouble / And make the daylight sweet once more."

With the tower's central position in its immediate landscape consolidated, the speaker's imagination radiates outward to the larger territory
which Gregory, as in "Shepherd and Goatherd," synthesized through
his actions and art (VIII, IX). Remembering his horsemanship with a
vivid intimacy reinforced by the casual lapse of memory, the speaker
implicitly compares that consummate control over physical action with

22 B. L. Reid, *The Lyric of Tragedy*, p. 113.

23 Yeats possibly intended his description to resemble Gregory's sepia drawing of
the tower and its environment (reproduced in Joseph Hone, *W. B. Yeats* [1943; rpt.
London: Macmillan, 1965], facing p. 319).

Pollexfen's gradual enervation. Pollexfen "could have shown" that human passion is subject to an impersonal order, but Gregory mastered from within himself the passion of his aristocratic quest, created his own form, revealed an inimitable *sprezzatura:*

> At Mooneen he had leaped a place
> So perilous that half the astonished meet
> Had shut their eyes . . .

Unlike Johnson, *"fall*ing," and Synge, who reached the Aran Islands only "Towards night*fall*," Gregory was above disaster: his symbolic action, a connection between opposites, is a leaping of the abyss of failure.

Gregory's art is public legend binding society in common recognition of its epical territory. His art, for the speaker's "small circle," is private legend:

> We dreamed that a great painter had been born
> To cold Clare rock and Galway rock and thorn,
> To that stern colour and that delicate line
> That are our secret discipline
> Wherein the gazing heart doubles her might.

Gregory's art would have given the West of Ireland its fullest articulation. Yet the speaker is concerned less with his output than with his temperament, the visionary power he himself has felt in evoking the tower. Yeats's obituary notwithstanding, Gregory knew tragic passion without undergoing personal estrangement, "tragic war"; he remains in Yeats's work the sole example of an artist who achieves that condition without pain and exile. Gregory was "born" to a landscape which the speaker has but recently occupied, a terrain like that which Synge discovered only after "long travelling." He came instinctively to "our secret discipline," the formal means of containing passion until it all but bursts. Their humanistic art, "Wherein the gazing heart *doubles* her might," is a repudiation of Johnson's dream of a "measureless" consummation; yet the speaker, despite his profession of kinship, recognizes how hard he has labored to achieve that same *sprezzatura.* Here, imperceptibly, his later self-deprecation (XI) originates. Gregory the Renaissance humanist is his superior, a man who could have realized the speaker's own ambition of transforming his regional experience at Kiltartan into a microcosm of joy: "he had the intensity / To have published all to be a world's delight." In a stanza whose explicit concern with measurement is quietly reinforced by paired images and countable elements, the word "all" resounds with the speaker's immense awe.

"A world's delight": the latent memory of Sidney[24] marks the outermost boundaries both of Gregory's impact and of the speaker's imagination. Recalling his own "delighted" vision of the tower (VII), he turns back to explore the interior of his home:

> What other could so well have counselled us
> In all lovely intricacies of a house
> As he that practised or that understood
> All work in metal or in wood,
> In moulded plaster or in carven stone?

Combining the craftsman's skill with the aesthetician's taste for the arts of living, Gregory is responsible for revealing the tower's "secret" beauty, interior as well as exterior; not until "Meditations . . ." will the speaker consider himself his tower's creator. The faintly Augustan verse reflects both the speaker's contentment and Gregory's poise. But the syntax expands dynamically, multiplying rather than enumerating elements, suggesting the increasing range of Gregory's abilities. The refrain, instead of exploding into "all" (IX), indicates his power to channel that complex totality into simplicity: "As though he had but that *one* trade *alone*." The versification of the two stanzas reenacts the central paradox of Gregory's intensity: multiple unity, unified multiplicity.

Knowledge of Gregory's perfection inevitably crushes the sense of shared community stressed throughout; the speaker must admit the crucial difference (XI):

> Some burn damp faggots, others may consume
> The entire combustible world in one small room
> As though dried straw, and if we turn about
> The bare chimney is gone black out
> Because the work had finished in that flare.

The smolder, like the "fire of turf" (I), is the speaker's life, his imagination: mere survival, an art without creative passion. Enclosed in stone, he realizes that Gregory, in passionate vision, has transformed all

---

24 The phrase is from the Countess of Pembroke's elegy on Sidney, "Astrophel" (or "The Lay of Clorinda"), 1. 49. Yeats plainly knew not only Spenser's *Astrophel* but all the other elegies on Sidney published in the same volume with *Colin Clout's Come Home Again* (1595). In the essay on Spenser (*Essays*, p. 381), he cited 11. 103–6 of Matthew Roydon's "An Elegie, or Friends Passion, for his Astrophill."

external architectures into "the divine architecture of the body."[25] Ms. Witt states that in the act of death, "for a moment only," Gregory achieves unity of being.[26] But the unity of Gregory's entire life is evident throughout. His destruction, his last creation, is not the achievement of a totality previously unattained but the final, inevitable expression of a complete selfhood not to be judged by ordinary standards: "What made us dream that he could comb grey hair?" His death, once a baffling "discourtesy" (VI), now makes sense. Gregory was already a "complete arc"; "the work had finished in that flare." As Yeats had eulogized Shawe-Taylor, "his work is as fully accomplished as though he had lived through many laborious years."[27]

Ms. Perloff argues that Yeats, criticizing Gregory for wasting his passion, claims his own slow, damp fire to be the proper emblem of the creative imagination. Her evidence is not the poem, but a passage in *The Tragic Generation* derived from the poem: "They [Dowson, Johnson, Horne, Symons] had taught me that violent energy, which is like a fire of straw, consumes in a few minutes the nervous vitality, and is useless in the arts. Our fire must burn slowly . . . ."[28] But despite the same central image of fire burning through straw, the poem speaks not of Gregory's "nervous vitality" but of an energy everywhere controlled by judgment and courtesy. Hardly a wasted passion "useless in the arts," his intensity has produced a perfection both personal and aesthetic; the speaker's romanticism makes Gregory's deep visionary understanding more significant than its embodiment in paintings.[29] The poem acknowledges what the prose ignores: Gregory belonged to a different order of humankind. And instead of showing a Yeats deliberately burning a slow fire to avoid early exhaustion, it depicts a speaker who feels condemned to his "damp faggots" and is, if anything, jealous of

---

[25] W. B. Yeats, *Mythologies* (New York: Macmillan, 1959), pp. 332–33.

[26] Witt, "The Making of an Elegy," p. 121.

[27] *Essays*, p. 345.

[28] Perloff, "The Consolation Theme," pp. 310, 319–20; *Autobiography*, p. 271. Perloff further argues that "The speaker . . . of the poem is consistently presented as one who has heroically survived the turmoil and temptations of the fledgling artist to achieve the Unity of Being denied to Robert Gregory in his lifetime" (pp. 307–8). But in light of stanza XII, which is the only point at which the speaker considers his youth directly, "heroic" seems the very last word he would apply to his process of maturation. The speaker's pain is precisely that his survival gives him so little consolation.

[29] Perloff rightly corrects Witt and Kermode for not seeing that "the speaker regards Gregory's achievement in painting as potential, not actual" ("The Consolation Theme," p. 319); but she uses that notion of potentiality to derogate Gregory's accomplishment and argues that "The passionately warm praise of Gregory is undercut by a slight tinge of skepticism" (p. 316).

Gregory's blaze. Tonally, however, his remorse remains muted. He considers Gregory's death neither the sign of failure nor the beckoning symbol of the "artist's escape": part of a stupendous glory, it justifies the struggle of the speaker's aristocratic community to achieve that inimitable nobility. It proves that the aristocratic ideal is real.

But the unifying aesthetic calm of tragic elation cannot persist. Panged thoughts of ageing swirl the undercurrents of rueful self-irony (IX) into shame, hollowness, inexpressible self-doubt. Stanza XII is startling not merely because, in formulating the poem's structure, it admits so much more than the introduction; it points to feelings about his friendships which the commentaries themselves conceal. When you think you may have touched bottom in a Yeatsian dramatic mono-logue, he will always carry you down further. "I had thought . . .

> to have brought to mind
> All those that manhood tried, or childhood loved
> Or boyish intellect approved . . .

What is new here, and made poignant by the decorous phrasing, is the raw self-loathing, the complete lack of self-sympathy which retrospec-tion has engendered. Again he apologizes for his inhospitable welcome: he can *bring* no more friends, for "a thought / Of that late death *took* all my heart for speech." No voice remains to counteract the raging storm. His desolation, extending beyond Gregory's death, is a grief for the futility of his life, now bitterly revealed in Gregory's splendor. Its "lovely intricacies" forgotten, the tower again stands chill and cavern-ous upon barren ground. The resurgent hopes of new fruition, gained from ceremonial mourning in "Shepherd and Goatherd," are here absent.

IV

"A Prayer for My Daughter" (1919) is the emotional sequel, not simply the theoretical complement, to "In Memory of Major Robert Greg-ory."[30] To be sure, Yeats remembered the opening portraits in *The Courtier,* Jonson's epistles to the nobility in *The Forrest* and *The Under-Wood,* and intended his two poems as paired aristocratic images in the Renaissance tradition. Yet the prayer, properly construed, is a continuation of the internal drama sparked by Gregory's death. It

---

30 Cf. Alex Zwerdling, *Yeats and the Heroic Ideal* (New York: New York Univer-sity Press, 1965), p. 84.

begins in exactly the same environment of brute noise which closes the elegy: the connection is an unstated memory of disaster. As a compensatory poem, it attempts to create in Anne the Renaissance courtesy and joy which the elegy claims irrevocably lost; continuing to transfer the aristocratic culture from Coole to Thoor Ballylee, it asserts amidst many hesitations that the tower may nurture the genesis of a new dynasty.

As "To be Carved on a Stone . . ." (first version) suggests, Yeats had endowed his children with intellectual and social identities long before they were born. But "The Second Coming," composed just before Anne's birth and strategically placed before the prayer, indicates her central importance as a symbolic counterimage to historical catastrophe. The frenetic background of Yeats's apocalypse encompassed thoughts of the Russian revolution, the arrest of Con Markiewicz and Maud as conspirators in the "German Plot" against conscription, Sinn Fein's victory over the moderates in the election of December 1918, England's imposition of military rule in Ireland, and the retaliatory guerrilla campaign waged by the IRA. In "The Second Coming," natural upheaval echoes political and moral decay: "The best lack all conviction, while the worst / Are full of passionate intensity." The judgment achieves a complex understanding: Yeats's speaker can watch in passive horror the inevitable demise of a once noble aristocracy and yet admit, despite his historical determinism, the ineradicable fault of that order in surrendering its traditional intelligence to mass tyranny. The prayer reiterates the criticism of a debased aristocracy: Helen (Maud) and Aphrodite (Iseult) have wasted their aristocratic natures; as in "To a Wealthy Man . . .," individual bearing is directly responsible for a nation's health. Through Anne the speaker seeks to reinstate the "ceremony of innocence"; even if it can flourish only in isolation, the mere knowledge of its survival may stave off confusion. Transforming the falcon into the linnet (VI), opposing the hulking nativity of some vague "rough beast" with Anne's birth, Yeats sought his only available sanctuary, the creation of a vision antithetical to the dread convulsed genesis of the new historical cycle.

The prayer opens with the speaker's bleak recognition of vulnerability. The landscape, despite his unspoken prayer for an "obstacle" against elemental fury, offers somber tokens of his defenselessness: the master of "Gregory's wood" is dead; the "one bare hill" endures without fertility. The sea-wind, which had left his tower a shambles before he rebuilt it, ravages harvested crops and tower alike. Anne, "*half* hid" in her cradle, is an index to his ambivalence. He envies her tranquillity, feels selflessly relieved that she is innocent of historical adversities, yet knows her cradle an insufficient protection:

And for an hour I have walked and prayed
Because of the great gloom that is in my mind.
                              [I]

I have walked and prayed for this young child an hour . . .
                              [II]

The repetition, despite its measured cadence, mirrors his aimless, agitated attempt to control a violent despair. Coherent syntax nearly collapses, imaging both the mind unhinged and the storm's terrific power:

> I have walked and prayed for this young child an hour
> And heard the sea-wind scream upon the tower,
> And under the arches of the bridge, and scream
> In the elms above the flooded stream.

The discordance results from the jarring, helplessly erratic interweaving of three grammatically different coordinate constructions. The use of "and" in the first two lines to join three main verbs sets up expectations which are twice violated in the third line. "And under" replaces the expected verb with a preposition. With "and scream," the reversal of expectations is compounded: "and" is followed by neither of the previously established norms but by a repetition of the verb in the noun clause. Compare this passage with "In Memory of Major Robert Gregory" (VII), where the speaker conceives his environment as an aesthetic unity resolving conflict. Here, what had been a mutually dependent group of objects breaks into a multitude of discrete units; the wind attacks each object individually, and the speaker, enclosed,[31] cannot discern a sequence in its tumult. He has only the dismal yet strangely exhilarating consolation of having predicted this frenzied historical chaos. Yet recognition of the sea's intolerable "murderous innocence"—his own "flooded stream" apocalyptically magnified into a brute force, outrageously innocent because unknowing and predestined—comes as a shock. For himself as well as Anne, the speaker now seeks a countervailing image of innocence—not the accidental, power-

---

[31] Cf. Jon Stallworthy, *Between the Lines: W. B. Yeats's Poetry in the Making* (Oxford: Clarendon, 1963), p. 43. Stallworthy thinks the speaker "on the top of Thoor Ballylee." But the poem's persistent emphasis on sound and the marked suppression of visual perception of the outside world suggests enclosure; compare "In Memory of Major Robert Gregory." In terms of Yeats's iconographic use of the tower in the entire series, Yeats's speaker does not reach the top of Thoor Ballylee until "Meditations . . ." (VII); in dramatic terms, it makes no sense for a speaker fearful for his daughter's safety to drag her into the midst of a storm.

less innocence of infancy which Wordsworth extolled, but that aesthetic innocence of the soul's self-created beauty which can transcend natural generation, here as elsewhere symbolized by water.

The prayer for Anne's beauty (III), no mere convention, reflects on an aristocratic radiance which, like Gregory's physical control, manifests the mind's "deliberate shaping of all things."[32] Although seemingly theoretical, the vision is a retreat from private disaster. Latent memories of Maud, triggered by cosmic destruction, trouble him; Yeats has disguised himself as both the "stranger" and the "friend," "distraught" by Maud's beauty and kept from true friendship by the selfishness of her apparent independence. Self-protectively, he imagines a beauty which cannot deceive or destroy; as he wishes for Anne's "right" choice of a husband, he vicariously enacts the marriage to Maud which never occurred. The autobiographical allusion embodies an analysis of individual freedom: unflawed beauty, fostering an immoderate pride in surface, portends an isolating, narcissistic self-destruction; an impenetrable "mask of burning gold" ("The Mask") hides the interior self and denies the individual and social harmony which should be life's true "end." The speaker prays for Anne what Yeats felt he and Maud lacked: a "heart-revealing intimacy," open, gracious, bred from the humbling knowledge of imperfection. Without such knowledge, free and intelligent choice is impossible. The secularized paradox of the "fortunate fall," remembered from "Adam's Curse," anticipates stanza V: the road to innocence must pass through the experience of human frailty.

The danger of bodily perfection is aristocratic degeneration (IV). Helen and Aphrodite, considering beauty "a sufficient end," wasted their natural gifts, recklessly turned self-governing freedom into license, undid "the Horn of Plenty." Helen, desiring nothing, allowed herself to be "chosen" and become the victim of a tragedy which the speaker, caught in his own chaos, evades naming: "The broken wall, the burning roof and tower / And Agamemnon dead."[33] With Helen's suspension of the will, the speaker pairs Aphrodite's folly of willful choice. Who, after all, he asks with a touch of self-deprecation, would willingly choose "a bandy-legged smith," an artist, for a husband?[34] Her failure is a bitter irony: having accomplished the triumph of personal form over the formless waters of generation ("that great Queen, that rose out of the

[32] *Essays*, p. 253.

[33] "Leda and the Swan."

[34] Compare Yeats's remark in *A Vision* (New York: Macmillan, 1961), p. 140: "Venus out of phase chose lame Vulcan." As usual, the poetry shows a much greater stress on individual freedom than the determinism of the system permits.

spray"), she then "drowned" her own "ceremony of innocence." Although Helen and Aphrodite veil Maud and Iseult, the unexpected jump
into myth is itself crucial to the poem's emotional development. Tonally,
the stanza operates through a felt discrepancy between the speaker's
actual experience and the myths he employs. Precisely because stanza
III touches painful memories too directly, he must now translate those
realities into mythological, fictional shape, treat the whole matter as a
joke: instead of the romantic melancholy of "A Woman Homer Sung"
or the tragic irony of "No Second Troy," this poem mocks a Helen who
is the dubious heroine of petty domestic comedy and a flighty Aphrodite whose life is tinged with bawdy. The speaker handles classical myth
with Jonson's casual, irreverent urbanity; although his sometimes ebullient wit, like Jonson's scorn of Vulcan,[35] conceals a "great gloom,"
stylistic decorum itself demands that the theme of aristocratic dissipation be imaged in a debased treatment of myth. The sudden excursus
on Helen and Aphrodite, moreover, suggests that the speaker thinks of
Anne, with self-consciously paternal elation, as an unfallen myth: if she
achieves "the sort of beauty that I have approved" (VII), she will be
exalted above beauty queen and goddess alike.

The stanza prepares with superb felicity for the important fragment
from the myth of Daphne and Apollo (VI): the myth of Aphrodite
mediates structurally between the violent sea (I–II) and the dry land,
"one dear perpetual place" where the self, a "hidden tree," may
flourish in ordered tranquillity. In stanza V, the speaker gives his
daughter the very counsel of which Aphrodite, "fatherless" (IV), was
deprived: "In courtesy I'd have her chiefly learned." The judgment,
prompted by myth, dark memories of Maud, his own discourtesy in "In
Memory of Major Robert Gregory," is authoritarian but not pat.
"Chiefly" suggests a multitude of previously considered virtues which
have gradually ceded place to courtesy, the self's triumph over nature
and "the growing murderousness of the world."[36] Typically, the precision of courtesy must include the heart's indispensable passion:

> Hearts are not had as a gift but hearts are earned
> By those that are not entirely beautiful.

Natural blemish, paradoxically valued, fosters the quest for interior
radiance, teaches humility and discipline; the richly humanistic asser-

---

35 See Jonson's "An Execration upon Vulcan"; Donald Davie has also noted the
stylistic similarity in the treatment of myth (*'Michael Robartes and the Dancer'*, in
An Honoured Guest, p. 84).

36 *Autobiography*, p. 168.

tion is tempered by knowledge of the suffering in passionate quest. That knowledge, the fruit of his own experience, is once again recalled obliquely:

> Yet many, that have played the fool
> For beauty's very self, has charm made wise,
> And many a poor man that has roved,
> Loved and thought himself beloved,
> From a glad kindness cannot take his eyes.

Once deluded into thinking that "beauty's very self" could reciprocate his neurotic adulation, the speaker has ultimately "settled" for the stabilizing warmth a wholly courteous woman confers. As in "Solomon to Sheba," he quietly pays tribute to his wife, no less a ritually central, civilizing figure than Elizabetta Gonzaga, Lady Gregory, Mabel Beardsley, and presumably Anne in her maturity. His act of acceptance is unique in Yeats's work. Having *"played* the fool," scorning Paris-MacBride for simply *being* one, he repudiates the obsessive quest for the women lost whose behavior, in stanzas III and IV, seems so discordant.[37]

   This psychological reconstitution explains the imaginative freedom, the selflessness in the speaker's visionary prayer for Anne's transformation into a laurel tree (VI). Only because he himself has ceased roving can he envisage her unperturbed joy in "one dear perpetual place." He can create, for the first time, a luminous Edenic image to oppose his antipastoral world. "One bare hill" becomes a fertile bower; the swaying "elms above the flooded stream," a protected inland tree; the screaming wind, a composed music of songbirds; and the "frenzied" dance of the "future years," a lithe and elegant neoclassical gambol. Through the allusion to Daphne and Apollo, the speaker transmits his poetic identity to Anne:[38] her poetry, surpassing his, is as naturally

---

[37] Harold Bloom (*Yeats* [New York: Oxford, 1970], p. 326) overlooks the importance of this unusual moment when he generalizes about the vicarious marriage to Maud which he believes Yeats represented in the last stanza. The comparable emotion in "Meditations . . ." (IV) lacks the full joy present here.

[38] The allusion has its weaknesses as well as its strengths. Despite its unobtrusive smoothness, its content—once recognized—jars. Apollo seeking sexual and marital bliss with Daphne is one thing; Yeats-Apollo seeking Anne-Daphne for the same reasons is quite another. The incest motif is inappropriate; the allusion encompasses more than Yeats meant it should, or shows too blatantly what he felt. He was out of control here, the servant of his own sexual anxieties—as in so many other instances in this poem of exquisite images imperfectly subsumed to a complete whole. Beryl Rowland, "The Other Father in Yeats's 'A Prayer for My Daughter,' " *Orbis Litterarum* 26 (1971): 289, has objected to the image on other grounds: "since Daphne was doomed to perpetual virginity, the allusion can have only limited reference."

joyous as the song of "golden king and silver lady"; like Gregory, who could have "published all to be a world's delight" (IX), Anne will generously create communal harmony by "dispensing round / [Her] magnanimities of sound." These transformations, as in "In Memory of Major Robert Gregory" (VII), complete the recurrent Yeatsian pattern: generated nature (the self unformed) transmuted by art into a "golden" nature which is innocent precisely because the art has been practiced with such *sprezzatura* that its civility seems natural. The importance of Anne's perfection, as in all Yeats's images of aristocracy, is that it is a transcendence within time and space of earthly limitations, not the absolute and sometimes negative transcendence stipulated in "Sailing to Byzantium."

The speaker's vision is a warm ecstasy of hope. Yet as in "In Memory of Major Robert Gregory" (XII), the very nobility he imagines induces a Wordsworthian "falling off," a stinging awareness of separation from the image he has created. Implied recognitions of personal failure gall him; as stanza VI closes, the metaphoric equation of Anne and the refulgent laurel weakens into simile. His deepest depression follows:

> My mind, because the minds that I have loved,
> The sort of beauty that I have approved,
> Prosper but little, has dried up of late.
>
> [VII]

"My mind" recalls his historical "gloom" (I). The vision of a continued aristocratic tradition is mere fantasy: neither Synge nor Lane nor Gregory has survived to change a world desperately in need of their guidance.[39] Lacking the independence he later wishes for Anne, symbiotically bound to the fates of his friends (as the deterministic syntax indicates), he is defeated. What meager strength he retains is bitter: having consolidated his identity as the Jonsonian arbiter of excellence, he finds himself the celebrant of a dead order. Preying in contempt upon his own debility, he converts the evergreen laurel into a metaphor of his withering. An intimate knowledge of hatred, bred from repeated confrontations with "the worst," lurks within his indirect caution to Anne: "to be choked with hate / May well be of all evil chances chief." "Choked with hate" suggests the gagged muffling of "magnanimities of sound," his own condition; "chief" polarizes hatred not against love

---

39 A. Norman Jeffares, *A Commentary on the Collected Poems of W. B. Yeats* (Stanford: Stanford University Press, 1968), p. 246, believes that Yeats was alluding to Maud in these lines; but the implicit criticisms of Maud in stanzas II and III make this identification unlikely.

but against the courtesy which flowers in love (V), showing him almost by linguistic accident the self-discipline necessary for freedom:

> If there's no hatred in a mind
> Assault and battery of the wind
> Can never tear the linnet from the leaf.

Deliberate self-purgation can bring a joy which violence cannot touch: the mind is its own worst enemy. Tree and bird once more appear sacred emblems, now signifying the speaker's partial recovery from despair. The imagery, its delicacy matched only by "the right twigs for an eagle's nest" in "To a Wealthy Man. . . ," bespeaks an eloquent faith that brutality cannot prevail.

Increasingly, the speaker believes that Anne's freedom entails his own liberation: his injunction that she eschew "opinions," "intellectual hatred" (VIII), is sharply self-critical. Yet paradoxically he pursues hatred with a vengeance; in doing so, he purges his own repressed violence, enacts the cleansing required by the hypothesis, "If there's no hatred in a mind . . .":

> Have I not seen the loveliest woman born
> Out of the mouth of Plenty's horn,
> Because of her opinionated mind
> Barter that horn and every good
> By quiet natures understood
> For an old bellows full of angry wind?
>
> [VIII]

Casting aside the masks of mythology, he finally confronts his hatred of Maud directly: instead of wry jocularity, infuriated outrage; in place of casual rumination, exclamatory sharpness edged by personal pain. Having acknowledged the demise of true aristocracy, he excoriates her self-righteous wastage of aristocratic heritage for the sake of a misguided demagogic agitation "content to attack," as Yeats wrote in "Poetry and Tradition," "little persons and little things."[40] Judging her by Platonic standards of knowledge, he damns her discourteous capitulation to opinion with the familiar metaphor of democratic commerce. Anne, by comparison, "will have no *business*" but dispensing her "magnanimities of sound." But Maud has traded that Pythagorean music for "an old bellows full of angry wind." That vituperative epithet for MacBride, who remains too bathetic to justify serious treatment, measures the speaker's progressive recovery: by personifying the "hay-

---

[40] *Essays*, p. 249.

stack- and roof-levelling wind" (I), he simultaneously transcends private animosity and mocks the storm into comic insignificance.

The cathartic liberation from hatred brings a recapitulation of stanza VI. Yet the themes of innocence and joyous autonomy possess a might redoubled because the speaker has so vigorously examined the dangers of the soul's perversion:

> Considering that, all hatred driven hence,
> The soul recovers radical innocence
> And learns at last that it is self-delighting,
> Self-appeasing, self-affrighting,
> And that its own sweet will is Heaven's will.
>
> [IX]

The Edenic condition, Yeats wrote in *The Stirring of the Bones,* "is no longer a mere accident of nature, but the human intellect's crowning achievement."[41] The prose, however, refers to a purification gained after death; the speaker of the prayer, threatened by disasters, can countenance no such postponement. As in "In Memory of Major Robert Gregory," he requires an earthly incarnation of sanctity. Anne's recovery of a total correspondence between desire and destiny will depend not on a Wordsworthian recollection of youth but on progressive aesthetic labor; the discipline of courtesy implied by the word "learns" is carefully transposed from stanza V.[42] The speaker posits in her unimpeded maturation an ideal sequence that bypasses the middle-aged "despondency and madness" which Yeats no less than Wordsworth feared. He prays for Anne an ultimate *condition* of Edenic joy which Yeats's speakers constantly seek yet never hope to gain; the experience of transcendence recounted in "Vacillation" (IV) is inexplicable, unearned, momentary.[43] Only through Anne, a surrogate, can he achieve a similar happiness. Yet in bestowing such joy, he participates

---

41 *Autobiography,* p. 320.

42 Donald T. Torchiana, *W. B. Yeats and Georgian Ireland* (Evanston: Northwestern University Press, 1966), p. 298, states that the stanza embodies Yeats's "ideal of Protestant patriotism"; the interpretation seems excessively sectarian and unnecessarily political for a poem whose true ideal is to steer clear of both extremes.

43 Cf. James H. O'Brien, "Self vs. Soul in Yeats's *The Winding Stair,*" *Eire* 3, no. 1 (1968): 36: "As the poet sits in a London restaurant, he reaps the fruit of his discipline." But the fact that the speaker now tests "every work of intellect or faith" hardly means that his vision necessarily comes as a consequence. Indeed, one of the poem's central problems is the impossibility of being assured that a secular joy will follow struggle. The disconnection between sections III and IV, of course, further intensifies the "accidental" nature of the vision.

in that emotion of sanctity and is elevated by it. The strength of his associative recovery is his empathetic capacity to imagine another's joy without experiencing personal anguish or envy. Through his love, he becomes unified with the person he has created; and with a quietly defiant exuberance in Anne's happiness, he barely deigns to acknowledge the imminence of his own defeat.

Thus, with poignant tranquillity, the speaker can recognize that he must lose the child he has made, the Daphne his Apollo has sought. As his chaste marriage to the image of his self-perfection dissolves, he envisages an actual marriage which both fulfills Anne's development and reinstates the "ceremony of innocence" by insuring aristocratic continuity. Like the end of "Shepherd and Goatherd," the image joins the Jonsonian themes of organic fruition and spiritual beauty:

> How but in custom and in ceremony
> Are innocence and beauty born?
>
> [X]

The rhetorical question, replete with radiant but baffling abstractions, paradoxes of generation, testifies to the speaker's rapt assurance; so too, the originative act of naming which he performs with such mellow grace:

> Ceremony's a name for the rich horn,
> And custom for the spreading laurel tree.

The stanza, however, raises questions which the speaker avoids because he so desperately needs to protect Anne and preserve aristocratic innocence. The insuperable poetic difficulty in his final vision—quite apart from Yeats's chauvinist attitudes toward women—is that it contradicts everything which has preceded: having just extolled Anne's independent self-delight, he now places her in a dependent position where she becomes, as a breeder, merely the instrument of Yeats's social theory.[44] Yeats tried very hard to hide the contradiction by making the beginning of stanza X ("And may . . .") echo stanza VI ("May she become . . ."), thus creating verbally the impression of consistency; but nowhere in his work are the opposing claims of individual aristocratic freedom and the historical coherence of the aristocratic order so unresolved as here. Nor can the effulgent assertions obscure the fact that the speaker has created for Anne's innocence an Edenic environment even

---

[44] Bloom (*Yeats*, p. 327) has made a related charge: "One wonders how or why these souls will need one another, and how each will manage after learning the exuberant lesson that its own sweet will is Heaven's will?"

more sequestered than her cradle. If such perfection can survive only in hot-house isolation, do "innocence and beauty" exist at all?

Had this country house environment been less rarified, the transition from Anne's individual development to social recrudescence might have been more credible. But a real country house, its veil of romance stripped away, would be subject to dissolution; as Yeats anxiously showed in his cancelled drafts, Anne's happiness in such a potentially disrupted environment would be uncertain.[45] Yeats understood the problem; caught between fidelity to social realities and fidelity to his paternal feelings, he chose the latter. Nowhere else in his poetry does Jonson's magical demarcation between outside world and country house prevail so absolutely. The house, removed from the urban "thoroughfares" of arrogance and hatred, is wholly Jonsonian: an unthreatened shelter for the poet's child, whose self-created "magnanimities of sound" are the music of the revived aristocratic ritual. In placing Anne within it, the speaker vicariously accomplishes his own escape from the tower, where he must suffer the quest for purity amidst the discourtesies of historical and psychological turmoil. Despite the unresolved problems of the last stanza, Yeats's conceptual design is plain. The imaginative movement from tower to country house summarizes all courses of progress in the poem—from childhood to maturity, from unconscious peace to conscious innocence; the education which leads from turbulence to civilized stasis, and the speaker's own recovery from despondency to joy.

V

The chimerical nature of this country house is Yeats's tacit admission that the world Gregory's death destroyed could not be reconstituted. Yet his speaker achieves, through Anne, an undeniable serenity. This vicarious resolution is not an isolated phenomenon but a prominent feature of Yeats's poems about aristocracy through "A Prayer for My Daughter." Thereafter, he radically altered this characteristic dependence of his *personae* and, with it, the identity of the tower.

The vicarious resolution, although found in Wordsworth, is the method typical of Coleridge's conversation poems, "Frost at Midnight"

---

45 See Stallworthy, *Between the Lines*, pp. 38–42. The original drafts of stanzas X–XIII, whose conception derives largely from "Tintern Abbey," present Anne walking alone through Coole. Yeats, addressing her from beyond the grave, repeatedly wonders "if you be happy & yet grown" (p. 41) or variants thereof, and asks her to "cry / That all is well" (ibid.). The very need for reassurance conveys his doubt.

in particular—a work Yeats almost indisputably had in mind when he composed "A Prayer for My Daughter."[46] Here is Coleridge:

> The inmates of my cottage, all at rest,
> Have left me to that solitude, which suits
> Abstruser musings: save that at my side
> My cradled infant slumbers peacefully.
>
> [11. 4–7]

Intending to create a tradition of fatherhood, Yeats recalled this passage in several intermediary drafts to stanza I, e.g.:[47]

> Considering that this cradle old may be
>
> Some other father has had like reverie
> When the wind rose . . .

Although Yeats borrowed his weather from the "Dejection" ode, there remains—among many other specific debts—a strong resemblance in the general structure of psychological relationship between Coleridge and Hartley on the one hand, and Yeats and Anne on the other. Coleridge, struggling against the perturbations of an intellect which "makes a toy of Thought," prays that Hartley possess the sensuous and immediate consciousness of nature's universal harmony of which he himself, "reared / In the great city," was deprived. Seeking, like Yeats in "The Wild Swans at Coole," a "companionable form" which is no mere solipsistic self-reflection, he prays that Hartley instinctively perceive such correspondences everywhere (11. 54–64). As he imagines Hartley's joy, he achieves vicariously a new happiness, a quieting of frustration and an indirect recovery of innocence. None of this differs radically from "A Prayer for My Daughter." The city has become the tower, the countryside a country house, and Yeats has given his speaker's anxiety a historical dimension; but the fundamental pattern of vicarious resolution is the same. Both children are emblems of personal desire whose happiness their troubled fathers nevertheless manage to visualize without envy, Coleridge in terms more generous and less prescriptive than

---

[46] Rowland ("The Other Father," pp. 285–86) has reached the same conclusion. Yeats's references to Coleridge before the late twenties are deceptively scanty; and the question of Coleridge's influence on Yeats—especially through the "conversation poems"—remains to be studied in full. It is likely that Yeats also had in mind Henley's mawkish poem on his infant daughter, "When You Wake in Your Crib" (in Rhymes and Rhythms), a portion of which Yeats cited in The Tragic Generation (Autobiography, p. 253).

[47] See Stallworthy, Between the Lines, pp. 29–30.

Yeats; precisely this capacity for disinterested contemplation of another's joy is what brings the restoration of internal order.

The vicarious resolution is directly analogous to the relationship
between Yeats's speakers and the aristocrats they praise. Its basic
components recur constantly: the speaker's emotion of incompletion,
deprivation; his separation from the image of his desire, often conjured
in compensation for personal failure; his dependence on surrogates for
his own momentary joy; his gradual sublimation of desire into disinterested love. The speaker's tranquillity in "In the Seven Woods" comes
from the Great Archer. His courage in "The New Faces" depends on
Lady Gregory's survival and his recognition of her dignified assurance.
In the epilogue to *Responsibilities,* the rancorous poet can muster the
moral stamina to forgive only when he imagines Coole's decorous
aristocratic life. Shepherd and Goatherd—divided aspects of Yeats—
approach self-completion by envisaging Gregory's totality. The despondent speakers of "In Memory of Major Robert Gregory" and "A Prayer
for My Daughter" experience vicarious joy by discovering distant
images of perfection. Both poems, like "Pardon, Old Fathers," exalt
their heroic figures at their speakers' expense. In short, Yeats's *personae*
do not corroborate his remarkable assertion in "If I Were Four-and-
Twenty" (1919): "I have become a cultivated man."[48] Instead, they
persistently refuse to make claims for themselves, deny the illusion of
having mastered an aristocratic bearing—as if any hint of personal
success would destroy the dream of unflawed perfection. Against themselves they summon a host of criticisms: discourtesy, emotional turbulence, moral failure, cowardice, sexual impotence, hatred, imaginative
torpor. Virtue, achievement, the balance of "passion and precision"—
these belong to others.

Compare Jonson, whose speakers in the epistles to the aristocracy
attempt not to expose but to conceal their failures. Although part of
Jonson's design is to create perfect images to imitate, he speaks as an
independent man who assumes an equality with those he praises, acts as
an intimate who practices their values. You never find him, as you find
Yeats in the epilogue to *Responsibilities,* acknowledging with ruthless
self-criticism that he needs a "sterner conscience" to instruct him: the
authoritative role of adviser is one of his chief masks. In the "Epistle.
To Katherine, Lady Aubigny," for example, Jonson never divulges his
desire to share Katherine's life of virtuous, tranquil isolation from "the
maze of custome, error, strife" (1. 60). He presents her retirement
impersonally, as an ideal model of spiritual courage and humility.
Although attacked by the corrupt, who "sinne onely for the infamie"

48 *Explorations,* p. 263.

(1. 86), Jonson shows himself refusing to flee; his steadfastness, he
implies, is perhaps more admirable than Katherine's because it survives
the tests of calumniation. His integrity and his judgment, strategically
published in the initial self-portrait, validate his praise:

> I, therefore, who professe my selfe in love
> With every vertue, wheresoere it move,
> And howsoever; as I am at fewd
> With sinne and vice, though with a throne endew'd;
> And, in this name, am given out dangerous
> By arts, and practise of the vicious,
> Such as suspect them-selves, and thinke it fit
> For their owne cap'tall crimes, t'indite my wit;
> I, that have suffer'd this; . . .
> . . . .
> I, Madame, am become your praiser . . .
>
> [11. 7–15, 21]

The passage is Yeatsian in attitude, but not in tone. Yeats's speakers, no
less embattled against the mob, lack the tough resilience and poise
Jonson summons so majestically. Instead of asserting their immunity
from detraction, they confess their hurt ("all my priceless things /
Are but a post the passing dogs defile"). Instead of claiming self-sufficiency,
they acknowledge dependence, as in stanza VII of "A Prayer for My
Daughter." They praise not their equals but their superiors, and validate
that praise not with claims to comparable excellence but through the
perspicuity of their self-criticism and the intensity of their desire for
the personal beauty they lack.

  Not until the valediction of "The Tower" (III) does Yeats's speaker
claim to embody the aristocratic pride of self-mastery:

> It is time that I wrote my will;
> I choose upstanding men
> That climb the streams until
> The fountain leap, and at dawn
> Drop their cast at the side
> Of dripping stone; I declare
> They shall inherit my pride,
> The pride of people that were
> Bound neither to Cause nor to State,
> Neither to slaves that were spat on,
> Nor to the tyrants that spat,
> The people of Burke and of Grattan
> That gave, though free to refuse—

> Pride, like that of the morn,
> When the headlong light is loose . . .

This is not a vicarious joy gained through displaced quest; the speaker invokes Burke and Grattan not to expose his own deficiencies but to declare full kinship. Yeats's alteration of his *persona* was certainly hastened by Ireland's political turbulence, his new alignment with Anglo-Ireland, and the disintegration of the aristocratic order, whose healthy survival might have tempted him to public celebrations along Jonsonian lines. But principally the revolution was inward: the enervating habit of attributing to others what he did not possess distracted him from creating his own destiny. The self-critical tendency persists, of course, long after "A Prayer for My Daughter"; but instead of augmenting others' glory, it functions as a method of self-purgation. The cathartic stanza on "intellectual hatred" in the prayer (VIII), although it deflects the ensuing joy to Anne, foreshadows the later technique. The subsequent poems seek what virtually none of the earlier work envisages, much less accomplishes—self-mercy, forgiveness, the capacity to confer blessings in a world whose "sheltering sacredness" physical and mental violence have destroyed. The history of the 'tower' poems after the prayer is Yeats's painful attempt to make his own void grow fruitful.

CHAPTER

SIX

An Acre of
Stony Ground

You know too that a period of 2000 years was also given to me for the complete circle, but one must of course not insist too literally on the figure. It has only an ideal existence. . . . All this however is too remote to help us in our Irish Crisis.

—Yeats to AE[1]

A month after Yeats finished "A Prayer for My Daughter," Ireland was wracked by the guerrilla war against the Black and Tans which ended with the 1921 Treaty granting Ireland dominion status. Yeats's response to the Terror, although ambivalent, was not the heroic pose Henn implies: "Was not that war on the Renaissance model: compact, perspicuous, a war for liberty, and he its only poet?"[2] What Yeats saw was a frighteningly unconventional conflict without gentility, marked by gratuitous cruelty, indiscriminate violation of innocents. "Reprisals" and "Nineteen Hundred and Nineteen" (1919–22) thus jettison the heroic paraphernalia of war in poems like "The Valley of the Black Pig" and "Reconciliation." Military action now means victimization. Despite Robartes's brash injunction to "Love war because of its horror, that belief may be changed, civilisation renewed,"[3] Yeats sometimes feared to face the war at all. Lecturing in America in 1920, he wrote to Lady Gregory asking if it was safe to return to Ireland and Thoor Ballylee.[4] When he ended his tour, he went to Oxford. Lady Gregory, angered by

[1] W. B. Yeats, *The Letters of W. B. Yeats*, ed. Allan Wade (London: Hart-Davis, 1954), p. 666.

[2] T. R. Henn, "W. B. Yeats and the Irish Background," *Yale Review* 42 (1953): 362.

[3] W. B. Yeats, *A Vision* (New York: Macmillan, 1961), pp. 52–53.

[4] Joseph Hone, *W. B. Yeats* (1943; rpt. London: Macmillan, 1965), p. 323.

"Reprisals," chastised his escape: Yeats had dragged her son from his grave to make an insincere poem, for he knew only by hearsay of the Irish troubles.[5] But Yeats felt deep remorse. His occasional sense that he had foreseen Ireland's tragedy was a merely intellectual solace which concealed a confluence of troubled responses: staunch patriotism, defensive jocularity, thoughts of permanent self-exile. Most especially, doubts about his poetic identity haunted him: the Terror exacerbated fundamental questions concerning the relation between art and action, art and violence, and compelled him to examine the validity of poetry in a time of acute national crisis.

"Nineteen Hundred and Nineteen," "Meditations in Time of Civil War" (1921–22), and "The Tower" (1925) constitute an extended, oblique anlaysis of the imagination; new turmoil following the Treaty rekindled the series. "Nineteen Hundred . . . ," Yeats's most nihilistic work, explores without recoil the artistic and spiritual chaos his later speakers must combat. The poems chronicle Yeats's gradual recovery of constructive imaginative power, his increasing consciousness of his tower's strength and his territory's fertility. When Yeats arranged them in The Tower, however, he reversed the order of composition. Thus, tempting himself to a further crisis of nothingness, he implied that the victories of personal and poetic identity won in "The Tower" and "Meditations . . ." were lies which could not avail against the inexorable historical violence and corrosive knowledge of guilt represented so vividly in "Nineteen Hundred. . . ."

Although not overtly concerned with Coole Park and Thoor Bally-lee, "Nineteen Hundred . . ." takes its chief image of military terror from Kiltartan, the Black and Tans' slaughter of Lady Gregory's tenant Ellen Quinn:

> a drunken soldiery
> Can leave the mother, murdered at her door,
> To crawl in her own blood, and go scot-free.
> [I.iv]

In "Reprisals" (11. 15–22) the same gruesome event symbolizes the collapse of feudal aristocracy in the West of Ireland: allusions to Kiltartan and Coole, and the definition of Ellen Quinn as a cottager's

5 Lady Gregory, Unpublished Journals, Book X, November 28, 1920 (Berg Collection, New York Public Library). For Lady Gregory's account of the Terror, see, in addition to her Journals (ed. Lennox Robinson [New York: Macmillan, 1947]), the series of articles she wrote for The Nation: "A Week in Ireland," October 16, 1920, pp. 63–64; "Another Week in Ireland," October 23, 1920, pp. 123–24; "Murder by the Throat," November 13, 1920, pp. 215–16; "A Third Week in Ireland," December 4, 1920, p. 333; "A Fourth Week in Ireland," December 18, 1920, pp. 413–14; "A Fifth Week in Ireland," January 1, 1921, pp. 472–73.

wife, limit its scope. "Nineteen Hundred . . .," vastly more comprehensive, refuses to localize the event, dispenses with the aristocratic context, and scrupulously avoids partisanship. Ellen Quinn is, simply, "the
mother," an emblem of dead love. Flanked by surreal images of
nightmare, the incident epitomizes universal lawlessness and derangement. The catastrophe of yet another British invasion—after the promise of Home Rule—is general. So too the speaker's inexpiable guilt.
" 'There will never be another war,' that was our opium dream," Yeats
later castigated his youthful myopia.[6] Failing to recognize that England
remained a political enemy, he had indulgently contented himself with
the shadow fruit of

> Public opinion ripening for so long
> We thought it would outlive all future days.
> O what fine thought we had because we thought
> That the worst rogues and rascals had died out.
>
> [I.ii]

Mocking a cultural nationalism which blindly assumed uninterrupted
progress, the derisive repetition of "thought" connects the speaker's
failure to perceive impending evil with the present disaster. Now

> The night can sweat with terror as before
> We pieced our thoughts into philosophy,
> And planned to bring the world under a rule,
> Who are but weasels fighting in a hole.
>
> [I.iv]

Blind to all but "culture," he had disregarded the prophetic warning of
"culture" itself:

> When Loie Fuller's Chinese dancers enwound
> A shining web, a floating ribbon of cloth,
> It seemed that a dragon of air
> Had fallen among dancers, had whirled them round
> Or hurried them off on its own furious path.
>
> [II]

This sensuous reminiscence initially conjures an illusion of aesthetic
freedom, but actually insists that the autonomy of art is a fiction:

---

[6] Quoted by Richard Ellmann, *Yeats: The Man and the Masks* (1948; rpt. New
York: Dutton, n. d.), p. 244; Donald Torchiana, *W. B. Yeats and Georgian Ireland*
(Evanston: Northwestern University Press, 1966), pp. 317–18, prints another
portion of the same speech.

historical necessity forces the powerless dancers to enact the sinister image of their era, a crazed dance of puppets:[7]

> So the Platonic Year
> Whirls out new right and wrong,
> Whirls in the old instead;
> All men are dancers and their tread
> Goes to the barbarous clangour of a gong.
>
> [II]

That conflict between freedom and determinism, imaging the poet's struggle to define his responsibilities, is the poem's principal tension. The speaker constantly seeks an impersonal, detached vision of what can only be personally horrifying. He would possess Robartes's cold calm in "The Phases of the Moon," with its casually domestic metaphor of the second coming. As in *A Vision,* he exploits philosophy to place demented experience within a preordained scheme of cosmic fragmentation. He resorts to seeming factuality of tone, invokes epochal and mythic concordances to salvage the dark consolation that all apocalyptic convulsions are similar: "Herodias' daughters have returned again" (VI). Comparing Ireland to Phidian Greece, he dramatizes himself as an Athenian who witnessed the Persian invasion, pretends that the present Irish crisis is really another.[8] Yet even as he seeks objectivity, he finds panoramic vision unendurable. Images of preordination, though they may mirror truth, mechanize him, cancel his selfhood—even if the only selfhood he can cherish is his guilt. However consolatory, these images evade self-confrontation, like the dodge in "Easter 1916":

7 John Unterecker, *A Reader's Guide to William Butler Yeats* (New York: Farrar, Straus, 1959), p. 183, finds a consolation in the metaphor "All men are dancers": "those men move as artists." What Yeats means, however, is brutally ironic: "all men" suffer the same imprisonment as Loie Fuller's dancers. Unterecker writes that the dancers "had *transformed* strips of gauze into 'a dragon of air' " [italics mine], but that willed metamorphosis is exactly what they did not accomplish. The dancers "enwound"—and then, "It seemed. . . ."

8 Cf. Thomas R. Whitaker, *Swan and Shadow: Yeats's Dialogue with History* (Chapel Hill: North Carolina University Press, 1964), p. 223, who considers the comparison simply the speaker's "retrospective view" of a past event. See also Thomas Parkinson, "The World of Yeats' 'Nineteen Hundred and Nineteen,' " *University of California Publications in English Studies,* 11 (1955), p. 214; Parkinson accepts the poem's cosmology as a given, and does not see the speakers appeal to philosophic structures as an attempt to evade responsibility: "As poet and prophet he has the unsettling chore of displaying his world in the process of surrender, of dramatizing the ultimate inadequacy of the will and reason when faced with an apparent solidity that suddenly emerges as a whirling flux, only to take the form of a new circular reality, moving from pole to pole, that underlies flux and is its nonhuman motivator" (p. 212).

>   our part
>   To murmur name upon name,
>   As a mother names her child.

The poem paradoxically asserts that the operation of historical necessity cannot absolve the individual of responsibility. Although Yeats
elsewhere expounded a rigorous determinism mollified only by the
unexplained "work of the *thirteenth sphere* or cycle which is in every
man and called by every man his freedom,"[9] the speaker's typical
gesture is the hard moral judgment of presumably free acts.

  Thus the speaker everywhere brandishes his complicity in ruin.
Anarchic, he would rather will his own destruction through merciless
self-criticism than succumb to external forces presaging the same end.
This is not Cuchulain's heroic, suicidal defiance but the diseased rant of
a man who knows that his defiance is futile and ugly, yet cannot cease
until exhausted; Yeats's skill in the poem is his control over his
speaker's madness. The masochistic self-examination produces multiple
indictments: inaccurate vision, political naiveté, precious refusals to act.
Reiterating the public pronoun "we," the speaker makes himself the
scapegoat of an entire coterie.[10] With bitter irony he construes himself
a trapped Daedalus, "lost amid the labyrinth that he has made / In art
or politics" (III.ii): the doomed reverie spawns a comprehensive metaphor of historical violence which measures his knowledge of responsibility:

>   Herodias' daughters have returned again,
>   A sudden blast of dusty wind and after
>   Thunder of feet, tumult of images,
>   Their purpose in the *labyrinth* of the wind.
>   [VI]

As in "The Cold Heaven" and "Parnell's Funeral," the "thirst for
accusation" is insatiable. Jealously, he guards the "ghostly solitude"
(I.v) his folly has created, finds sensual titillation in suffering (IV). No
less than the Irish countryside or Loie Fuller's dancers, he is "dragon-
ridden" (I.iv) by the minotaur in his mind's labyrinth. His youthful
supposition that "All teeth were drawn, all ancient tricks unlearned"

---

9 Yeats, *A Vision*, p. 302.

10 Thomas Parkinson, *W. B. Yeats: The Later Poetry* (Berkeley: University of
California Press, 1964), p. 47, argues that Yeats adopted "the editorial 'we' with
the motive of appealing to the experience of his contemporaries who have suffered
the same historical set of events." Doubtless; but Yeats's further motive was to
show his contemporaries the pain of recognition they *should* feel. Parkinson adds
that the predominantly "extrahistoric spirit" in the poem is "malicious and sadistic" (pp. 48–49); but the malice is so internalized that it has become masochism.

(I.iii) merely concealed a self-destructive urge. Like the sudden unleash-
ing of sexual perversion and military terror, that suppressed violence
now explodes in a ceremony of hate so virulent that it can only end in
nauseated self-loathing:

> Mock mockers after that
> That would not lift a hand maybe
> To help good, wise or great
> To bar that foul storm out, for we
> Traffic in mockery.
>
> [V.iv]

The end of satire is the satirist's vindictive demand for his own blood,
the only means of recovering honesty. In a time of extreme dislocation,
what else can the artist rightly peddle but his entrails? In an awesome
paradox, the speaker becomes the symbol of his world: self-denuncia-
tion, *chosen* as a brutal but necessary means of retaining identity in the
face of a tempting determinism, is itself predetermined. By the end of
section V, the only significant difference between the Irish speaker and
the Athenians who survived their city's rape is that he has "dared
admit" (I.vi) what they felt, yet lacked the honesty to confess: destructive invasion by an external agent satisfies his inner desire to "end all
things" (III.iii).

This public exhibition of suicidal impulse derives from the profound crisis of vocation in section III. From Spenser and Shelley the
speaker resurrects an emblem of the soul or poetic imagination to
counter the nightmarish mechanical dance visualized in section II. The
swan, though floating on the "troubled," mirroring waters of history,
has the capacity for choice, is free:

> The wings half spread for flight,
> The breast thrust out in pride
> Whether to play, or to ride
> Those winds that clamour of approaching night.
>
> [III.i]

Yet the borrowed metaphor, for all its comforting splendor, creates a
false analogy. The speaker's imagination has deluded him into thinking
that he, like the swan, retains control. But he soon acknowledges his
imprisonment within "the labyrinth that he has made," and from this
recognition the self-annihilating impulse crowds fast upon him:

> Some Platonist affirms that in the station
> Where we should cast off body and trade
> The ancient habit sticks,

> And that if our works could
> But vanish with our breath
> That were a lucky death,
> For triumph can but mar our solitude.
>
> [III.ii]

Earlier (I.v), the speaker had regarded the inevitable transience of "master-work of intellect or hand" with bleak resignation. Here the argument is more frightening: since "our works" do not "vanish with our breath," *it would be better if they did.* This is the will to deny and wreck the limited eternity of artifice. Because his work is a trap, it should not survive; because the pain of knowing it would survive only to be destroyed by others is unendurable, he would destroy it now, leaving no trace of having lived. Who other than the creator should be privileged to annihilate his work? Thus killing his tragic love for "what vanishes" (I.vi),[11] the speaker enters a frenzy of obliteration:

> The swan has leaped into the desolate heaven:
> That image can bring wildness, bring a rage
> To end all things, to end
> What my laborious life imagined, even
> The half-imagined, the half-written page . . .
>
> [III.iii]

Here, finally, the solitary swan seeking its own negation images truthfully the speaker's "state": he would destroy what he has not yet made. From this willed denial of the shaping spirit of the imagination, the poem offers no reprieve.

II

Self-sacrifice could not kill the dragon. Before Yeats returned to Thoor Ballylee in the spring of 1922, civil war had interrupted Ireland's new independence. Repudiating the nominal allegiance to England stipulated by the Treaty, the Irish Republican Army began a vehement terrorism designed to intimidate the Irish Free State government, retaliate against its countermeasures, and cripple the feudal system. Near Gort, as elsewhere, conditions were bad. The IRA raided, comandeered, or sacked the Anglo-Irish country houses. Roxborough, Lough Cutra,

11 See Whitaker, *Swan and Shadow*, p. 228: "The speaker exhibits what Rachel Bespaloff has seen in Achilles, a Dionysian 'passion for destruction growing out of a hatred for the destructibility of all things.' "

and Castle Taylor—all houses with strong Gregory connections—were harrassed throughout the summer; Roxborough was burnt to the ground in November.[12] Anglo-Irish landowners either endured or made their exodus to England. "Lord Lascelles has given up the idea of coming to Portumna," Lady Gregory wrote, "and Lord Kenmare may be driven to leave. . . . Furniture vans engaged for nine months ahead are taking goods from the country to England."[13] Coole was raided in early June; during the week of June 8, which Yeats spent at Coole, he began "Meditations . . ."; aside from Coole and Tillyra, he wrote Olivia Shakespear, "other houses of the gentry stand empty."[14] Despite Yeats's belief that his own territory would remain unscathed, as it had during the Terror, the IRA blew up the Thoor Ballylee bridge around midnight on August 19.[15]

What Yeats witnessed was not merely fresh evidence of cultural fragmentation in the West of Ireland but the enforced demise of an entire class. Coupled with Catholic acquisition of political power, the tumult brought him to a crisis he had evaded for years: examination of his Anglo-Irish birthright. The suffering, seemingly in retribution for a hegemony of cruelty or benign neglect, gave Yeats a sympathy for the dying aristocracy such as he had previously felt only for Coole. If he had never wasted affection on houses like Lough Cutra and Roxborough, where "all had lacked intellectual curiosity until the downfall of their class had all but come,"[16] he nevertheless understood that the "soil" of "Leisure, wealth, privilege" needed to produce the "most living" had been salted. In the Protestants he now met in the Dail and Senate he found what the Anglo-Ireland of his youth had lacked, courage and "hereditary passion": ". . . two or three went in danger of their lives; some had their houses burnt; country gentlemen came from the blackened ruins of their houses to continue without melodrama or complaint some perhaps highly technical debate in the Senate. Month by month their prestige rose."[17] Yeats's new allegiance was typically paradoxical: he championed the Anglo-Irish tradition only as it verged

[12] Lady Gregory, *Journals*, pp. 172, 174; Unpublished Journals, Book XIX, June 21, 1922, July 5, 1922; Book XX, October 1922, passim, November 12, 1922.

[13] Lady Gregory, *Journals*, p. 180.

[14] *Letters*, pp. 683, 686; Lady Gregory, Unpublished Journals, Book XIX, June 21, 1922.

[15] *Letters*, p. 680; Lady Gregory, Unpublished Journals, Book XX, August 20, 1922.

[16] W. B. Yeats, *The Autobiography of William Butler Yeats* (New York: Macmillan, 1938), p. 335.

[17] W. B. Yeats, "Ireland, 1921–1932," *The Spectator*, January 30, 1932, p. 137. Donald Pearce, ed., *The Senate Speeches of W. B. Yeats* (Bloomington: Indiana

toward its doom. Without risking opprobrium he could now explore his heritage.[18] "Freedom from obsession," the achievement of national liberty, "brought me a transformation akin to religious conversion. I had thought much of my fellow-workers—Synge, Lady Gregory, Lane— but had seen nothing in Protestant Ireland as a whole but its faults, had carried through my projects in face of its opposition or its indifference, ... but now my affection turned to my own people, to my own ancestors, to the books they had read."[19] Had Yeats not sought that tradition, he would have courted new alienation. He was not returning to a familiar world.[20] His avid study of Berkeley, Swift, and Burke was the new discovery of an ethnic identity which, despite his pride in family, he had never possessed in any positive way, a selfhood which his participation in Ireland's "hereditary political aim"[21] had compelled him to deflect into Celtic or Renaissance myth. His intensity in embracing what he had once called, cautiously, "that splendid misunderstanding of the eighteenth century,"[22] seems proof of his earlier deprivation. Now, in "that one Irish century that escaped from darkness and confusion,"[23] Yeats found an indigenous culture—like Swift himself "the last passion of the Renaissance"[24] —which embodied the ideals for which he had previously crafted foreign symbols, foreign heroes. He discovered imaginative freedom defined nationally: Swift had fiercely served intellectual liberty, scorned the tyranny of democracy; Berkeley had asserted the mind's domination over external reality and defiantly claimed that Ireland possessed a philosophical tradition which opposed Cartesian logic and Lockean materialism; Burke, Swift's heir in hatred, had evolved an organic conservatism to counter anarchic modernity. Yeats could now justify Roxborough for having helped create Lady Gregory's sense of kinship with heroic legend: "Looking back, *Cuchulain of Muirthemne* and *Gods and Fighting Men* at my side, I can see that they were made possible by her past; semi-feudal Roxborough, her

---

University Press, 1960), pp. 50–51, n., gives a partial listing of property damages sustained by senators.

[18] Yeats told Lady Gregory that he had refrained from vaunting the intellectual and ethical superiority of Protestant Ireland while the Anglo-Irish remained an oppressive power; with Catholic Ireland now in control, he felt free to assert that greatness (Lady Gregory, Unpublished Journals, Book XXX, June 22, 1925).

[19] Yeats, "Ireland, 1921–1932," p. 137.

[20] Cf. James D. Boulger, "Yeats and Irish Identity," *Thought* 42 (1967): 194.

[21] W. B. Yeats, *Essays and Introductions* (New York: Macmillan, 1961), p. 411.

[22] W. B. Yeats, *Explorations* (New York: Macmillan, 1962), p. 28.

[23] Ibid., p. 345.

[24] *Letters*, p. 773.

inherited sense of caste, her knowledge of that top of the world where men and women are valued for their manhood and their charm, not for their opinions."[25] For the first time Yeats could place Coole's continued energy and decorum within their proper historical context—as at the end of *The Stirring of the Bones* (1922), in "Coole Park and Ballylee, 1931," *Dramatis Personae*, and the story of John Bond and Mary Bell (*A Vision*). As he learned that he could establish Parnell's spiritual descent from Swift more powerfully than he could claim Hugh Lane's kinship with Cosimo de' Medici, he understood the need to make the Anglo-Irish tradition a guiding presence in contemporary culture. Its latitude of vision, governmental expertise, and aesthetic sophistication might save Ireland from barbarism: "we alone had not to assume in public discussion of all great issues that we could find in St. Mark or St. Matthew a shorthand report of the words of Christ attested before a magistrate."[26] If Ireland, having finally triumphed over its conqueror, repudiated these values simply because they had flourished in an Anglo-Irish soil, the catastrophe would be no less national than Anglo-Ireland's own indifference to the "civilisation full of religion and myth"[27] it overwhelmed.

Yeats, naturally disinclined to see his new heritage relegated to obscurity, advocated Anglo-Irish culture with a genuine concern for Ireland's future. But he also feared Catholic retaliation: "what resolute nation permits a strong alien class within its borders?"[28] Thus, the conflicting tonalities of the Divorce Speech (1925):

> I think it is tragic that within three years of this country gaining its independence we should be discussing a measure which a minority of this nation considers to be grossly oppressive. I am proud to consider myself a typical man of that minority. ... We are the people of Burke; we are the people of Grattan; we are the people of Swift, the people of Emmet, the people of Parnell. ... If we have not lost our stamina then your victory will be brief, and your defeat final, and when it comes this nation may be transformed.[29]

What begins in noble opposition to religious intolerance, tragic consciousness that one of Ireland's chief disasters may be repeated, ends in

25 *Autobiography*, pp. 389–90. Compare Lady Gregory's own explanation of her desire to understand indigenous Irish life in *The Kiltartan Poetry Book* (Dublin: Cuala, 1918), p. i.

26 Yeats, "Ireland, 1921–1932," p. 137.

27 *Explorations*, p. 347.

28 Ibid., p. 350.

29 Donald Pearce, ed., *The Senate Speeches of W. B. Yeats*, p. 99.

a vituperative war-cry as sectarian as the bigotry Yeats sought to denounce. The fury externalizes problems Yeats could not resolve. In this speech, as nowhere else, Yeats extolled the present reality of Anglo-Ireland *as if* it were the ideal itself; the eloquence conceals his knowledge of the discrepancy. Yeats knew too well that the disinterested intellectual passion which Burke and Grattan had inherited from Swift and Berkeley had subsequently dimmed. Anglo-Ireland had sunk into torpor, failed to transcend class interest, opposed land reform and Home Rule. "Our upper class," Yeats charged in 1934, "cares nothing for Ireland except as a place for sport."[30] Were these really the "people" of Burke, Swift, and Parnell? Despite his assertions of class toughness in the speech, Yeats knew that Anglo-Irish "stamina" had been irrevocably dissipated. The intimate conversations which Lady Gregory conducted with the ancient ghosts of Anglo-Irish excellence— she would imagine Burke's pleasure in knowing that Ireland had cultivated its waste places, Peel's satisfaction in learning that the peasantry now possessed their own land—were atypical instances of the tradition retained intact.[31] Contemporary Anglo-Ireland could not sustain the boasts Yeats made on its behalf. To validate them, he would have to create his own world.

III

With "Meditations in Time of Civil War," Yeats began arduously crafting a universe to incorporate his Anglo-Irish identity. He started by analyzing the central issue of cultural "stamina" which the Divorce Speech blinks. "Ancestral Houses" (I) constitutes Yeats's thorough, and agonized, rejection of the contemporary Anglo-Irish aristocracy, Coole excepted. To measure his criticism you have only to see that, in this most complex manipulation of Jonson's form, Yeats was dealing for the first time with an entire social class; that the structural relationship between "ancestral houses" and Thoor Ballylee duplicates the relationship between houses of other "lords" in "To Penshurst" and Penshurst itself makes the character of Yeats's judgment plain.

Lady Gregory's witty comments on the unfinished poem help focus Yeats's approach; the uprooted landowners, she said, would employ Yeats to write poems showing that they moved from their estates not out of necessity, but virtue.[32] Yet the crucial poetic fact about "Ances-

---

30 W. B. Yeats, *The Variorum Edition of the Poems of W. B. Yeats*, eds. Peter Allt and Russell K. Alspach (New York: Macmillan, 1966), p. 836.

31 Lady Gregory, MS to *Coole*, Book X.

32 Lady Gregory, Unpublished Journals, Book XIX, July 8, 1922.

tral Houses" is that Yeats chose to avoid all reference to the burnings. He was concerned with a more internal and tragic conception of historical necessity: "every civilisation," he later summarized an obviously congenial aspect of Swift's political philosophy, "carries with it from the first what shall bring it to an end."[33] Like the "dragon of air," the burnings were but the outward confirmation of the subverting labyrinth within. In "Ancestral Houses," as in "Nineteen Hundred . . ." and the greatest of Yeats's work, the felt pressure of an historical determinism cannot negate human responsibility. Had Yeats desired to whitewash the Anglo-Irish aristocracy of all complicity in its own demise, including an unwitting will to self-destruction, he could easily have pinned the blame on IRA depredations. Yet he spurned such melodrama; the loss of "stamina" and psychic strength preoccupied him, not the physical collapse of buildings. Mr. Torchiana, interpreting the Anglo-Irish as noble victims of the burnings, offers an analysis of social change less trenchant than Yeats's.[34]

Yeats's criticism of the Anglo-Irish was part of a large design. A class subverted from within is the social version of the imagination turned self-destructive, the desperate theme of "Nineteen Hundred. . . ." In "Meditations . . ." he combatted his own nihilism, sought sanctuary from a world without walls. Further, he intended to free himself from earlier poetic modes, knowing that recent history had rendered obsolete any conception of a joy vicariously achieved. "Ancestral Houses," dramatizing that purgation, self-consciously reverts to the manner of "In Memory of Major Robert Gregory" and "A Prayer for My Daughter" in order to dismiss the personal myth of vicarious participation in a rich abundance created by others. By the time Yeats crossed the "ancient bridge" to Thoor Ballylee (II.i), he had traversed an immensity in his poetic development. However ill-equipped he often found himself, he had finally accepted the responsibility of becoming his own hero.

The initial problem in "Meditations . . ." is where and how, in such politically turbulent times, the aristocratic myth can survive. Standing gloomily "amid" his own barren "emblems of adversity" (II.iii), the speaker conjures elsewhere a deliberately contrived but sensuously aristocratic Eden.[35] Art and nature collaborate perfectly in this Anglo-

[33] *Explorations*, p. 314.

[34] Torchiana, *W. B. Yeats*, pp. 311–12: Yeats "is simply lamenting the fact that great ancestral country houses and their traditions in modern Ireland have been rejected (in fact often burned down) not only by the Irregulars but, in spirit, by the new democratic Ireland that was everywhere victorious."

[35] Whitaker (*Swan and Shadow*, p. 171) believes the poem opens in "pale abstractness." Heather Glen, "The Greatness of Yeats's *Meditations*," *Critical Review* 12 (1969): 30, complains that "Besides Jonson's rich, immediate images [in "To

Irish landscape: the fountain seems an organic form, a sacramental image of the soul's bountiful "self-delighting" freedom. A dynamic Great Chain of Being, governed only by internal law and thus immune to historical danger, it symbolizes an ecstatic equilibrium, the "courtesy and self-possession . . . [which] are the sensible impressions of the free mind."[36] Too proud to "stoop to a mechanical / Or servile shape," it also has the humility not to suffer "ambitious pains." That absence of personal ambition is the final seal of a mind superbly trained to objective discernment. Yet here, even as the speaker surrenders to his ideal, is the seed of subsequent criticism: can such completeness sustain itself in the absence of need for further accomplishment?

"Mere dreams, mere dreams!" (I.ii)—the self-castigation suddenly challenges the assumptions behind the word "Surely" (I.i). As with the initial image of the swan in "Nineteen Hundred . . ." (III.i), the speaker's imagination has again spawned a deluded fantasy. A rapturous indulgence in pathetic fallacy (e.g., "As though to choose whatever shape it wills") has obscured the discrepancy between the symbol of the fountain and the culture it purportedly represents. The craving to know that joyous life exists somewhere has falsely connected personal abundance with vast inherited properties. Yet because imaginative fertility depends on "beautiful life at which we look as old men and women do at young children,"[37] the speaker cannot sacrifice his vision, though he must discard its present embodiment. Thus, he counters his own savage attack, invoking a titanic antiquity beyond that of ancestral houses:

> Yet Homer had not sung
> Had he not found it certain beyond dreams
> That out of life's own self-delight had sprung
> The abounding glittering jet . . .
>
> [I.ii]

In reaffirming the indispensable reality of that sacramental fountain, he carefully prunes his language of pathetic fallacy, avoids the dishonest blurring of actuality and symbol. Changed language alters the symbol: it now signifies internal creative joy, not a social order. The crucial shift, detaching the fountain from its manicured landscape, makes possible the speaker's later attempt, still an unconscious hope, to

---

Penshurst"], Yeats's flowering lawns . . . seem curiously distant and artificial." The images are hardly lacking in richness; the sense of distance is the logical consequence of Yeats's stationing his speaker elsewhere.

36 *Essays*, p. 253.

37 *Autobiography*, pp. 404–5.

establish that joy within his own territory. Here, however, the tena-
ciously declared faith prompts to rueful admission that

> now it seems
> As if some marvellous empty sea-shell flung
> Out of the obscure dark of the rich streams,
> And not a fountain, were the symbol which
> Shadows the inherited glory of the rich.
>
> [I.ii]

In this difficult, ambivalent revaluation of Anglo-Irish aristocracy, the
speaker cannot wholly spurn what he loves: sensations of rare, exquisite
intricacy mingle with those of sterility and darkness.[38] Yet here is no
Aphrodite who "*rose* out of the spray" but her mere Botticellean shell,
passively "flung" from its element, the "rich streams" of tradition
which generate "The abounding glittering jet." Simultaneously, the
symbol "Shadows" forth (see II.ii) and darkens the glitter of the
"rich." Has passion deserted precision? Has the aristocracy, having lost
Eros, become only a trivial decoration?

Guided by the memory of Homer to question the past for answers,
the speaker reverts to the historical genesis of the house:

> Some violent bitter man, some powerful man
> Called architect and artist in, that they,
> Bitter and violent men, might rear in stone
> The sweetness that all longed for night and day,
> The gentleness none there had ever known.
>
> [I.iii]

---

38 Torchiana (*W. B. Yeats*, p. 313) replaces Yeats's image of "rich streams" with
his own image of a "stormy sea"; he can thus regard "that empty shell as another
symbol of the Horn of Plenty undone by civil rancor and personal ill-breeding" in
democratic Ireland—that is, by a force external to the aristocracy. The cluster of
images in "Ancestral Houses" is not the same as in "A Prayer for My Daughter" (I,
IV), although their structural relationship appears similar. The assumption governing Torchiana's argument—that all of Yeats's shell images carry the same meaning
(p. 312)—is fallacious. He cites, for example, the introductory song from *Fighting
the Waves*, without perceiving how radically its tone of embittered adoration differs
from the more critical, less enthusiastic passage in "Ancestral Houses." The Blakean
description of the shell in *Fighting the Waves*, moreover, makes it a symbol of
intense mental struggle, a quality wholly absent from the "marvellous empty
sea-shell." Torchiana correctly associates the shell with the country house; but his
claim that "such a house will rise again" (p. 313) clearly violates the substance of
the image: fountains revive, but empty shells do not. Ormonde Plater, "Water
Imagery in Yeats's 'Meditations in Time of Civil War,' " *Style* 2 (1968): 61, goes to
the other extreme by disregarding the speaker's anguished sense of loss, the product
of Yeats's delicately gauged tone.

Like Dante, suffering "A hunger for the apple on the bough / Most out of reach," these rough eighteenth-century founders sought an image of their opposite. They craved a permanent monument to their own transience; an alien power among reputed barbarians, they raged for simplifying emblems of Platonic idealities, and reared "in stone" not a house but "sweetness," "gentleness": forms of personal and social order. That tempestuous passion is exactly what the contemporary aristocracy has forgotten:

> But when the master's buried mice can play,
> And maybe the great-grandson of that house,
> For all its bronze and marble, 's but a mouse.
>
> [I.iii]

The real threat to aristocratic identity is not crumbled stone but the degeneration of personality, the failure to understand that the aristocratic dream proclaims its reality only in constant creation.

Yet the violation may be unconscious, dictated by the dynamics of the aristocratic institution itself. Yeats here treated his recurrent theme of betrayal with a tragic compassion not found in the handling of Helen and Aphrodite. His speaker entertains the appalling hypothesis that originative aristocratic achievement, by bestowing such great gifts upon succeeding generations, necessarily saps the future of its strength. Birth begins death: violent bitterness, once expended in creating a consummately equilibrated Augustan civility, must leave in its wake baffled men who may unconsciously seek to pervert what they cannot improve. How, if the past has usurped their creativity, can they imitate the passion of William Connolly, who in the 1720s "could still call out a posse of gentlemen to design the façade of his house"?[39] What is left but false pride lacking toughness, "slippered Contemplation" lacking the complement of action? The obverse of these questions terrifies: "what if" greatness can return only with a resurgent internal violence which must destroy "inherited glory" in order to create afresh?[40]

---

[39] *Explorations*, p. 358. Cf. James H. O'Brien, "Yeats' Dark Night of Self and *The Tower*," *Bucknell Review* 15 (1967): 15: "But the designers and landowners approached 'sweetness' and 'gentleness' from different perspectives. The landowners ... did not understand that escutcheoned doors and galleries of family portraits arise from the suffering of the artist." The distinction between types of men is not Yeats's, as his treatment of Gregory in the famous elegy indicates. Gregory, although compared with Sidney, was Yeats's prototype for the ideal eighteenth-century hero, a man who "practised" *and* "understood" his arts (X). Yeats's paralleling of "Some violent bitter man" with "Bitter and violent men" makes plain that he saw no difference in esthetic sensibility between landowner and artist.

[40] Torchiana (*W. B. Yeats*, p. 313) explains these stanzas (I.iv–v) as follows: the speaker "asks that the magnificence symbolized by those houses accept the modern

Inhabiting a landscape whose very beauty seems insidiously destructive of selfhood, the Anglo-Irish aristocrats appear the victims of Yeats's romantic mythology, which requires them to make when all is made. But compare Coole, whose "levelled lawns" also allure: there, from "Upon a House ..." through "Coole Park and Ballylee," making continues unabated. In "Ancestral Houses" it is not the landscape which is "inadequate" but the men.[41]

These criticisms inhere in the form of "Ancestral Houses"—a country house poem which, instead of fulfilling expectations of an ideal universe, presents an image of degeneration. Despite his inveterate contempt for Pope, Yeats was employing Pope's method of satirizing Timon's villa (*Epistle to Burlington*, 11. 99—176)—a passage which itself manipulates the design and themes of "To Penshurst" to expose Timon's corruption. Yeats shared Pope's understanding of the genre: reality had invalidated the form as Jonson had used it—to compliment existing greatness. Now, it could only measure historical and moral decline. Knowing how distant the ideal had become, Yeats stationed his speaker at Thoor Ballylee, where he can but dream. Compare Jonson, the putative observer of an Edenic reality; and Pope, the begrudged, daytime guest of a deterioration which satire may still rectify. Yeats's speaker, his imagination traveling in conventional pattern from "flowering lawns" to terraces, through "escutcheoned doors" to "great chambers," sees a hypothetical landscape belonging to no one. This distanced vagueness produces a sweeping double-edged commentary: all Anglo-Ireland now suffers enervation; all eighteenth-century Anglo-Irish culture displayed imagination, power, fierce craving for joy. The "buildings that a haughtier age designed" express the sensuous strength of Augustan architectural harmonies and expose the debility of the present. Violation of the tradition inverts the ethical and intellectual correspondences between house and inhabitant. The heir merely occupies a "marvellous ... shell" whose vast spaces once symbolized public magnificence, family pride. The real inhabitants of this ghostly mansion, represented in "famous portraits of our ancestors," are dead;

---

violence and bitterness of civil war in Ireland along with her continued greatness." Although "toleration is most often found beside ornamental waters, upon smooth lawns, amid conversations that have no object but pleasure" (*Essays*, p. 488), what Torchiana unintentionally attributes to the Anglo-Irish aristocracy is really a perverse masochism bred of spinelessness and eroded identity. Yeats is not likely to have pleaded for the honor of such an order, nor thought that such an aristocracy deserved to have its estates protected. Torchiana, because he seeks to preserve the innocence of Anglo-Ireland, regards the violence and bitterness as external elements; but how can he account for the reiterated pronoun "our" (in the last line of each stanza), by which the speaker admits his kinship with Anglo-Ireland and indicates that bitterness and violence are indigenous to his class?

41 Cf. Whitaker, *Swan and Shadow*, p. 172.

but as Yeats asserted in "The New Faces," "The living seem more shadowy than they."

"Ancestral Houses" presents the disillusioned speaker with a clear lesson: since aristocratic joy comes only from struggle, he must reject Anglo-Irish decadence and make his own world. Thus the autonomous

Courtesy of M. Frances MacNally

THOOR BALLYLEE
seen from the east

An ancient bridge, and a more ancient tower,
A farmhouse that is sheltered by its wall . . .

founding of the tower, "My House." But "House," enlarging the tower, intimating dynasty, echoes the title of section I to indicate the speaker's true intent: he will reenact the creation of eighteenth-century Anglo-Irish culture, transpose the original country house ethos to his own "acre of stony ground." As in "The Tower" and "Blood and the Moon," he has "two eternities, / That of race and that of soul" ("Under Ben Bulben," II): he cannot quest for his own identity without exploring his ethnic traditions.

Becoming his own spiritual architect, he combines the earlier influences of Dante and Gregory, and reverts to the sole image in "Ancestral Houses" which offers direction, the creation of the mansion. Imitating that process, confronting that adversity, he may regain an eighteenth-century toughness and joy. Tentative hope mixes with determination as he gazes upon a landscape barren of the civilized, inherited "gentleness" which has ruined modern Anglo-Ireland. It invites what he grimly wishes: effort and sacrifice, not casual delectation on sensual delights (I.iv). The austere terrain is a potential world not yet realized, a list of objects lacking active verbs:

> An ancient bridge, and a more ancient tower,
> A farmhouse that is sheltered by its wall,
> An acre of stony ground,
> Where the symbolic rose can break in flower . . .
>
> [II.i]

With "break," implying the painful ecstasy of the completed quest, his world enters time. But the action is future, and the reverie on "*Il Penseroso's* Platonist" (II.ii) concerns the past: the speaker still has no present. Yet by the time he states, "Two men have founded here" (II.iii), he has become an actor, has completed the creation of his world. His seemingly disorganized meditation on the landscape is his founding: walking from bridge to study, he has named the elements in his world, become Adam. The passage illustrates Mr. Holloway's astute remarks on the style of *The Tower*: "The *forming ritual* of these poems . . . is the solemnised calling-up of objects by the poet to people the world of his imagination. . . . [The poems] do not offer to depict and describe things which the reader is invited to envisage as having prior, independent existence. On the contrary, the reader is invited to see them as called into being by the *fiat* of the poet, peopling a world *ab initio* as part of the creative act."[42]

42 John Holloway, "Style and World in 'The Tower,' " in *An Honoured Guest*, eds. Denis Donoghue and J. R. Mulryne (London: Edward Arnold, 1965), p. 97.

Yet, in a crucial paradox, this autonomous creation is derivative. Making the tower, he has remade the country house, internalized its values, and deliberately duplicated the centripetal movement toward the building which "Ancestral Houses" takes from "To Penshurst." This movement, however, does not end in a public feast; it is a psychic act of self-definition. At the center of the tower, as at the center of himself, the speaker finds his emblems of poetic quest, "A candle and written page"—the emblems which Robartes had mocked in "The Phases of the Moon." Claiming them as his own, he accepts the bitter isolation which prodded his ancestors to "rear in stone" what they did not possess. Yeats's transformation of the conventional movement into a romantic quest may appear foreign to Anglo-Irish neoclassicism; yet he persistently interpreted Swift and Berkeley as solitaries, and showed the modern corruption of that creative solitude—an exhausted loneliness—in the hollow "galleries" of the composite country house (I.v).

This return to Anglo-Ireland's creative source typifies the first two stanzas of "My House." The images the speaker names all derive from the landscape of "Ancestral Houses":

Theme or Motif	"Ancestral Houses"	"My House"
Founding	"Some violent bitter man . . ./ Called architect and artist in"	"Two men have founded here."
Estate	gardens "levelled lawns and gravelled ways"	"the symbolic rose" "An acre of stony ground" "Old ragged elms, old thorns innumerable"
Water	"The abounding glittering jet"	"stream"
Bird	"the peacock . . ./With delicate feet"	"The stilted water-hen"
Entrance to house	"the glory of escutcheoned doors"	"A winding stair"
Interior space	"great chambers and long galleries"	"a chamber arched with stone"
Interior materials	wood ("polished floors"), "bronze and marble"	"grey stone"
Mode of contemplation	"slippered Contemplation finds his ease"	"*Il Penseroso's* Platonist *toiled*" [second italics mine]

Theme or Motif	"Ancestral Houses"	"My House"
Personal symbol	escutcheons	"A candle and written page"
Ancestry	"famous portraits of our ancestors"	"Il Penseroso's Platonist toiled on/ In some like chamber" [second italics mine]
Legacy	"sweetness," "gentleness," "greatness"	"Befitting emblems of adversity"

No manipulation of imagery could better illustrate the speaker's appropriation of the aristocratic tradition. He has sloughed off the perfected landscape but found within his environment new symbols to embody the same central desires which motivated his forbears to create estates. What the Irish Augustans made and what the speaker makes differ in external details but not in their dominant values, for the concerns of aristocracies are constant. The eighteenth-century country house lives anew in the tower: the radical symbiosis measures needs as well as continuities. Without "hereditary passion" the speaker cannot attain complete self-expression; without the speaker's historical imagination the ideals of the eighteenth century must die.

But this twentieth-century heir does more than graft his heritage to the tower when it no longer survives in the country house. He actually founds it. His paired images have a distinct evolutionary design, like that of the closure to "A Prayer for My Daughter." Thoor Ballylee is, metaphorically, the situation which the Anglo-Irish first confronted when they conquered James II at the Battle of the Boyne (1690). Through the disciplined quest of the aristocratic imagination they transformed the Anglo-Norman tower into a neo-Palladian country house, cultivated "An acre of stony ground" into "flowering lawns," and replaced the "stilted water-hen" with the ornamental peacock. The speaker at the tower stands imaginatively at the beginning of Anglo-Irish history—and possesses the impossible awareness of consequences which "none there had ever known" (I.iii): the hindsight knowledge, now prophetic, of Anglo-Irish history itself. He thus can *choose* whether to reenact that history, civilize his landscape, and risk enervation—or pursue another direction. His judgment on Anglo-Ireland is plain; he has founded

> that after me
> My bodily heirs may find,
> To exalt a lonely mind,
> Befitting emblems of *adversity*.
> [II.iii]

Remaking Anglo-Irish history, he will preserve its momentary genius by denying that all has been accomplished. Beyond the physical order of "levelled lawns" lies a realm of art where "the *symbolic* rose" flourishes.

The choice of an internal art is hedged about by self-critical, monitory images. The speaker distrusts his commitment, must invoke future obligations to regulate his present behavior. The same suspicion of wavering purpose emerges as he observes the "Scared" water-hen—an "ironic self-image"[43] which suggests his timidity in coping with external shock. The psychic legacy of the tower's first founder is threatening: the "man-at-arms," lacking the stamina to endure adversity, declined like George Pollexfen and succumbed to oblivion.[44] If Yeats was satisfied that the two founders, swordsman and poet, were complementary types, his ambivalent speaker is typically unable to reconcile active and contemplative modes. Will the contemplation his quest demands become a pointless, debilitating exile from reality? In "Nineteen Hundred . . ." he had damned philosophical pursuit for the paralysis it induces—yet again he goes the route of solitude. This time, however, he seeks neither easy clichés nor the intellectual pastimes of "slippered Contemplation" but something more rugged, Homeric, akin to war:

> *Il Penseroso's* Platonist toiled on
> In some like chamber, shadowing forth
> How the daemonic rage
> Imagined everything.
>
> [II.ii]

Yet even at this illimitable verge of imaginative creation achieved through union with the anti-self, Robartes's mockery of "mysterious wisdom won by toil" resounds ("The Phases of the Moon"). That implicit self-criticism is justified. Strangely detached, the speaker observes:

> Two heavy trestles, and a board
> Where Sato's gift, a changeless sword,
> By pen and paper lies,
> That it may moralise
> My days out of their aimlessness.
>
> [III]

---

43 Whitaker, *Swan and Shadow*, p. 174.

44 Cf. ibid., pp. 173–74: "the comparison of founders ominously reduces the man-at-arms to the speaker's own proud and introverted isolation."

He has made his world; ironically, nothing happens. If the urge to destroy his work, so prevalent in "Nineteen Hundred . . .," has vanished, so also has the creative desire to explore "daemonic images" (VII.v). At the very least, the sword—a beautiful instrument of violence, a symbol of the tower's dual heritage—should make him examine his own dilemma or the world of physicality he has rejected. But most remarkably, it ironically tempts him to further aimlessness, an evasive daydream about Japan—far from his own aesthetic difficulties in a time of Irish crisis. He ignores the sword's intrinsic values, values as evident as those he realizes.[45] The artifact demonstrates, in terms of "Ancestral Houses," the tragic inseparability of "greatness" and "violence"; yet here on his work-table that truth lies too close. He shrinks from "adversity," contemplates the sword's origin, history, aristocratic beauty—but not its violent nature. Significantly, he sees it scabbarded. The self-deceiving evasion, disturbingly like that derided in "Nineteen Hundred . . .," persists throughout sections I–IV: the title, the unmentioned burnings (I), the phrases "this tumultuous spot" (II.iii) and "whatever flourish and decline" (IV.iii) all allude to the civil war without facing its reality. The price of such repression is the awakening trauma which the invasion of his territory initiates (V).

This emblem of beauty is nevertheless an object to imitate, like the furnishings in "A Prayer on Going into My House." With awed affection the speaker meditates upon a loveliness which, unlike the landscape of "Ancestral Houses," augments creative desire. Its artifactual permanence and the permanence of change it represents ("Curved like new moon") spark transcendental longings:

> only an aching heart
> Conceives a changeless work of art.
> . . . .
> Soul's beauty being most adored,
> Men and their business took
> The soul's unchanging look.

He reflects upon Japan's vital, long-sustained unity of culture; complacency never touched its "most rich inheritor," who

45 Cf. ibid., p. 175; Harold Bloom, *Yeats* (New York: Oxford, 1970), p. 353; Plater, "Water Imagery," p. 64; Glen, "Yeats's *Meditations*," p. 34; O'Brien, "Yeats' Dark Night of the Self," p. 16; John Unterecker, *A Reader's Guide to William Butler Yeats* (New York: Farrar, Straus, 1959), pp. 178–79. To know from Yeats's biography that Junzo Sato gave him a ceremonial sword not intended for use should only clarify Yeats's deliberate dramatization of his speaker's self-deception.

> Had such an aching heart
> That he, although a country's talk
> For silken clothes and stately walk,
> Had waking wits . . .

This is "inherited glory" (I.ii) at its best, justifying aristocratic privilege: the "rich streams" of family pride and inbred commitment to aesthetic excellence continually push the "abounding glittering jet" through the passionate heart. And what does the "inheritor" image but a refinement of the speaker's desire, the solitary quester about whom "Benighted travellers" (II.ii) gossip? The entire passage asserts the Homeric reality of joy which modern Anglo-Ireland has perverted. The new perspective on Anglo-Irish failure, together with the touch of self-irony, finally snaps the reverie: "It seemed / Juno's peacock screamed." That indecorous cry, remembered from artificed estates, heralds the dénouement of cyclical change, the breakdown of civilization.

Tolled back to the tower (IV), the speaker translates his meditations on aristocratic inheritance into excruciatingly intimate terms:

> Having inherited a vigorous mind
> From my old fathers, I must nourish dreams
> And leave a woman and a man behind
> As vigorous of mind . . .
>
> [IV.i]

This is a radical shift in self-definition. Once intent only upon his quest for joy, he now insists upon establishing a family tradition. The many parallels between "Ancestral Houses" and "My Descendants," including the verse form, underscore the difficulty: he forces the definition of his own aristocratic nature to depend on successful resolution of the one issue questioned throughout: *continued* vitality. Only if his descendants retain the fragile flower of aristocratic greatness will he have proof that his own identity is not fraudulent. Pressures from the future are balanced by debts to the past: only if he spawns children "as vigorous of mind" as his "old fathers" will his ancestors be satisfied that he has not violated their legacy. Caught by these intolerable, self-imposed conditions, he is bound to fail. Violence wrecks the potentially consummated marriage of transcendental rose and "morning beams"—the moment of joy, sexual, religious, aesthetic, the barely secular transfiguration which the speaker seeks through art. His anguished complaint is poignantly understated:

> and yet it seems
> Life scarce can cast a fragrance on the wind,

> Scarce spread a glory to the morning beams,
> But the torn petals strew the garden plot;
> And there's but common greenness after that.
>
> [IV.i]

Recalling "though now it seems" (I.ii), "and yet it seems" measures the historical dimensions of that defeat: the speaker cannot renew Anglo-Irish greatness. Further, while the sudden metamorphosis of the rose into "torn petals" parallels the fountain's transformation into the sea-shell (both changes symbolize death), they differ qualitatively: the aristocracy retains a "marvellous" form; the speaker ends with nothing, unredeemed earth.

A terrible aberration follows (IV.ii): the speaker, unable to accept such failure, must blame his descendants for desecrating the "flower" which he himself cannot "nourish" into being. His horrified suspicion that the soul's "natural declension" may overtake them slides quickly into allegation: they, like Helen and Aphrodite, may consciously squander their inheritance.[46] The speculation has the same rhetorical form as stanzas iv–v of "Ancestral Houses": "And what if. . . ?" In this galling parental tyranny, he punishes his young offspring for the pain of inadequacy *his* "old fathers" inflicted on him. But the psychological violence boomerangs: he feels his children's future guilt as his own, now. His mind unhinged by preoccupation with coming historical doom, he accuses himself of lacking omnipotence; as in "Nineteen Hundred . . .," this inhuman self-judgment emanates in execration against his own symbol:

> May this laborious stair and this stark tower
> Become a roofless ruin that the owl
> May build in the cracked masonry and cry
> Her desolation to the desolate sky.
>
> [IV.ii]

Like the willed negation of his art, the curse gains power from his tragic courage to destroy what he most dearly loves; the possessive gestures— "*this* laborious stair and *this* stark tower"—intensify the pain of loss. His descendants' perversion attacks himself and thus the world he has made; knowing their decline his fault, he will destroy it. The neurotic logic shows the intimacy of his relation to stone. Unlike the country house, which remains to mock betrayal, the tower must unambiguously display failure: physical ruin must answer internal decay.

---

46 Cf. Holloway ("Style and World," p. 100), who over-rates the importance of "natural declension" and misses the speaker's underlying concern with personal responsibility.

As in "Nineteen Hundred . . .," withdrawal to a comprehensive vision of destiny forestalls further experience of nothingness. He knows his suicidal curse an egotist's assertion: "The Primum Mobile that fashioned us / Has made the very owls in circles move" (IV.iii). Accepting the satisfactions of present survival, he consecrates the tower to the memory of Lady Gregory, his wife, and himself. He escapes the impending horrors of time by disclaiming any concern, scraps his "dreams" of recreating an aristocratic Anglo-Irish culture. The phrase "And I," self-consciously transposed from "My House" (II.iii), no longer rings with the founder's defiance; he muses that he simply "*chose* the house," "And *decked* and *altered* it. . . ." Those verbs of reconstruction are unquestionably the weakest in all Yeats's poetry about Thoor Ballylee; they are nearly disengagements from pain and risk. The mind's sphere having contracted, the speaker finds a new self-definition—less majestic, more realistic, and more complacent.

Nowhere else does a Yeatsian speaker so readily accept his present condition; his sudden lapse into nostalgia, his ease in ordering his chaotic imaginings should rouse suspicion. His explanation for feeling "most prosperous"—"Seeing that love and friendship are enough"— simply does not satisfy, hardly because the emotions are not genuine but because the minimalism he so glibly embraces belies everything else in the poem thus far. Are all his quests for aristocratic excellence to be so casually abandoned? Can domestic tranquillity so rapidly placate the "aching heart"? When you consider that the speaker's withdrawal is prompted only by the imagined hypothesis of decay, his contentment does not seem worth the price. This pivotal stanza, far from being "poetically dishonest,"[47] is Yeats's careful dramatization of false quiescence; precisely because he valued so highly the bitter fruit of the void, he was prepared to expose his speaker's moral sham. Minimalism, unless it is the actual salvaging of something from nothing, is a neurotic self-defense against risk, and the nothingness of the preceding stanzas does not justify the speaker's pose. The passive retreat into consolatory determinism or cozy insularity is as invalid a response to existential history as the assumed omnipotence of the curse. Dramatically, this fine passage is the lull before the storm in "The Road at My Door" (V) and after. That storm, shattering the absurd illusion of cloistered contentment, is Yeats's fresh variation on the problem of "adversity":if his speaker recoils from imaginary violence, how will he react when forced to confront the real thing?

Civil war finally breaks upon a self-enclosed mind (V). As lone Irregular and Free State soldiers intrude, the speaker faces an experience which completely alters his overall perception of Thoor Ballylee:

[47] Glen, "Yeats's *Meditations*," p. 36; see also pp. 37–38.

the myth of the tower's immunity and the self's sanctuary which Yeats had maintained since "Ego Dominus Tuus" is wrecked. The ease with which these oddly reportorial stanzas dramatize the inevitable encounters as if they actually occur within the course of the poem should not obscure the fact that Yeats quashed his myth deliberately. He could have eliminated the invasions, or made them less threatening to his physical space; he could have had the incidents remembered—and thus reduced the reader's awareness of actual incursion. Yeats, however, needed to challenge his myth explicitly, not simply because anything less would have falsified his experience of history but because he felt compelled to court dispossession, knowing that "A poet, when he is growing old ... cannot keep his mask and his vision without new bitterness, new disappointment."[48] As elsewhere, Yeats tightened his imaginative grasp of the tower by threatening himself with its loss.

The actual encounter, ironically harmless, renders ludicrous the speaker's squeamish fears of violence and causes a shamed self-recognition. Filtered through a complex self-irony, comic incongruities belie the national tragedy he intuits: a biting sense of his displacement, "small talk," jaunty rhythms, the allusion to Falstaff (V.i). Dry understatement conceals his gloomy awareness of widespread destruction:

> I complain
> Of the foul weather, hail and rain,
> A pear-tree broken by the storm.
> [V.ii]

Civil war exists *because* it has come to Thoor Ballylee, once again "this tumultuous spot" (II.iii). Yet although the tower's fragile environment now symbolizes Ireland disrupted, the speaker blandly—and evasively—discusses the metaphor literally. For the first time, however, he acknowledges *real* loss.[49] The psychological contact with specific violence is salutary: the maker of the tower discovers that his realm reflects, beyond his control, the world he had rejected.

He responds ambivalently to exposure:

> I count those feathered balls of soot
> The moor-hen guides upon the stream,
> To silence the envy in my thought;
> And turn towards my chamber, caught
> In the cold snows of a dream.
> [V.iii]

---

48 W. B. Yeats, *Mythologies* (New York: Macmillan, 1959), p. 342.

49 See Whitaker, *Swan and Shadow*, p. 178.

If the "cold snows" have buried the flower of aristocratic beauty, does his vocation have any value? The issue is not whether to join Free Staters or Republicans, but whether to act at all. His "envy," a craving to slough off isolation, is a dark temptation: if all men dance "to the barbarous clangour of a gong," he would rather join a community of violence seemingly lacking purpose than suffer the poet's helpless irrelevance. The desire prefigures the ghastly lure to destroy in section VII (ii). To quell these desperate emotions, he seeks distraction: "I count. ..." The act is numbly mechanical (compare "The Wild Swans at Coole," I–II), yet encompasses more than the speaker intends.[50] The "balls of soot" channel a violent image of "gunshot" into ordered form. No longer a timid, "stilted water-hen" (II.i), the fowl has a tranquil, assured control which the gun-shy speaker finds as attractive as the soldiers' affability and roughness. Free from moral dilemma, she navigates with perfect instinct, impervious to the destructive waters—"foul weather, hail and rain"—which have left the speaker's pear-tree broken. Like the fountain (I.i) and the pool (VII.iii), the stream is "companionable" to its own kind alone. The moor-hen's world is the natural embodiment of his dream: like the ram and ewes in "Shepherd and Goatherd," the hen with her chicks implies the aristocratic ideal of family coherence he has just relinquished (IV.iii). Closed off from such impossible tranquillity, equally estranged from military action, he shuffles inward to his uninviting refuge. The physical and emotional retreat is not a choice: "caught," he is a man defeated and confused.

The consequent need for sanctity brings him closer to his eighteenth-century ancestors' experience than any other in the poem. Their dire yearnings for "sweetness" and "gentleness" (I.iii) become, in "The Stare's Nest by My Window" (VI), intimately his. Avoiding his worktable, he moves to the window, where he had once felt Gregory's visionary joy transform his landscape. He focusses on immediate, small details, as if again seeking self-distraction. But again he sees his preoccupations imaged. The unashamed prayer for regeneration answers, in its rhyme-scheme as in its ritual, the chaos of section V:

> The bees build in the crevices
> Of loosening masonry, and there
> The mother birds bring grubs and flies.
> My wall is loosening; honey-bees,
> Come build in the empty house of the stare.
>
> [VI.i]

---

[50] Cf. Glen, "Yeats's *Meditations*," p. 39: "The response is an active one . . . *done simply for its own sake*" [italics mine].

As all aspirations to create a house (I, II, IV) culminate in this imagery of construction, the speaker resigns his role as architect, submissively confesses that only a providential force can rescue his world.[51] What replaces the earlier humanistic sense of mastery is an absurd, religious faith that beeswax can cement his cracked, "loosening masonry." Appalled bewilderment suffuses the tense recognition: "My wall is loosening." He might as well have said, "my mind, my body, all structures which make existence intelligible." The poem's tragic irony is that only in the spirit of total fragmentation does the speaker approach his long-cherished goal of establishing an absolute identity between self and tower. The agony is selfless: "Come build in the empty *house of the stare.*" For all the pained transparency of the house/nest metaphor, he fears to ask too much; he can pray only on behalf of something other. He suffers the tragic derangement in which everything that is not-self becomes infinitely precious, sanctified. The stare's nest acquires broad values through the refrain: it is a house without inhabitants, the mere "shell" of existence, the body without the soul, the heart so choked with hate that it is emptied of love. Only a transcendental sweetness can heal that nearly impersonal *horror vacui.*

The speaker's imprisonment parodies the creative isolation earlier vaunted. No longer "caught" by "mere dreams" (I.ii), he belongs to a community of victims; the tower has become the mind's dungeon:

> We are closed in, and the key is turned
> On our uncertainty.
>
> [VI.ii]

The craving for facts is satisfied by knowledge of particular barbarism:

> A barricade of stone or of wood;
> Some fourteen days of civil war;
> Last night they trundled down the road
> That dead young soldier in his blood:
> Come build in the empty house of the stare.
>
> [VI.iii]

The indignation against murder in "Nineteen Hundred . . ." (I.iv) turns to flat recitation: what can emotion add to the atrocity itself? Yet a

---

51 Glen ("Yeats's *Meditations*," p. 41) finds this "self-abrogation . . . disturbing," chiefly because she wishes Yeats or his speaker to be perpetually heroic in self-confrontation; she consequently overlooks the significance of the surrender itself and permits Yeats less than he for once permitted himself, a merciful relapse into an *unashamed* confession of inadequacy.

barely voiced self-taunt emerges: that shambles of a barricade may be a
surreal metamorphosis of his own ruined landscape, cracked masonry
and broken pear-tree—creativity ironically maimed into the ugly ac-
coutrements of guerrilla war, "Bitter and violent men" (I.iii) erecting
not a country house but an image of their violent selves. If his tower is
implicated in the terror, how can he pretend a victim's innocence?

> We had fed the heart on fantasies,
> The heart's grown brutal from the fare.
>
> [VI.iv]

The language of bestiality prepares for the terrible apocalypse: "*Monstrous* familiar images," "Trooper belabouring trooper, biting at arm or
at face" (VII.i–ii). The self-indictment, encapsulating the hard conclu-
sions of "Nineteen Hundred . . .," shuns all appeal to a comprehensive
vision of history. Knowledge of brutality, shocks of invasion have
shown him the moral irresponsibility which predestination insidiously
offers. Only a complete recognition of complicity can suffice: "More
substance in our enmities / Than in our love" (VI.iv). The autophagic
pun—"substance"/"meat"—is ghoulish. The entire stanza is Yeats's
acceptance of Swift's justified rebuke in *The Battle of the Books*; the
bee addresses the spider:

> *Whether is the nobler Being of the two, That which by a lazy
> Contemplation of four Inches round; by an overweaning Pride,
> which feeding and engendering on it self, turns all into Excrement
> and Venom; producing nothing at last, but Fly-bane and a Cobweb:
> Or That, which, by an universal Range, with long Search, much
> Study, true Judgment, and Distinction of Things, brings home
> Honey and Wax.* [52]

> O honey-bees,
> Come build in the empty house of the stare.
>
> [VI.iv]

But neither his prayer nor the harsh naming of sins breaks his
claustrophobic despair.[53] Revulsed by the blood-sodden ground of

---

[52] Swift, *Gulliver's Travels and Other Writings*, introd. Ricardo Quintana (New
York: Random House, 1958), p. 377. Whitaker (*Swan and Shadow*, p. 179)
explicates Yeats's other sources, in Porphyry and Blake.

[53] Cf. Plater, "Water Imagery," p. 67: "The lyric of the birds and the bees thus
engenders truth. After writing the lyric, Yeats 'began to smell honey in places
where honey could not be, at the end of a stone passage or at some windy turn of
the road, and it came always with certain thoughts' [*The Bounty of Sweden: A*

human activity, the speaker climbs to the "tower-top"—and suffers, exhausted, a panoramic vision of his earthly experience (VII). The title indicates his condition: possessed of nothing, he cannot say "*My House*"; rather, "*I See* Phantoms of Hatred and of the Heart's Fullness and of the Coming Emptiness." This waking nightmare, unlike the fanciful dream of "Ancestral Houses," distills known realities; the speaker can no more control its horror than prevent invasion. Despite its pseudo-Hegelian dialectic, its real movement is the spontaneous, dislocated procession of "reveries." Symbols and significant vocabulary culled from the entire meditation merge, split asunder, acquire distorted meanings. "A bit of an embroidered dress" (III) is perverted into the "cloud-pale rags" worn by the "rage-driven, rage-tormented" troop (VII.ii). The language of artistic creation is debased by "senseless tumult":

> Life scarce can cast a fragrance on the wind,
> Scarce *spread* a glory to the morning beams . . .
>
> [IV.i]

> [the] rage-hungry troop,
> Trooper belabouring trooper, biting at arm or at face,
> Plunges towards nothing, arms and fingers *spreading* wide
> For the embrace of nothing.
>
> [VII.ii]

In this vicious metamorphosis of the rose, animal lust-hate supplants the speaker's ideal of sacramental marriage. The felt connection between the "abounding glittering jet" (I.ii) and "Sato's sword" (III) now becomes explicit, but the composite form—"A glittering sword out of the east" (VIII.i)—is not an image of aristocratic self-delight but a twisted emblem of destruction, its intrinsic violence finally evident. Equally frightening: instead of comparing the sword to the moon (III), the speaker now sees that the moon is like the sword, "unchangeable." Historical time halts in a period of total disruption; and "if no change appears" (III), there can be no redemption from the condition of hatred.

Caught in that nothingness, the speaker cannot distinguish his own experience from past history: all versions of anarchy coalesce. The

---

Meditation, and a Lecture (Dublin: Cuala, 1925), p. 51] . . . . This lyric, generating imagination in an interplay of rhythm and symbol, enables Yeats to experience his vision." It makes little sense to base an interpretation of section VI, not to mention the dramatic transition to section VII, on a passage from the prose. Simply because Yeats actually experienced such a sweetness, it hardly follows logically that the poem must therefore represent the same infusion of joy.

murder of Jacques Molay, like the outrageous derangement of the "insolent fiend Robert Artisson" in "Nineteen Hundred . . ." (VI), fuses medieval madness with present disaster to objectify the tradition of hatred from which the Irish civil war springs. Molay becomes identified with "That dead young soldier in his blood" (VI.iii),

> and I, my wits astray
> Because of all that senseless tumult, all but cried
> For vengeance on the murderers of Jacques Molay.
> [VII.ii]

Hysterical mob brutality again tempts the speaker: to act in a terror is less terrifying than to observe it. Behind the flooding of violent desire lies a horrendous moral paradox: would retributive justice for Molay, burned at the stake, have been any less an irrational crime than the atrocity it purported to avenge?

In the antithetical fantasy of "Magical unicorns" bearing "ladies on their backs" (VII.iii), the ladies seemingly "close their musing eyes" on that chaos; the speaker would imitate them if he could. Overwhelming wish rarifies motifs not only from "Ancestral Houses" but from "Nineteen Hundred . . ." (VI):

> Violence upon the roads: violence of horses;
> Some few have handsome riders, are garlanded
> On delicate sensitive ear or tossing mane . . .

By contrast, unicorn and lady, male and female, spirit and body fuse in the *hortus conclusus* of the speaker's mind to symbolize a transcendental, languid self-delight:

> Nothing but stillness can remain when hearts are full
> Of their own sweetness, bodies of their loveliness.

Fountain (I) and stream (II, V) culminate in limpid calm: "their minds are but a pool / Where even longing drowns under its own excess." In this inhuman, unobtainable oblivion, joy exists despite the death of desire: instead of modern Anglo-Irish stagnation (I) and Lethean doom (II.iii), a serenely beautiful stasis. The sensuous fantasy has no correlatives in the landscape (compare the moor-hen in V.iii). It is characteristic of "Meditations . . ." that as the threats of disorder intensify, the speaker's images of normative aristocratic greatness become progressively removed from human realities—until finally, here, unicorns prance upon air.

Because this discrepancy has widened to an abyss, the fragile vision dissolves. The swirls of cloud

Give place to an indifferent multitude, give place
To brazen hawks. Nor self-delighting reverie,
Nor hate of what's to come, nor pity for what's gone,
Nothing but grip of claw, and the eye's complacency,
The innumerable clanging wings that have put out the moon.

[VII.iv]

Subjected to new vision, the speaker recognizes the aerial counterpart
of the apocalytic "rough beast" heralded by peacock (III) and owl
(IV.ii): not even the brutality is passionate. In effect, "The swan has
leaped into the desolate heaven"—metamorphosed into a "gloomy bird
of prey," its "bell-beat" made into cacophony.[54] Exhausted by the
various shapes of "nothing," the speaker shuts the door (VII.v), for the
second time, against the outside world. Yet he hesitates, wondering not
if but

how many times I could have proved my worth
In something that all others understand or share.

[VII.v]

This is a far more searching judgment on renewed isolation than in
"The Road at My Door." If "how many" measures a new self-confi-
dence, it also registers the intensity of his guilt. "Traffic" in self-
mockery now seems too easy; instead, as he seeks without heroic
pretense to salvage some minimal value for his poetic vocation, he
weighs his psychic needs:

But O! ambitious heart, had such a proof drawn forth
A company of friends, a conscience set at ease,
It had but made us pine the more.

[VII.v]

This, in part, is a recognized cowardice: involvement would have
augmented his grief in seeing Ireland wrecked; the evasion of painful
remorse is worth the price of loneliness and an uneasy conscience. The
brutal analysis recalls the *dementia* of treasuring "solitude" in "Nineteen Hundred . . ." (I.v) and verges perilously close to an acceptance of
"the eye's complacency." But cowardice, paradoxically, is the hardest
way. The real complacency, like that in "My Descendants," would be
the grim satisfaction, supported by the egocentric gratification given by
communal approbation, of believing that because he had acted he was
absolved from blame.

---

[54] The quotations are from, respectively, "Nineteen Hundred and Nineteen"
(III.iii), "Tom O'Roughley," and "The Wild Swans at Coole" (II).

He rejects that fraudulent ambition for a deeper one: the need to reassert continuities, redefine the foundation of his existence. The quest, deflected and questioned throughout, begins afresh:

> The abstract joy,
> The half-read wisdom of daemonic images,
> Suffice the ageing man as once the growing boy.
>
> [VII.v]

In the broad spectrum of Yeats's progress, the retrieval of any constructive purpose from the debris of civil war represents a tangible gain; it is the crucial link between the nihilism of "Nineteen Hundred . . ." and the proud closure of "The Tower." But the poem itself is less optimistic. In this quiet statement of faith, doubt qualifies every word. What "suffice" are the minimal imaginative properties needed for existence: belief in the possibility of a joy that is not "abstract," a wisdom that is not partial; in the endless interim, the endurance of limitation. He has had to jettison much in order to discover these indispensable remnants of his original plan. He has recognized the impossibility of restoring an aristocratic ideal and surrendered his design of revising Anglo-Irish history; he has given up family, heirs, the dynastic dream; he has been compelled to acknowledge self-deceits, glibness and histrionic posings, timidity in the face of adversity and horrifying temptations to violence, the mind's uncontrol and the heart's emptiness. "Meditations . . .," defined in the last line as a rite of passage, is an apocalypse, a stripping away of paraphernalia down to the bedrock—"broken stone" (VII.i)—of identity. The endurance of attrition finally confirms a new resilience, an unexpected capacity to turn deprivation to advantage. From hard self-knowledge and his world's disintegration, the speaker wrests not merely a consolation but reasons for going on. The minimal affirmation, which Yeats later symbolized in the scarecrow-skeleton of "Sailing to Byzantium" and "Among School Children," comes not from weariness[55] but from the plain will to prevail.

IV

It is the natural consequence of Yeats's mode of dramatic lyric—"I study every man I meet at some moment of crisis"[56] —that "The

[55] Cf. Plater, "Water Imagery," p. 70.

[56] *Letters*, p. 675. Yeats went on to add, in a mood similar to that which closes *Reveries*, "I alone have no crisis": the poems seek to show otherwise.

Tower" should test so incisively the resolution gained in "Meditations. . . ."

> What shall I do with this absurdity—
> O heart, O troubled heart—this caricature,
> Decrepit age that has been tied to me
> As to a dog's tail?

[I]

The "ageing man" becomes a thing of hatred. If the speaker can "shut
the door" on military violence, he cannot so easily block out nature, his
bodily image. "*Daemonic* images," remote, do not "suffice." As he
withers into skeleton, his imagination gains in passionate fecundity: the
discrepancy appalls, disgusts him.

Yeats had handled the irreconcilable conflict between sexual poten-
cy and imaginative capability in "Pardon, Old Fathers," the middle
poems about Maud, and elsewhere; his Nobel Prize medal had rekindled
the obsession: "It shows a young man listening to a Muse, who stands
young and beautiful with a great lyre in her hand, and I think as I
examine it, 'I was good-looking once like that young man, but my
unpractised verse was full of infirmity, my Muse old as it were; and now
I am old and rheumatic, and nothing to look at, but my Muse is
young.' "[57] This account of psychological antinomies, as in Blake's "The
Mental Traveller" and *A Vision,* dooms the poet to perpetual quest,
unrequited desire. But its most damaging consequence, as the anguished
speaker of "The Tower" knows, is that the Muse, a *belle dame sans
merci,* may turn termagant and mock her helpless lover. Because the
imagination works through concrete sensuous embodiment, not "abstract things," it constantly exposes the particulars of human form,
however debilitated. In "Sailing to Byzantium" (1926, but placed
before "The Tower"), Yeats evaded this dilemma by creating a realm
where the imagination, encased in "gold enamelling," could dwell
immune from the tortured self-consciousness of decrepitude yet still
freely sing the temporal world. "The Tower" rejects that solution as
cowardly, meretricious, and sterile. The choice is not between an art
which accepts the body and an art which ignores it, but between an art
which accepts the body and no art at all:

> It seems that I must bid the Muse go pack,
> Choose Plato and Plotinus for a friend
> Until imagination, ear and eye,
> Can be content with argument and deal

[57] *Autobiography,* pp. 459–60.

In abstract things; or be derided by
A sort of battered kettle at the heel.

[I]

These alternatives, spat out with such colloquial, sardonic bitterness, [58]
both require enormous sacrifice. To break off the treacherous affair
with the Muse is to conquer death by making nature "but a spume that
plays / Upon a ghostly paradigm of things";[59] yet this perverse al-
chemy insists that he surrender what he has barely salvaged from
"Meditations . . .," his vocation and identity. Conversely, if he affirms
the imagination he must endure humiliation, self-contempt in the world
of matter. The *tertium quid* of the conclusion, the imagination's capacity to make death palatable, is not yet visible on the poem's horizon.

The quandary shows Yeats's purpose: "The Tower," taking sight of
all personal follies wrought in the history of the Rising, the Black and
Tans, and the civil war, is Yeats's most self-demanding revaluation of
the imagination. The temptation to alter the tower's ancestry—from *"Il
Penseroso's* Platonist," the questing poet, to the Plato of the *Ion* and
Republic—renders the traditional philosophical debate in terms of the
territorial myth. Despite his exuberant, Wordsworthian sense that the
"fantastical" imagination (I) both perceives and half creates its universe, the speaker seriously entertains Plato's charge that imagination,
imitating an imitation, distorts truth. If imagination produces only
illusion, why pursue its lures? "Nineteen Hundred . . ." and "Meditations . . ." have caustic comments on its falsehoods:

> O what fine thought we had because we thought
> That the worst rogues and rascals had died out.
>
> A man in his own secret meditation
> Is lost amid the labyrinth that he has made
> In art or politics . . .
>
> Mere dreams, mere dreams!
>
> We had fed the heart on fantasies,
> The heart's grown brutal from the fare . . .

After that last condemnation, "fantastical" is a risky praise of imagination's virtue. If the speaker in section II sometimes appears to grant

[58] Cf. Daniel Albright, *The Myth Against Myth: A Study of Yeats's Imagination in
Old Age* (London: Oxford, 1972), p. 10: "This descent into abstraction is surely a
last resort for a poet, especially for a poet with Yeats's intense hatred of abstractions; but it is all treated with good humour, almost too gently to be the gallows
humour of old age."

[59] "Among School Children," VI.

Plato everything, his torrential outburst is also a defiant defense of imagination's splendor, climaxing in the firm declaration of faith (III). Between these two extremes, puzzlement: Was it liquor *or* poetry which maddened Mary Hynes' brawling lovers (II.iv)? Was Hanrahan drunk *or* sober when, crazed, he sought Mary Lavelle's ghost (II.vi–viii)?[60] The strained ambivalence, the wildly rocking vacillations between wry wit and desperation signify his persistent questioning: is the imagination worth affirming?

Failure to perceive the pressing reality of this debate will obscure the poem's structure.[61] In contrast to "Meditations . . ." (VIII), the speaker neither flees experience nor suffers uncontrolled vision. He deliberately ascends to the tower-top, a place of energetic defiance ("battlements" against the battering "kettle" of age), and organizes his mortal world. With the panoramic perspective his promontory offers, [62] he stares upon a landscape whose psychic legacy he will compel to yield him guidance (II.i). Craving some community with whom to share his isolate pain, he will ask, when his historical imagination has provided "Images and memories" with new bodies,

> Did all old men and women, rich and poor,
> Who trod upon these rocks or passed this door,
> Whether in public or in secret rage
> As I do now against old age?
>
> [II.xi]

But the structural complexity of section II is that, as in the opening portraits of "In Memory of Major Robert Gregory," the specters serve a thematic function quite different from what the speaker initially purposes. The summonings focus not on the "absurdity" of "Decrepit age" (as section I and the question of section II [xi] might suggest),[63] but

---

60 Cf. Sarah Youngblood, "A Reading of *The Tower*," *Twentieth Century Literature* 5 (1959): 77–78. Youngblood, speaking of the "drunken admirers who are betrayed by their excited imaginations," obscures the question. Cf. also Albright, *Myth Against Myth*, pp. 15–16.

61 Cf. Torchiana, *W. B. Yeats*, p. 305: the speaker is "*pretending* to abandon" poetry for philosophy [italics mine]. See Albright, *Myth Against Myth*, p. 13.

62 Youngblood ("A Reading of *The Tower*," pp. 78–79) argues that the tower (as a physical emblem) has little prominence in this poem because it is a "phallic symbol *manqué*." Quite apart from that distressingly mixed metaphor, it seems plain that the real reason for Yeats's lack of direct attention to Thoor Ballylee is that he was concerned with its function, not its nature.

63 Cf. Albright, *Myth Against Myth*, p. 12: "By summoning the images of the old, Yeats is summoning his own rage against old age." Bloom (*Yeats*, p. 350) apparently thinks that the speaker intends both questions from the very beginning; Whitaker (*Swan and Shadow*, p. 194) thinks that the "question" (II.i) leads only to II.xi.

on the nature of the imagination. The specifically aesthetic concerns of section I cannot be repressed; each episode becomes a miniature version of the problem of fantasy. The second, more crucial question;

> Does the imagination dwell the most
> Upon a woman won or a woman lost?
>
> [II.xiii]

is one which the speaker initially has no intention of asking: evolving subconsciously and spontaneously from the meditation itself, it constitutes a structural refutation of abstract "argument."

The specters reveal a world where imagination and fact are perpetually confounded, sunlight outshone by the moon. Thus, the metaphorical language of Mrs. French, a type of the poet, sparks victimization (II.ii): "I wish the fellow's ears were cut off! that might quiet him."[64] Unlike Salome, whom she distantly resembles, she does not intend her wish fulfilled; but the sly, devoted "serving-man" imaginatively interprets her outburst literally. The speaker's wry, understated tone contains this explosive anecdote with fine dramatic tension yet leaves his response obscure. As the arch ironies show, he delights in the outrageous admixture of passion and courtesy, the intrusion of grotesque, barbaric comedy upon late eighteenth-century Anglo-Irish ceremony. But, ominously, he is not only spectator but vicarious actor in his literary memory: as a poet, unable to control the consequences of his language, he too must "make men mad" (II.v). Beyond that nagging ethical concern, he senses an affinity with Mrs. French's victim. What if *he* lost his "ears"—the metaphorical ears by which the poet perceives and half creates? Obliquely, "deafness" links the double threats of decrepitude and waning imaginative power.

The mythic plot of this anecdote is reiterated in the Raftery and Hanrahan episodes (II.iii–v; II.vi–viii). Its basic form describes the magic and madness of art: the poet, sitting at a table where liquor is served, creates a poem or metaphor so captivating that its hearers, their "wits astray," confuse aesthetic illusion with reality; they quest after the subject of the poem; disaster, however comically treated, follows. The superimposition of narratives demonstrates the homogeneous experience of aristocrat, peasant, and poet which the tower's inhabitant inherits by reviving. What holds his attention, as he explores a legend of poetic fame all but carved on the stones of Thoor Ballylee, is Raftery's vision of the peasant Mary Hynes, as mythical as Homer's of Helen: an

---

[64] Sir Jonah Barrington, *Sketches of his Own Times*, 3rd ed. (London: Lynch, 1871), I: 27. Barrington narrates the episode as proof of "the devotion of servants in those days to their masters."

emblem of unobtainable beauty and sexual fulfillment. The poet's song, living beyond his death, binds the community in a frenzy which is also the tower's foreboding legacy. Mary Hynes, because she exists only in the imaginative illusion created by blind poets, must always lure her lovers in vain pursuit: "one was drowned in the great bog of Cloone." Like Hanrahan possessed by the "horrible splendour of desire" (II.vi), they must return tormented to a deathly world whose "prosaic light of day" can no longer illumine. This is why the speaker, despite his gauged comic detachment, suddenly speculates on "the tragedy" and affirms an archetype indigenous to Western culture, local history, and private biography alike: "And Helen has all *living* hearts betrayed." Implicitly, he names himself a victim, and not simply Maud's. The lover's sexual anguish mirrors the poet's desire for his Muse: he may envisage but not possess her. Like Coleridge's mariner, the speaker now knows the dark suffering his vocation entails. Tormented by his Muse, he must, whether he seeks catharsis or displaced revenge, create images which inflict his anguish upon others. The passionate cry,

> O may the moon and sunlight seem
> One inextricable beam,
> For if I triumph I must make men mad,
>
> [II.v]

voices the harrowing plea that poetry be other than it is.[65]

Thus, amalgamating sadistic pride and hideous self-loathing, the speaker proclaims his creation of Hanrahan, acknowledges his self-compensatory cruelty. The Hanrahan episode, gleaned from the speaker's past, not from history or public legend, is possibly Yeats's most complicated allusion anywhere. In the *Stories of Red Hanrahan* (1897), Yeats had saddled Hanrahan with his passion for Maud and projected that turmoil upon the territory around Thoor Ballylee. Announcing his proprietary role in elaborating the tower's mythology by alluding to those tales, the speaker simultaneously recovers an earlier phase in his consciousness, the "barren passion" which memory of the stories enables him to examine from the dual perspectives of youth and age. But he seemingly cannot recall much of what he has written (II.viii). What does his apparent lapse of memory mean?

In an episode which encompasses autobiography and present drama, ancient myth and allegory of the daemonic intricacies of the imagination, the speaker takes all parts at once. Despite his tirade against ageing, his focus is not Hanrahan's "curse on his own head because it

65 Cf. Albright, *Myth Against Myth*, p. 18.

withers grey,"[66] but the reenactment of his own unrequited passion. As the *Stories* indicate, a ghostly trickster from the faery Sidhe of Celtic mythology hypnotizes Hanrahan from his earthly love of Mary Lavelle and sends him off in dizzy pursuit of an immortal beauty he scarcely knows exists. Bewitching fact into phantom, the trickster is a poet; his "juggleries" are indistinguishable from the present (and past) machinations of the self-mocking, self-recognizing speaker. The interfusion is clear:

> And I myself created Hanrahan
> And drove him drunk or sober through the dawn
> From somewhere in the neighbouring cottages.
> Caught by an old man's juggleries
> He stumbled, tumbled, fumbled to and fro . . .
>
> [II.vi]

Hanrahan is essentially victimized by his own imagination, symbolized by the poet-trickster figure; in the *Stories* Hanrahan confuses him with "his own shadow." Hanrahan, "the learned man and the great song-maker," makes a poem "in praise of Venus and of Mary Lavelle," [67] modeled on Raftery's vision of Mary Hynes as Helen. The poem, seductive, tempts him to make his life imitate his art. As he mistakes his poem for reality, an uncontrollable passion compels him to seek—not Mary Lavelle, but the metaphor he has made for her—Venus. His quest derives from the Grail legend. If, when he enters the "shining house" of the Otherworld,[68] he can ask the proper questions about the Grail symbols, he will win the love of Echtge—the spiritual form of Mary Lavelle. In learning the mystery, he will gain the self-completing understanding of Pleasure, Knowledge, Courage, and Power, redeem himself from death, and inhabit—not merely "dream"—"Translunar Paradise" (III). But Echtge's supreme loveliness paradoxically terrifies Hanrahan the poet into muteness. The vision breaks; he awakes into mortality and soon ages into madness. Failure to complete the quest haunts him until death.

This whole adventure underlies the tremendous crisis which explodes when the speaker dramatically truncates his narrative:

> Hanrahan rose in frenzy there
> And followed up those baying creatures towards—

---

[66] *Mythologies*, p. 243.

[67] Ibid., pp. 219, 216, 215.

[68] Ibid., p. 220.

> O towards I have forgotten what—enough!
> I must recall a man . . .
>
> [II.vii—viii]

This is too impassioned, the "enough!" too desperately willed, the excursus too deliberate for anyone to believe that the speaker has really forgotten the goal of Hanrahan's quest.[69] He knows, but *will not* remember beyond the journey's beginning, as if full verbal expression could itself entail some terrible consequence. By repressing Hanrahan's confrontation with Echtge and his subsequent derangement, the speaker hopes to dissociate himself from Hanrahan's fate. He shrinks from vicariously reliving his own anguished, "horrible splendour of desire" for Maud, recoils from renewed knowledge of failure. In this intricate symbiosis between creator and creation, what Hanrahan does or thinks commits the speaker to virtually identical behavior. The creator, now nearly his creation's slave, can wrest his freedom from a doom which appalls him only by denying that the main substance of Hanrahan's quest—and his own—ever occurred.

The denial is a crucial rejection of the imagination's odyssey toward beauty and wisdom. Without quite choosing "Plato and Plotinus for a friend," he turns from "a great labyrinth" (II.xiii) to the more tangible landscape of the tower, grasping the ignoble but honest consolation that his disaster hardly matches the unending calamity of its mid-nine-teenth-century tenant:

> I must recall a man that neither love
> Nor music nor an enemy's clipped ear
> Could, he was so harried, cheer.
>
> [II.viii]

Despite its bleakness, the memory subtly counterbalances the negative interpretation of the imagination. The "master of this house," though he *became* "fabulous," lacked the delight in fable, aesthetic distance, which would have eased his misery;[70] his true bankruptcy was imagina-tive. The notion that the imagination can "cheer," heal as well as maim, is the speaker's first positive judgment on art since his praise of Raftery's song (II.iii); his vacillation, following so suddenly his dissocia-

---

[69] Youngblood ("A Reading of *The Tower*," p. 76) has reached the same conclu-sions about the psychological implications of the language.

[70] Cf. Whitaker (*Swan and Shadow*, p. 195), who argues that the "ancient bank-rupt master" is "parallel to the speaker himself, save that he has 'finished his dog's day.' " More important is the speaker's gradual self-differentiation from this un-imaginative creature who is beyond "cheer."

tion from Hanrahan's quest, measures a new detachment from his trepidations. Behind it lies the faith of "Lapis Lazuli": the imagination, for all its horrors, can also transfigure raw suffering into aesthetic shape and thus permit a transcendental gaiety.

Rejecting a life untouched by art, the speaker returns to his Anglo-Norman heritage (II.ix): resilient earth-bound warriors whose clanking ascent of the "narrow stairs" warns him that, in pacing "upon the battlements" (the metaphorical extension of their movements), he has symbolically committed himself to mortal struggle. Even more cautionary, in a poem which values so highly the conscious power to summon spirits, are the "men-at-arms"

> Whose images, in the Great Memory stored,
> Come with loud cry and panting breast
> To break upon a sleeper's rest
> While their great wooden dice beat on the board.

As in "Meditations . . ." (VII), these spirits come uncalled. The dead, not done with life, intrude into the unconscious mind; their imaginations mingle with those of the living.[71] To "choose" Plato and Plotinus is a metaphysical and psychological impossibility; to exclude the Muse, an indulgence in pernicious fiction. In that unspoken recognition of the independence of the imagination the speaker will ultimately discover his freedom.

To the tower the speaker now summons directly the specters he has meditated into being (II.x). The postponed question (II.xi), coming in tense fury, is painfully rhetorical. The cumulative *genius* of his territory condemns him not only to imagination's thralldom but to a bitter ageing. Imperiously, yet with sympathy for the specters he has forced to relive their rage, he releases all but Hanrahan, his own image.

The spontaneously generated, climactic questioning of Hanrahan (II.xii–xiii) is an excruciatingly transparent self-judgment. Unlike Hanrahan at the end of the Grail quest, the speaker is not mute in confronting his own purgatorial "shadow":

> Does the imagination dwell the most
> Upon a woman won or a woman lost?

The question *is* the answer. Through it the speaker "remembers" what he had "forgotten," accepts his own experience: the "woman lost," Maud, Hanrahan's quest for Echtge. The courageous act of remembrance commits him, irrevocably, to imaginative quest, however

[71] See *A Vision*, pp. 221, 228–29, 233–34.

dreaded. But the risks of *not* questing are as dangerous: the energetic lechery of Hanrahan's old age is but a surrogate activity designed to assuage the violent remorse of his failure;[72] the pain of unfulfilled desire, as the warriors' "loud cry" implies (II.ix), does not end with death. Thus, the self-castigating speaker attacks his double:

> admit you turned aside
> From a great labyrinth out of pride,
> Cowardice, some silly over-subtle thought
> Or anything called conscience once . . .

By way of displaced accusation the speaker encompasses not only his guilt about Maud, but, with stunning critical insight, his withdrawal from imaginative quest in section I: the Hamlet-like vacillations, the cowardice masking as compliance with natural law, the vain fear of decrepitude, the casuistic belief that imagination could be satisfied with "abstract things." In this ruthless stripping away of masks, the speaker breaks loose from his haunting "near-identity with Hanrahan,"[73] frees himself to prevail where Hanrahan failed. As in "Little Gidding" (III), "This is the use of memory: / For liberation." The speaker thus becomes Theseus, seeking to liberate himself, the trapped Daedalus of "Nineteen Hundred . . .," the creator of the *Stories* caught in his own artifice. The labyrinth through which he must wander, armed with nothing but imagination, is the symbolic body of the Muse. Passionate pursuit of the Muse and battle against death's tyranny have become one: "only an aching heart / *Conceives* a changeless work of art" ("Meditations . . .," III). The metaphor of mystical sexual union, as in the "Crazy Jane" sequence, here reconciles the realms of body and imagination. But the quest's conclusion remains ambiguous: the conflation of the Grail legend with the Theseus myth makes plain that the figure at the center may be either "a woman, the most beautiful the world ever saw,"[74] or the chthonic, devouring minotaur.

Having accepted mortality, the speaker accomplishes by design the surrender which time will require:

> It is time that I wrote my will;
> I choose upstanding men
> That climb the streams until
> The fountain leap, and at dawn

---

[72] See *Mythologies*, p. 239.

[73] Bloom, *Yeats*, p. 351.

[74] *Mythologies*, p. 220.

Drop their cast at the side
Of dripping stone . . .

[III]

Imagery and diction from section I emphasize his decision: he
"chooses" not "Plato and Plotinus" but "upstanding men" who will
continue the quest he began in "boyhood." His shrewd pun on "upstanding" saves this powerful naming of heirs from sentimentality—and
compactly defines his visionary men: they are "upright" physically, as
well as morally and intellectually; they neither drown "in the great bog
of Cloone" (II.iv) nor, like Hanrahan, stumble on "broken knees"
(II.vi).[75] Mr. Bloom has questioned the fishing imagery as being "inappropriate if not silly";[76] but its symbolic value is plain from the
allusions to "The Song of Wandering Aengus" (1893), "The Fisher-
man" (1914), and the Grail legend, as well as from the link between
fishing and apocalyptic vision (I). The fishermen are Yeats's aristocrats:
indomitably searching for beauty and perfection, intent upon "contact
with the soil," skilled in *sprezzatura*—the effortless flick of the wrist.
Yeats, having learned in "Meditations . . ." that the "abounding glittering jet" cannot truly "leap" amidst artificed gardens, has moved it to a
lonelier, less accessible terrain. His speaker does not say "until *they see*
the fountain leap"; the omission, together with the subjunctive mode,
makes the landscape visionary. The fountain is the internal joy which
the climbing, the quest itself causes. These seekers alone are fit to
receive the speaker's pride,

> The pride of people that were
> Bound neither to Cause nor to State,
> Neither to slaves that were spat on,
> Nor to the tyrants that spat,
> The people of Burke and of Grattan
> That gave, though free to refuse—
> Pride . . .

All this departs radically from the preceding sections. Expansive joy
replaces a morbid fascination with victims. From possessing nothing but
a "caricature" (I), the trick of "mocking Muses" (II.x), he now knows

---

[75] See also the "half-mounted man" (II.x). Torchiana, (*W. B. Yeats*, p. 306, n. 42),
citing Jonah Barrington (*Recollections of Jonah Barrington* [Dublin, n. d.], p. 90),
restricts the meaning of "half-mounted" to a designation for the lowest category of
gentry; but Yeats was doubtless wittily aware of other and more visually dramatic
implications in the phrase.

[76] Bloom, *Yeats*, p. 351.

himself the "rich inheritor" of an autonomous aristocratic culture whose values he can transmit without the fear of corrosion evident in "Meditations . . ." (IV). The confidence, matched by no other 'tower' or Coole Park poem, reflects more than the liberation from Hanrahan. While vacillating between Plato and the Muse, he gradually recognizes the cultural synthesis his territory embodies; his awareness confers new strength. What had been a dramatic background for the debate now becomes foreground. Mrs. French, Raftery, the Anglo-Normans, and the rest—studied as examples of the imagination's intricacy, *not* as symbols of the imagination in a particular historical epoch—now epitomize "that one Irish century that escaped from darkness and confusion." Many critics, confounding Yeats with his speaker, have seen the speaker consciously reconstructing his eighteenty-century world; but the poem does not support the interpretation. The speaker inhabits an Anglo-Irish landscape only after he accidentally makes it; its identity is not fully known until he utters the triumphant, collectivizing epithet, "the *people* of Burke and of Grattan." Typically, Yeats chose to define his territory not by presenting conclusions but by dramatizing a revelation.

Through the revelation Yeats countered the debacle of "Meditations . . .," with its frank admission of modern Anglo-Irish enervation, and buttressed his mythology by revising his poetic approach to the eighteenth century. "Meditations . . ." judges Augustan and Georgian greatness partly by its consequences: barren inheritors sapped by its genius. In "The Tower" that standard vanishes: the speaker celebrates the genesis of his tradition for its own sake. Yeats also discarded his concern with the radiant creative *moment* which, like the "symbolic rose," dies as it flowers: the speaker can thus dwell unrestrained upon the imaginative richness of an extended period more completely fleshed out in panorama than any other in Yeats's poetry. And because contemporary history does not darken his mind, he feels no compulsion to assert the present "stamina," social and political, of the Anglo-Irish tradition. Although his language recalls the Divorce Speech, his meaning differs. Instead of claiming present class-power by association ("We *are* the people of Burke . . ."), "The Tower" specifically turns its back on modern Anglo-Ireland and extols "people that *were* / *Bound* neither to Cause nor to State."[77] Less parochial than the speech, the poem dispenses with political and religious warfares. It suffices both Yeats and his speaker that they have internalized their eighteenth-century

77 Both Torchiana (*W. B. Yeats*, p. 308) and Whitaker (*Swan and Shadow*, p. 198) assume that the prose (*Senate Speeches*, p. 99) and the poetry carry the same meaning.

heritage, brought that world in procession before the tower, and implicitly pronounced the West of Ireland the place of its most characteristic—and last—expression.

Nor is the speaker's cultural synthesis exclusively Anglo-Irish. Its epic spectrum includes the tower's Anglo-Norman founders, Protestants, Catholics, pagans, aristocrats and peasants alike. The history encapsulated extends explicitly back to the fourteenth century and implicitly back to Homer. It is Ireland "Before that ruin" (II.ix) of O'Connell's cheap, demagogic nineteenth century, and Western culture before

> Locke sank into a swoon;
> The Garden died;
> God took the spinning-jenny
> Out of his side.
>
> ["Fragments," I]

Yeats, in his introduction to *The Words upon the Window-pane,* sought from the Anglo-Irish eighteenth century "an image of the modern mind's discovery of itself"[78] to oppose that mechanistic catastrophe; but the conceptual design of "The Tower" differs. The speaker, like Yeats in his earlier understanding of the Renaissance, finds in Burke and Grattan not something new but the florescence of the old: their "written tradition . . . has been established" on the customary, imaginative, oral culture of the countryside;[79] their self-possessed dedication to liberty, their magnanimity bred of Roman and Renaissance decorum are the grave public counterparts to its flamboyant and spontaneous independence.

This legacy the speaker has received directly from his ancestors. The word "Pride" (1. 14) is *either* apposite to "my pride" (1. 7) *or* the direct object of the verb "gave" (1. 13). The marvelous syntactic ambiguity embodies his deep Burkean faith in cultural continuity. His understanding is not merely intellectual; he has been given his "pride" personally, in the course of the meditation, by "the people of Burke and of Grattan"—who have reached out from history to name him heir, as he in turn chooses "upstanding men." This pride is not the arrogance of a powerful minority but the exuberant sense of creative activity in history. It has the purity of natural fruition and the disinterest of courtesy. It is described in similies whose very cleanness of diction radiates, in perfectly blended fusion, amplitude and sanctity:

[78] *Explorations,* p. 345.
[79] *Essays,* p. 6.

> Pride, like that of the morn,
> When the headlong light is loose,
> Or that of the fabulous horn,
> Or that of the sudden shower
> When all streams are dry,
> Or that of the hour
> When the swan must fix his eye
> Upon a fading gleam,
> Float out upon a long
> Last reach of glittering stream
> And there sing his last song.

This vibrant, sensuous chiaroscuro, imitating the organic cycle of the entire poetic artifice, culminates in the swan's artless artistry. The speaker becomes what he beholds: a selfless creator, knowing death imminent, in love with the productions of time, singing. At the poem's end he will seek to emulate the serenity he images: the swan no longer leaps "into the desolate heaven" ("Nineteen Hundred . . .," III.iii).

Anyone privileged to perform this poem must pause, as the speaker certainly does, before beginning afresh. Exhilaration and elegy, tragic joy, subside momentarily into a delicate object-less reverie. The dramatic recovery, thus accentuated, follows:

> And I declare my faith:
> I mock Plotinus' thought
> And cry in Plato's teeth,
> Death and life were not
> Till man made up the whole,
> Made lock, stock and barrel
> Out of his bitter soul,
> Aye, sun and moon and star, all,
> And further add to that
> That, being dead, we rise,
> Dream and so create
> Translunar Paradise.

The passage resonates with full humanism. As the speaker chants his spiritual regeneration, the capacious and ever-generating human mind replaces God as the organizing center of experience. Matter is real; yet its particularities are real in that they are symbolic emanations of human passion and psychology, as Yeats thought Berkeley (despite his orthodoxy) had discovered. Only the human imagination, independent, even wayward, can transmute these material reflections of dreams into the "Mirror-resembling dream" of art and thus confer Edenic release from "Dull sublunary lovers love"—even if the art it creates, "makes

up," is an emblem of its own violence, a rifle. The fall into matter and
time is not only necessary but fortunate; as Stevens has it, "Death is the
mother of beauty" ("Sunday Morning").

The rhapsodic affirmation ebbs in tranquil reconciliation to mortality. For the first time since section II, the speaker focusses on the
tower, his own "proud stones" (III) that will outlast his death:

> As at the loophole there
> The daws chatter and scream,
> And drop twigs layer upon layer.
> When they have mounted up,
> The mother bird will rest
> On their hollow top,
> And so warm her wild nest.

The movement from anxiety to serenity and the construction of a
natural house (as in "To a Wealthy Man . . .") mirror the speaker's own
evolution, harmonizing it with cyclical regeneration in nature. The
construction counterbalances both the bitter awareness of "ruin" (II.i,
ix) and the swan's death; an earthly answer to the cry for transcendental sweetness in "Meditations . . ." (VI), it symbolically rebuilds the
"broken stone" battlements in "Meditations . . ." (VII.i). The imagery
of ascent, fused by pun with the fishermen's quest ("Climbing the
*mount*ain-side"; "When they have *mount*ed up"), produces a cluster of
values nearly Jonsonian: imaginative excellence, consummate physical
control, architectural wholeness.

These concrete physical images remind the speaker of his waning
stamina. Nostalgic envy tinges his last, almost involuntary bequest to
"young upstanding men." The metrical weakness of "I leave both faith
and pride" and the slack word "leave" make the regret unmistakable.
For an instant, as self-pity tempts him, he wavers in his new faith that
imagination may triumph over death; the exasperated turbulence of
section I nearly erupts afresh. The vacillation, like the *pianissimo*
preceding a Bethoven *finale,* intensifies the flat resolve to master bitter
experience:

> Now shall I make my soul,
> Compelling it to study
> In a learned school . . .

This is no appeal to "sages standing in God's holy fire" nor an attempt
to cast off "bodily form" ("Sailing to Byzantium," III–IV) but a hard
testing of his rhetorical claim: "Death and life were not / Till man made
up the whole." His intellect remains too muscular to succumb to Plato

and Plotinus. The schoolmaster is his autonomous imagination, teaching natural passion to obey; the "learned school," his mortal world;[80] the end of education, the transmutation of death's slow agony into aesthetic beauty. The gruff irony in "a learned school," acknowledging the difficulty of disciplining the recalcitrant heart to disinterested vision, slyly debunks philosophy's vaunted superiority by dressing the Muse in academic garb. If the phrase misses the lightness of the "grammar school of courtesies," it is because the stakes are higher, not because the intent of fundamentally revising the self has changed.

The packed, appropriately entropic subordinate clause which completes the speaker's self-command is one of Yeats's finest bravura performances. One by one the speaker summons the disasters of old age—and then neutralizes them all with a placidity which scarcely seems possible. That he even magnifies his impending ruin, seeks the most difficult confrontation—"*wreck* of the body," "*Slow* decay," "*Testy* delirium," the death "Of *every* brilliant eye"—makes the imagination's triumph all the more spectacular. If this victory appears meretricious, compare the exactly reversed relation between fact and metaphor in "Easter 1916":

> What is it but nightfall?
> No, no, not night but death.

The final metaphors in "The Tower" are not escapist euphemisms [81] but mirroring emblems permeated by the sensation of oncoming death. As aesthetic beauty transfigures experience, fact and metaphor mingle inextricably—without distortion, without engendering madness. What the speaker sees from the tower—"the day's declining beam" (II.i), "the clouds of the sky / When the horizon fades" (III)—are indistinguishable from the "fading gleam" on which "the swan must fix his eye" (III); the swan's "last song," the "sleepy cry" of the "mother bird" (III), and the poem's end are the same. The entire landscape, for all the speaker's visionary perception, is but reality observed, the spiritualized world of the tower accurately delineated. Such observation, like the self-transcending gaiety in "Lapis Lazuli," comes from the courteous discipline to become spectator of oneself. This saving capacity to conceive experience as aesthetic drama is precisely what the "ancient bankrupt mas-

---

80 Whitaker (*Swan and Shadow*, p. 202) observes that "The speaker approaches Keats's view that the world is the 'vale of Soul-making,' a 'School' in which each soul learns its 'Identity' " (*The Letters of John Keats*, ed. Hyder Edward Rollins [Cambridge: Harvard University Press, 1958], II: 102 [April 21, 1819]). Torchiana (*W. B. Yeats*, p. 310), however, believes that the speaker capitulates to philosophy.

81 Bloom, *Yeats*, p. 352.

ter"—and the speaker remembering Hanrahan—lacked. It is also the death of selfhood from which Hanrahan turned aside and the darkness which the speaker now accepts: "detachment / From self and from things and from persons," as Eliot has it.[82] Finally, within time, time collapses: the speaker's goal of creating the soul's future peace is what he achieves now. Having gathered history into the present world of the tower, he thus completes the process of eternizing that mutable landscape by fusing the language of prophecy with that of perception. For a moment of tragic exaltation, he realizes the dream of "A Tower on the Appenines": the poet is "not, as we say of many a one, speaking in metaphor, but as this were Delphi or Eleusis."[83] He sings "Of what is past, or passing, or to come," and they are the same.

[82] "Little Gidding," III, in *Four Quartets*.

[83] *Essays*, p. 291. Whitaker (*Swan and Shadow*, p. 202) writes that "as the metaphors suggest, with them ["evil and loss"] fades all that is temporal." But the content of the metaphors seems ultimately to contribute less to this fading of time than Yeats's method of spinning out his subordinate clause to such lengths that, by the end, the crucial conjunction denoting future time ("Till") has been forgotten.

CHAPTER

SEVEN

Tragic War

In "Vacillation" Yeats posed the central question of *The Winding Stair:*

> The body calls it death,
> The heart remorse.
> But if these be right
> What is joy?

[I]

"A Dialogue of Self and Soul" (1927) and "Blood and the Moon" (1926–27)[1] seek what "Meditations . . ." had failed to wrest from civil war, a tangible joy. Both poems tacitly acknowledge that "The Tower," for all its imaginative scope, is an insular poem whose joy is never tested against present history.

The poems share a background of political violence. On July 10, 1927, the IRA assassinated Kevin O'Higgins, the Minister of Justice, in retaliation for executions of their members. Yeats was shocked; O'Higgins had been a personal friend, "the one strong intellect in Irish public life,"[2] de Valéra's opponent and an intense conservative committed to Anglo-Irish ideals of integrity and service. Yeats, assuming personal responsibility for the tragedy, placed his guilt within so universal a context that it signified the Fall: political experience and

---

1 Richard Ellmann dates the poem July-December 1927 (*The Identity of Yeats* [1954; rpt. London: Faber, 1964], p. 291). Lady Gregory indicates that Yeats began the poem during the summer of 1926, just after he had started "Among School Children" (Unpublished Journals, Book XXXIII, May 28, 1926 [Berg Collection, New York Public Library]).

2 W. B. Yeats, *The Letters of W. B. Yeats*, ed. Allan Wade (London: Hart-Davis, 1954), p. 727.

Western mythology converged. Feeling "the helplessness of human life,"[3] he recounted to Olivia Shakespear certain premonitions he had disregarded the night before the ambush, and concluded: "Had we seen more he might have been saved, for recent evidence seems to show that those things are fate unless foreseen by clairvoyance and so brought within the range of free-will."[4] Yeats's guilt was not a neurotic self-laceration but a philosophic judgment on the inscrutable byways of the human psyche in relation to the totality of conscious and unconscious thought. Not the post-Treaty political morass but the epistemological failure of humankind to comprehend its own nature was the ultimate cause of O'Higgins's death. "Had we seen more he might have been saved": metaphysical blindness is sin.

That philosophical gloom suffuses the poems. In "A Dialogue of Self and Soul," Self claims that "A living man is blind and drinks his drop" (II.i); intrinsic blindness is less corrigible than the optimistic illusions castigated in "Nineteen Hundred . . . ." Soul terms existence the unredeemable "crime of death and birth" (I.iii); his call to escape the cycles of time reflects Yeats's revulsion. In "Blood and the Moon" the speaker smells "Odour of blood on the ancestral stair!" (III). Derangement and purification are obsessions: "What theme had Homer but original sin?" ("Vacillation," VII). The poem shows how Yeats transformed a public event into private drama. O'Higgins's death, completely assimilated into the tower's ecology, is invisible.[5] The emotions it prompted, the philosophical and religious issues it raised have been molded with intimate passion into generalization: Yeats attributed to the tower the contamination he felt, wrote in "Blood and the Moon" (III) *as if* the event had occurred at Thoor Ballylee, and used that implosive pressure to transmute his own experience into a crisis of the human spirit.

O'Higgins's death catalyzed the increasingly dialectical debate concerning the value of human life which Yeats had explicitly begun in *The*

---

[3] "Sympathy with Mrs. O'Higgins," *Irish Times*, July 14, 1927; quoted by Donald T. Torchiana, *W. B. Yeats and Georgian Ireland* (Evanston: Northwestern University Press, 1966), p. 184.

[4] *Letters*, p. 727.

[5] Cf. Torchiana, *W. B. Yeats*, pp. 179–80, 320–21. In "Blood and the Moon," the "blood of innocence" (III) is not identified. Had Yeats wanted the poem to assume an explicitly political cast, he would hardly have written so skimpy an introductory note (W. B. Yeats, *The Variorum Edition of the Poems of W. B. Yeats*, eds. Peter Allt and Russell K. Alspach [New York: Macmillan, 1966], p. 831); compare his extensive commentary on "To a Wealthy Man . . ." in the first edition of *Responsibilities.* Nor would he have first published the poem in America (*Letters*, pp. 728-29).

Tower and its title poem. Soul seeks to transform Self's architectural heritage, the "winding, gyring, spiring treadmill of a stair" ("Blood and the Moon," II.ii), into the spiritual staircase of mystical ascent. The radical repudiation of earthly sanctity, the chief goal of Yeats's speakers, is a logical development in Yeats's exploration of the tower. His architectural iconography shows a clear progression from the tower's earth-bound base to its top, a visionary promontory. "Ego Dominus Tuus" occurs outside; in "A Prayer on Going into My House," the speaker is at the tower's threshold; in "The Phases of the Moon," the poet has reached his second-floor study. The speaker of "In Memory of Major Robert Gregory" is in the ground-floor dining area. "Meditations . . ." contains more dynamic movement than any other of the poems: the speaker begins outside (I, II), goes to his study (III), descends to his doorway to meet the "affable Irregular" and Lieutenant (V), returns to his study (VI), and then—the move is crucial—escapes, for the first time in the poetry, to the tower-top (VII), where he ironically suffers a vision of history so terrifying that he must "shut the door" and "turn" downstairs (VII.v). On the battlements in "The Tower," he *seeks* a visionary understanding and gains, within time, a moment of transcendent joy. The mystical ascent proposed in "A Dialogue of Self and Soul" climaxes Yeats's fascination with the tower's top and what lies beyond it, the contemplative world of the spirit's perfection. Because the poem so emphatically polarizes the tower's base and top, Self's choice not to ascend appears all the more decisive. The poem is Yeats's most blunt, tragic affirmation of existence.

"A Dialogue of Self and Soul" is appropriately the most ethereal of the 'tower' poems. It originates *ex nihilo,* and the unexplained, ghostly beginning shocks. In Marvell's "A Dialogue between the Soul and Body," you accept a motiveless opening because the participants are abstractions. But in Yeats, Soul as well as Self has a body (e.g., "my tongue's a stone," I.v), and you quite properly want to know how he arrived at Thoor Ballylee.[6] The effect of that incongruous reification is spectral. When Soul summons Self (I.i), he explains *what* is happening, but not *why.* Even when he justifies his command (I.iii), he does not satisfactorily indicate why the alternative to earthly meditation should necessarily be a renunciatory devotion to mystical union. That it is

6 Cf. Harold Bloom, *Yeats* (New York: Oxford, 1970), p. 373. Bloom's approach to the poem's origin is biographical: "the poem's genetic impulse belongs to the Soul; Yeats has been very near the gates of death (having just experienced his first severe illness since childhood) and he turns to consider the Last Things in a very different spirit than that of *A Vision.*"

usually so in Christianity and sometimes so in Yeats (especially when he pits the swordsman against the saint) are arguments which do not diminish the inscrutability of this poem's drama.

Soul's mysterious visitation occurs because Self is in a trance, a semi-conscious reverie. Like the ghosts who "break upon a sleeper's rest" in "The Tower" (II.ix), he enters because the conscious will, which bars influx of the unknown, is half-asleep. Self, apprehending Soul only instinctively, never addresses him directly; trance produces a curiously diaphanous conversation whose logic of progression is almost always suppressed. Heightening the aura of reverie, Yeats deliberately obscured the spatio-temporal connections expected from earlier poems. The debate, a permanent human struggle, has no particular historical context. All references to weather and landscape at the tower's base, including the familiar storm of earthly complexities, have been omitted; instead, Soul alludes to a shimmering, "breathless starlit air" (I.i). The tower itself has lots its substantiality, and Soul mentions its "broken, crumbling battlement" (I.i) only to convince Self of transience. Compare "Meditations . . ." (VII.i): "I climb to the tower-top and *lean* upon broken stone." That crucial bodily pressure epitomizes the tactility which the dialogue eschews. Soul will not even deign to acknowledge Self's corporeal body; note the ellipsis in "I summon [you] to the winding ancient stair." Yeats, when he presented the tower, saw through Soul's eyes, included nothing to jeopardize an atmosphere conducive to Self's ascent.

Yet before the poem begins, Self has made his "choice of rebirth rather than deliverance from birth."[7] Seated in the tower's lower regions, he stubbornly refuses through his very posture to yield to Soul's temptation. The fact that he triumphs by belief rather than argument raises important questions about Yeats's purpose in writing a "dialogue." Yeats's subject was Adam's curse and the modes of responding to knowledge of sin, and not the *process* of self-affirmation. Dialogue obviously gained him a dual perspective; but the poem's form actually offers *three* opposed visions of temporal reality. Soul's asceticism is plain. Self, however, has two conceptions of his mortal state. The first, in section I, is induced by trance, a partial separation from

---

[7] *Letters*, p. 729. The poem's structure has been largely misunderstood. Denis Donoghue, "On 'The Winding Stair,' " in *An Honoured Guest*, eds. Denis Donoghue and J. R. Mulryne (London: Edward Arnold, 1965), p. 108, objects that the dialogue is not "an outstanding example of free democratic speech; the casting vote is delivered before the poor Soul has well begun"; he does not ask why Yeats planned it thus. John Untereker, *A Reader's Guide to William Butler Yeats* (New York: Farrar, Straus, 1959), at the opposite extreme, believes that Soul "eventually loses the debate" (p. 204).

reality which softens the vision of evil: it is a romantic, somewhat self-deluding fascination with the productions of time. But in his monologue (II), Self is rudely awakened into the purgatory of his own nature. In the passage of *Paradise Lost* to which Yeats alluded in "Under Ben Bulben" (IV), Adam tells Raphael how he dreamed Eden and then

> wak'd, and found
> Before mine Eyes all real, as the dream
> Had lively shadow'd . . .
> [VIII, 11. 309–11]

The discrepancies in vision between Self and Soul, and between Self dreaming and Self waking, result from the Fall, the loss of unitary perception. Through structure, Yeats illustrated within a very brief span the fragmentation which renders all psychic activity conflict and pain (the blindness Self derides in section II is partly his own in section I), and produced an increasingly ferocious account of the price one pays for living.

Unlike the speaker of "Meditations . . .," Self does not choose between poetic contemplation and action in the world, but between experience (which, as in "The Tower," includes poetry) and a mystical transcendence which denies art. The poet, because he takes his images from the sensuous world, cannot leave it without sacrificing his vocation; he must submit his soul to its chaos. These aesthetic principles are familiar. Yet Self, remarkably, nowhere employs them; nor does he identify himself as a poet. In this respect the poem is unique in the 'tower' series.[8] He neither mentions "pen and paper" ("Meditations . . .," III) nor invokes his literary ancestors ("Ego Dominus Tuus," "Blood and the Moon," II). He makes his choice as a human being. Art is no longer a detached "vision of reality" ("Ego Dominus Tuus") but an organic part of that reality; art and experience, though opposed in many respects, nevertheless join in common, guilty cause to reject the imageless infinite. A decade earlier, Ille had superciliously pitied the fate of the poet who identifies himself with humankind: "The struggle of the fly in marmalade." Self shows no such squeamishness masquerading as hieratic pride. He claims "as by a soldier's right / A charter to commit the crime once more" (I.iv). Soul may usurp the tower, but he

---

8 "The Black Tower," which might appear to share this distinction with "A Dialogue of Self and Soul," is in a class by itself; it simply does not raise the same kinds of questions, nor is the speaker's self-divestiture of his poet's pose an issue. Cf. Ellmann (*The Identity of Yeats*, p. xiii) and Unterecker (*A Reader's Guide*, p. 205), both of whom regard the speaker of the dialogue as an artist.

cannot erase Self's memory of ghostly "men-at-arms" ("The Tower," II.ix). He cannot, in short, combat the *genius loci* at Thoor Ballylee.

Thus, instead of the shapeless nothing at the "hidden pole" which Soul proffers (I.i), Self contemplates a changeless symbol of "love and war" which unites the world's antinomies in aesthetic form, "consecrated" to Self because it poses an "artifice of eternity" against eternity itself. Sato's sword, though still an emblem of aristocratic perfection, differs fundamentally from the same sword in "Meditations . . ." (III). There is no pretense of identifying the sword's permanence with the "soul's unchanging look." The sword, although "Unspotted" (I.ii), belongs to the fallen realm of blood; it is "razor-keen." Having seen the sword brandished in the apocalypse of "Meditations . . ." (VII.i), Self can no longer blink the tumultuous violence it implies. And compare "A bit of an embroidered dress / Covers its wooden sheath" ("Meditations . . .," III) with Self's fanciful embellishment, "That flowering, silken, old embroidery, *torn* / From some court-lady's dress . . . ." "Torn," alluding to murder or rape, is rhymed with "adorn"; the juxtaposition accurately defines the sword's mesmeric, "terrible beauty." Self seeks, as from a talisman, a reflection of its power. Lying not on his work-table but across his knees, it has merged with his total bodily figure in a posture of defense. And yet, the symbol continues to express more than Self, entranced, knows—although his evasions are less drastic than in "Meditations . . ." (III). Self recognizes the antinomies it embodies, but not their harshness. "Heart's purple" (I.iv) should be blood of the slain; instead, it is a badge of high passion and a refulgent epithet for the color of the embroidered flowers. Wistful but deliberate vagueness—"Flowers from *I know not what* embroidery"—blurs the truth of the earlier fancy, "torn / From some court-lady's dress." Flowing adumbration of adjectives and lush, incantatory repetition pastoralize the violence. All is seen as a remote chivalric drama.

Were Self less rapt, Soul might wittily have accused him of acting like Falstaff, wenching in his dotages. Instead, he makes an oratorical flourish:

> Why should the imagination of a man
> Long past his prime remember things that are
> Emblematical of love and war?
>
> [I.iii]

The impropriety of Self's egocentric fancy of his own juvenescence is the least of Soul's criticisms. Self has blindly embraced illusion (the sword) instead of reality (the "hidden pole"). Lacking that center of truth, Self's intellect must inevitably wander, as in the reverie itself.

Recognizing Self's penchant for antiques, Soul lures him with "ancestral night" (I.iii)—like Phase One of the Great Wheel, a condition of "complete passivity, complete plasticity,"[9] superhuman, amoral. Instead of mere trance, he offers total release from consciousness. Fixing upon Self's occasional longings for annihilation (as in "Nineteen Hundred . . .," III), Soul insidiously tempts Self with Self's own language of escape, drawn from "Meditations . . ." (VII.iii):

> Such fullness in that quarter overflows
> And falls into the basin of the mind
> That man is stricken deaf and dumb and blind,
> For intellect no longer knows
> *Is* from the *Ought,* or *Knower* from the *Known.*
>
> [I.v]

Soul's central promise is innocence, deliverance from the "crime of death and birth" (I.iii). Self has not fathomed the unreprieved horror of generation and destruction. Will and action have nothing to do with sin: existence is sin. The human power to sanctify—Self has called the blade "consecrated"—is a delusion.

> Only the dead can be forgiven . . .
>
> [I.v]

But Soul's stark pronouncement is ironically more than he had meant to say. He had intended to guide Self to a spiritual purgation which nevertheless left the body intact. Yet as his pessimism overtakes him, the premises of classical mysticism collapse. There is no way out except physical death,

> But when I think of that my tongue's a stone.
>
> [I.v]

Even Soul will not counsel suicide. The stone, hardly the fiery coal which purifies "unclean lips" (Isaiah 6:5; see "Vacillation," VII), symbolizes the spiritual vacuity of Soul's message. Defeated by his own inexorable logic, Soul recoils from despair, his tongue dehumanized; and Self's trance is broken.[10]

In plotting Soul's crisis, Yeats brilliantly hardened the lines of debate within the poem itself, closed off all alternatives to criminal

---

9 W. B. Yeats, *A Vision* (New York: Macmillan, 1961), p. 183.

10 See Bloom, *Yeats,* p. 375: "The poem's largest irony is that the Soul is an esoteric Yeatsian, and the Self a natural man."

existence except death *or* the affirmation of life despite its criminality. Yet Soul's reversal, while necessary dramatically, is psychologically gratuitous;[11] Self has already reasserted his commitment to the sword:

> and all these I *set*
> For *emblems* of the day against the tower
> *Emblematical* of the *night,*
> And claim as by a soldier's right
> A charter to commit the *crime* once more.
>
> [I.iv]

Self's subconscious assimilation of Soul's vocabulary (italicized) represents his complete acceptance of Soul's judgment on the world. Had he done less, the victorious bluntness of his "choice of rebirth" would have been vitiated. He makes absolutely no attempt to substitute a more palatable euphemism for Soul's piercing word "crime," and indeed uses it in a phrase—"commit the crime"—which evokes the very sexuality Soul abhors.[12] The paradoxical legal language suggests both that Soul's summons violates natural law and that natural law is chaotic: Soul has violated the institutionalized anarchy of existence. Finally, the repetition of "emblems," "Emblematical," scoffs at Soul's Philistinism and asserts the primacy of the imagination; for Soul has proposed questing for a "quarter" where symbol is both unnecessary and impossible.

Self now confronts—without benefit of chivalric fiction—the criminality he has chosen. He is "A blind man battering blind men" (II.iii) in furious flailings. Having willfully imprisoned himself, he executes a typically Yeatsian maneuver: he controls the grotesque absurdity of his experience by embracing it. The definition of humankind is cynically abrupt:

> A living man is blind and drinks his drop.
> What matter if the ditches are impure?
> What matter if I live it all once more?
>
> [II.i]

As he transforms imagery remembered from section I with dazzlingly illogical insight, Self mocks all thought of transcendence. Man, blind in daylight, needs no "ancestral night"; and, dizzy in compensatory stu-

---

11 Cf. Bloom (*Yeats*, p. 374), who thinks that Soul, as he begins his last speech, has already surrendered.

12 See *King Lear*, III.iv.81–82: "commit not with man's sworn spouse" (Edgar); see also "Consolation," in "A Woman Young and Old."

por, why should he need the trembling ecstasy of the saint? A "drop," moreover, ought to be a drink in a pub; but the snide rejoinder to such implied coziness—"What matter if the ditches are impure?"—twists the landscape into a phantasmagoria where the outcast, animalized, "drinks the green mantle of the standing pool" like Poor Tom (*King Lear*, III.iv.135–36). Soul's asceticism, although rejected, permeates Self's deepest thought. If Self repudiates the Platonic universe and any aesthetic which considers art the twice-removed shadow of an ideal type, he also recognizes that Sato's sword—fostering an illusion of secular purity—has protected him too well. In no other of Yeats's major works is the world's attraction so repugnant.

Unflinching, Self meditates not on a distant aristocracy but on his daily agony, knowing that he must

> Endure that toil of growing up;
> The ignominy of boyhood; the distress
> Of boyhood changing into man;
> The unfinished man and his pain
> Brought face to face with his own clumsiness;
>
> The finished man among his enemies [.]
>
> [II.i–ii]

The bitter variation on "Among School Children" (V) is no less than Self's criminal "delivery" into a new cycle. With terrific speed the anticipated future becomes the experienced present. As the crucial demonstrative adjective ("*that* toil") and the minutely sequential discrimination of pains indicate, the stages of what Eliot called "the rending pain of re-enactment"[13] are already vivid to the imagination. Although the passage corresponds to that portion of the afterlife Yeats designated *The Return*, it differs significantly in lacking a teleology.[14] Yeats's

13 "Little Gidding," *II*, in *Four Quartets*. Richard Ellmann, *Eminent Domain: Yeats among Wilde, Joyce, Pound, Eliot, and Auden* (New York: Oxford, 1967), pp. 93–95, thinks that Eliot was alluding in this passage (beginning "Let me disclose the gifts reserved for age") to Yeats's "The Spur" and "Vacillation." But this stanza in "A Dialogue of Self and Soul" seems a far more likely source.

14 Cf. Holloway, "Style and World in *The Tower*," in *An Honoured Guest* (p. 93): "Yeats is, in fact, conducting a rehearsal, in meditation during this life, of the stages of the Dreaming Back (part ii, stanzas 1–3) and the Return . . . ." From a technical point of view, there is no relation between these stanzas and the *Dreaming Back*, which is a nonsequential recapitulation of experience (*A Vision*, p. 226). Stanzas i and ii, in their strict chronology, do resemble the *Return*, but stanzas iii and iv are too generalized to be given precise labels from *A Vision*. The lumping together of stanzas i–iii, moreover, disregards the significant dramatic shift which occurs between stanzas ii and iii.

theory in *A Vision* sets forth a thoroughly organized process of expiation whereby the Spirit, variously recapitulating its life, finally casts out "remorse" and becomes—temporarily—innocent. The mental suffering entailed is consequently purposive. No such justification of agony graces the passage at hand ("What matter . . .?"). Not until the last stanza can Self discover a purgative value in the anarchy and guilt he confronts, the inescapable labyrinths of which Soul has warned. The searing revelation, parodying Paul (I Cor. 13:12), ends in a bleak admission of pointless doom. "Finished man," if it recalls Montashigi's completed aristocratic quest, cuts through such remote fictions with a morbid pun—"finished"/"dead"—which evokes a self-mocking parody of heroic combat. For the only time in Yeats's work, completion of the quest is irrelevant, useless.

Silently, Self remembers Soul's promise of deliverance, yet

> How in the name of Heaven can he escape
> That defiling and disfigured shape
> The mirror of malicious eyes
> Casts upon his eyes until at last
> He thinks that shape must be his shape?
> And what's the good of an escape
> If honour find him in the wintry blast?
>
> [II.ii]

The exasperation conceals a passion to renege on the choice. But the reiterated rhyme—"shape"/"escape"—defines the prison: even Soul could not surrender his body. Self, moreover, has no particular "shape" to "escape" from. The echoing repetition of "shape" makes nebulous what should be a circumscribed image. Self's shapelessness manifests physically his lack of identity, the lack of unitary self-perception which criminality imposes. Compounded of others' hatreds and his own, he resembles the Hunchback of Phase Twenty-six, nearly the exact opposite of the "perfectly proportioned human body" which signifies internal unity.[15] Only Sato's polished blade, "still like a looking-glass," retains its clear form; but Self has discovered that it reflects neither the world nor his own deformity, but something other and less obtainable. The culminating irony is that Self, spurning mystical ascent because it demands self-dissolution, finds himself already dissolved by irreconcilable perspectives. Yet the indomitable desire for "honour"—the illusion of selfhood—remains: farcical, tragic, hopelessly human. Unlike

---

[15] See *A Vision*, pp. 177–78; T. R. Henn (*The Lonely Tower* [1950; rpt. London: Methuen, 1965], pp. 184–85) has suggested additional relationships between the speaker and the Hunchback.

Yeats's ghost in "Little Gidding" (II), Self never learns that "fools' approval stings, and honour stains."

Superimposing self-pacification in the face of all that is humiliating and absurd, Self reasserts his "right," yet without vaunting any power to "claim": "I am content to live it all again." The contentment is minimal, vile; the galling qualification follows inevitably, quickening into a suicidal embrace of life,

> if it be life to pitch
> Into the frog-spawn of a blind man's ditch,
> A blind man battering blind men;
> Or into that most fecund ditch of all,
> The folly that man does
> Or must suffer, if he woos
> A proud woman not kindred of his soul.
>
> [II.iii]

The compulsive return to the double theme of love and war is the raw climax of the decision made in "The Tower" (II.xiii). Knowing no action can damage a "self" which is but an artificed construct, he plunges into crude generation, lured neither by noble passion nor by deceptive emblems of heroic glory.

Critics have often interpreted all of section II as Self's affirmation both of identity and of experience.[16] But not until the end can Self find valid reasons for his existence or begin what the mystical ascent precludes, the quest for self-understanding:

> I am content to follow to its source
> Every event in action or in thought;
> Measure the lot; forgive myself the lot!
> When such as I cast out remorse
> So great a sweetness flows into the breast
> We must laugh and we must sing,
> We are blest by everything,
> Everything we look upon is blest.
>
> [II.iv]

Contradicting for the first time Soul's judgment on human criminality, Self asserts imagination's power to confer absolution upon experience. Though he shares neither Satan's glibness nor his characteristic evasions of responsibility, Self claims in effect that "The mind is its own place,

---

16 See, e.g., James H. O'Brien, "Self vs. Soul in Yeats's *The Winding Stair*," *Eire* 3, 1 (1968): 27–28; Unterecker, *A Reader's Guide*, p. 205.

and in itself / Can make a Heav'n of Hell, a Hell of Heav'n" (*Paradise Lost,* I.254–55). Self-mercy—what Yeats's speakers so conspicuously lack—finally emerges. The desired consequence of such sweet purgation—a remarriage to Soul, suggested by the reiterated "we" and the concluding chiasmic structure—is the earthly re-creation of original Adamic unity. Unlike Coleridge's mariner, who blesses the water snakes before expiating his guilt and thus blesses "unaware" ("The Ancient Mariner," Part IV, 11. 272ff.), Self must cleanse himself first; his consecration will be fully conscious. Yeats's reversals of Coleridge imply his goal: an earned and controlled visionary joy, the capacity to experience in waking perception the awe with which Self initially contemplates Sato's consecrated blade.

What warrant has Self for his warm jubilation? None: the unexplained leap from the self-understanding of an interior hell to self-forgiveness, personal and cosmic blessedness, is essential to the stanza's design. Yeats somewhere cited Tertullian, *Credo quia absurdum.* Knowledge is not enough; Self affirms the consecration of earth because he must, not because it is logically permissible to do so. A strictly trochaic scansion of the counterpointed line, "We must laugh and we must sing," does not adequately render the obligatory force of "must." The time-structure emphasizes the greatness of his need. The future-oriented syntax (e.g., "I am content *to follow*") makes plain that the quest has barely begun.[17] Yet the vision of potential reunification so overwhelms Self that he switches tense:

> We *are* blest by everything,
> Everything we *look* upon *is* blest.

No rhetorically imposed solution, but the mirror of passionate desire, the shift has the suddenness of self-revelation.

Self's radical gesture toward his own secular beatitude is a critical moment in Yeats's career and the tower's history. No claim for the imagination's autonomy is so extensive as this. To create a sacred territory through ritual exclusions, to achieve a timeless moment through the study of history—these characteristic imaginative acts are not of the same order as Self's bestowing of absolution upon himself and "Everything."[18] When Yeats first explored Thoor Ballylee, his imagination—for all its daring—was in part imitative, receptive. He

---

[17]Unterecker (*A Reader's Guide,* p. 205), overlooking the way in which Yeats's verb tenses interact, regards the poem's conclusion as the moment of purification itself; he too remarks on the obligatory force of "must" but conceives it in terms of the poet's irrepressible creative energy.

[18] See Bloom's comments on the solipsism of this poem (*Yeats,* pp. 372–73).

followed Dante, accepted Gregory's counsel, prayed that he might handle nothing "But what the great and passionate have used" ("A Prayer on Going into My House"). The tower's stones were his model; he half expected wisdom, isolate strength, the richness in Irish tradition to emanate from the soil, and sought his own purification by sanctifying his territory. But repeated onslaughts against his space invalidated that imaginative mode. The realization which "A Dialogue of Self and Soul" encompasses is that blessedness cannot be absorbed by osmosis. This poem, consequently, has no territory to speak of, and the tower has nearly vanished. Self's beneficent joy depends upon nothing in the world which Yeats's earlier speakers have meditated into being; it has no objectifications such as the transformed landscape in "In Memory of Major Robert Gregory" (VII) or that in "The Tower" (III); nor is it localized in "a house / Where all's accustomed, ceremonious." The joy is a motion of the spirit which occurs in its own place and time, and no other.

II

"Blood and the Moon" follows the dialogue directly, as if in quarrel. Its speaker faces the difficult responsibility of validating, within historical particulars, Self's ahistorical faith in human sanctity. He understands all too clearly that his "choice of rebirth" compels him to relive more than personal memory. If he cannot exercise his consecrative imagination to redeem the confusions of his national experience, then he must acknowledge, with Soul, the bondage of his supposedly autonomous creativity. The drama thus played out at Thoor Ballylee involves exactly the problem of expiating cultural sin which drives the Old Man in *Purgatory* to kill (murder? sacrifice?) his father and his son.

The speaker begins with a brutally swift ritual of purification immeasurably distant not only from the serene elation in Self's "blest" perception of terrestrial glory but from the modest orthodoxy of "A Prayer on Going into My House":

> Blessed be this place,
> More blessed still this tower;
> A bloody, arrogant power
> Rose out of the race
> Uttering, mastering it,
> Rose like these walls from these
> Storm-beaten cottages . . .
>
> [I]

The consecration, even as it overwhelms all skepticism, anticipates the poem's dark conclusion: the profanation of ground initially made sacred by the speaker's own demand. The growling, dogmatic affirmation wars against a "time / Half dead at the top," strains against the mind's inveterate powerlessness to will sanctity. Flaunting a vengeful pride as he reclaims his usurped tower, the speaker blesses everything Soul had disparaged. He blinks no ugliness, exults in naked physical power (rhymed throughout with "tower"), revels in language designed to affront Soul's sensibilities and thus banish forever the temptations of infinity.

The tower's architectural evolution is Irish history itself, given compact mythological continuity in his own territory. As linear time dissolves in symbol, the Anglo-Norman, Anglo-Irish presence becomes a monolith, rising "like these walls." The tragic paradox, that such a violent mastery ultimately expressed most fully the ethos of the conquered Celtic aristocracy, is reiterated poetically in the speaker's own consecration: as he utters the tower's nature, masters its identity, he reenacts its founding; then, traversing seven centuries, he wheels about to scorn the worthless present:

> In mockery I have set
> A powerful emblem up,
> And sing it rhyme upon rhyme
> In mockery of a time
> Half dead at the top.

[I]

Seemingly, the tower immunizes him against all he despises: violations of aristocratic tradition ("In Memory of Eva Gore-Booth and Con Markiewicz," the opening poem in *The Winding Stair*), emasculation of the heroic ideal ("Statistics"), the decline of literature ("The Nineteenth Century and After"), the "levelling, rancorous, rational sort of mind" typical of modern Irish pettiness ("The Seven Sages"). Consequently deriding foulness, the speaker is hardly "content" to "pitch / Into the frog-spawn of a blind man's ditch."

Thus, Thoor Ballylee is both a consecrated place and the epitome of satiric hatred. These irreconcilably opposed definitions haunt the speaker: the mockery may turn corrosively inward, diminish his power to demarcate sacred ground. Is he not, as in "Nineteen Hundred . . ." (V), part of the world he condemns, perhaps its symptomatic figure? The poem dramatizes the appalling paradox of a man so tormented by the smell of mortality that he can seek a saving self-protection only by means wholly subversive of that end: "More substance in our enmities / Than in our love" ("Meditations . . . ," VI.iv). Even at the outset he hides in derision his fear that sanctuary may be impossible. "Half dead at the top," explicitly characterizing the corrupt "time," is also a vertical image of the tower: the image has psychological intensity precisely because it evokes the architectural analogy in ways which the speaker fails to recognize. Not until the terrifying rhetorical question (IV) does his suspicion of the tower's contamination become explicit knowledge:

> Is every modern nation like the tower,
> Half dead at the top?

Yeats marvelously calibrated these sole poetic uses of the tower's topmost Stranger's Room to show the drastic metamorphosis in understanding which finally renders tower and world indistinguishable. As the structure of this simile suggests, the tower has become the source and model of the world's deterioration. Corresponding to "Rose like these walls" (I), it completes the paradigmatic cycle of creation and dissolution which the tower incorporates. The attempt to consecrate ends in renewed consciousness of primal guilt.

As he faces that imminent knowledge, the fear of derangement burgeons. The ghost of Swift in his madness hovers like a fury over this poem even before the speaker names him. Consider Young's anecdote about Swift which spurred Yeats to make his architecture an image of *dementia*: ". . . [I] found him [Swift] fixed as a statue; and earnestly gazing upward at a noble elm, which in its most uppermost branches, was much withered and decayed. Pointing at it, he said, 'I shall be like that tree, I shall die at top'."[19] This ominous specter, the speaker's *genius loci* and that of Anglo-Irish culture, is subliminally present in the first use of "Half dead at the top." In Yeats's instinctive conflation of tree and tower, Swift's obsessive terror of insanity materializes. The tower, animated with his quietly hysterical prophecy, becomes a person helplessly losing control. The amalgamation of self and architecture is even darker than in "Meditations . . ." (VI.i): "My wall is loosening."

19 Edward Young, "Conjectures on Original Composition," in *Works* (London: Dodsley, 1798), III: 196. Young goes on in the next sentence: "As in this he seemed to prophesy like the Sybils . . . ." The comment would seem to be responsible for Yeats's image in section II, "Swift beating on his breast in sibylline frenzy . . . ." Dr. Thomas Sheridan, whose edition of Swift Yeats bought with his Nobel Prize money, cites part of Young's attack on Swift but stops just before Young narrates the incident from which the imagery of "Blood and the Moon" derives (*The Works of Jonathan Swift* [London: Strahan, 1784], I: 512). Mario Rossi and Joseph Hone also included the anecdote in *Swift, or The Egotist* (New York: Dutton, 1934), p. 364; but Yeats did not see their drafts until several years after writing the poem. A. Norman Jeffares, *The Circus Animals* (Stanford: Stanford University Press, 1970), p. 43, gives the allusion passing mention.

To evade it, the speaker turns to consider other towers (II.i), the architectural tradition symbolic of Western thought which Thoor Ballylee now threatens to end. "Alexandria's was a beacon tower" of unimpaired spiritual illumination; Babylon's symbolized not terrestrial convulsions but the rationalized order of the cosmos. Shelley's towers were "thought's crowned powers": the image of the head compensates for the dangerous allusion to Swift by emphasizing the strength of the intact mind; stark "power" is transmuted to "powers," the faculties of the exuberant intellect.

    None of these towers resembles the speaker's. Undeterred by the sinister discrepancies, he accepts his dwelling with bitter triumph:

> I declare this tower is my symbol; I declare
> This winding, gyring, spiring treadmill of a stair is my
>   ancestral stair;
> That Goldsmith and the Dean, Berkeley and Burke have travelled
>   there.
>
>   [II.ii]

This, Yeats's most radical possession of the tower, is also the most ambiguous. The last clause is self-consciously outrageous, a bizarre consolidation of his Anglo-Irish kin which deliberately contravenes history. Raftery and Mrs. French may well have "passed this door" ("The Tower," II.xi); Swift? Burke?—never. The act of populating Thoor Ballylee, far more compulsive than in "In Memory of Major Robert Gregory" or "The Tower," measures his need to house a quickly disappearing heritage within an impermeable bulwark. But his ancestors inhabit a dangerous environment. The stairwell is neither the defined space of the "narrow winding stairs" ("In Memory of Major Robert Gregory," I) nor the path of mystical ascent ("A Dialogue of Self and Soul," I). It is a maze and prison, the "treadmill" of human life. Its spirit is that of Piranesi or the "cunning passages, Contrived corridors" of history in Eliot's "Gerontion," not that of the diagrams in *A Vision*. Although "winding" refers to the unpredictable path of the Serpent, multiplicity; and "gyring," to the ordered intersection of antinomies in history; and "spiring," to release from the wheel of time—what matters about these adjectives is their cumulative visual effect: rapid, random, confused movement. The circular "treadmill," another conflicting pattern of motion, hoops the others together in an image of nonsensical, dehumanized labor. The stairwell is the physical form of madness.[20] What, then, does it mean that "Goldsmith and the Dean, Berkeley and Burke have travelled there"?

---

[20] Thomas R. Whitaker, *Swan and Shadow: Yeats's Dialogue with History* (Chapel

Yeats's prose does not much clarify the rhapsodic catalogue which follows (II.iii–vi). More than the speaker's enumeration of Anglo-Irish ideals and the substantiation of his initial "boast,"[21] it switches tone, point of view, and chronology so abruptly, welds together so many contradictory impulses that its ultimate dramatic character is that of an ecstatic mad-song, an extraordinarily distended sentence fragment which ends only when the speaker exhausts himself. With perverse joy he wrenches his ancestors from their rational Augustan couplets, flings aside their masks of courtesy and equipoise. As he celebrates, he imitates—not merely Swift's satiric energy or Burke's proud conservatism or Berkeley's pre-Romantic idealism but their passionate extravagance and wit, their "blood." He delights in Berkeley and Burke's absurd "proofs" which are really metaphors. Created in his image, they all become poets; their derangement is divine *afflatus*. These inspired men herald his own achievement; incorporating them, he stands "massed against the world" ("The Seven Sages").

But this maelstrom has other currents. In *The Words upon the Window-pane,* Mrs. Henderson transmits the following conversation:

> [*In Swift's voice.*] I have something in my blood that no child must inherit. I have constant attacks of dizziness. . . . I had them in London. . . . There was a great doctor there, Dr. Arbuthnot; I told him of those attacks of dizziness, I told him of worse things. It was he who explained. There is a line of Dryden's. . . . [*In Vanessa's voice.*] O, I know—"Great wits are sure to madness near allied."[22]

For Swift, and for the speaker as he envisages Swift, the alliance is too close for comfort:

> Swift beating on his breast in sibylline frenzy blind
> Because the heart in his blood-sodden breast had dragged him down
>   into mankind . . .
>
>   [II.iii]

"Blind" is syntactically ambiguous. Does it modify Swift or his frenzy? Is the frenzy truly "sibylline" or is it the "blind" chaotic utterance of madness? As Corbet asks in the play, "Was Swift mad? Or was it the

---

Hill: North Carolina University Press, 1964), p. 212, views the imagery more positively and speaks of the "compelling harmonies of life" in this stanza.

21 Torchiana, *W. B. Yeats,* p. 320; Bloom (*Yeats,* p. 377) has called the passage "rant."

22 W. B. Yeats, *The Collected Plays of W. B. Yeats* (1953; rpt. New York: Macmillan, 1966), pp. 383–84.

intellect itself that was mad?"[23] Is Swift the satirist so tormented by
his own fury that he can no longer conceive the "purity of the
unclouded moon" (III)? Or has the moon's very chastity goaded him to
rage against all impurities, himself included? The passion the speaker
celebrates is Swift's enslavement to corruption; yet Swift, had he not
despised his "blood-sodden breast," could not have risen to such
imaginative frenzy and prophesied the coming ruin. Swift, whose need
for sanctity counterbalances his satiric hatred, is clearly the speaker's
tutelary genius; yet like the tower in its later stages, he is also a nemesis
pointing toward self-destruction. The speaker is both attracted and
repelled; his ironic, affectionate portrait of Goldsmith, like Ariel
"deliberately sipping at the honey-pot of his mind" (II.iii),[24] seems a
suddenly calculated retreat from Swift's magnetic influence. Repeatedly he alters his distance from his ancestors, uncertain whether their
nonreturnable legacy of passionate imagination is a blessing or a curse.
All four suffer from solipsism, the recurrent danger of aristocratic
isolation and imaginative vigor; "God-appointed Berkeley" (II.v), despite the comic phrasing, seems like the speaker himself, threatened by
paranoia. With guarded satire the speaker fends off what his tower
presses upon him, the complete identification with his past that he half
desires. Behind the divine *afflatus,* actual madness remains; and behind
the speaker's satire lurks the foreboding that the real enemy to the
consecration of his territory is not external, but within the rich,
blood-sodden Anglo-Irish mind.

Upon these ambivalent, charged responses is imposed another. The
speaker takes his ancestors' masks, despite his misgivings, to gain
authority for his mockery. Yet the mockery shows no real hope of
redeeming Ireland from craven indignity. Like Parnell in "To a Shade,"
his ancestors return, in him, to preside in genuine grief and morbid
self-satisfaction over the last enervation of "The strength that gives our
blood and state magnanimity of its own desire" (II.vi). Swift's and
Burke's most dire prophecies of political decrepitude, loss of human
liberty, have been fulfilled. The stanza on Berkeley implies Stephen
Daedalus's gruesome, traditional judgment on Ireland: "the old sow
that eats her farrow."[25] As the summoning of eighteenth-century
Anglo-Irish vibrancy closes, the shadow of the assassinated O'Higgins,
who also kept faith with his tradition, passes before the speaker's eyes.

That undertow of pessimism climaxes in section III. The final

---

[23] Ibid., p. 387.

[24] See *The Tempest,* V.i.88. The image also refers to Goldsmith's editorship of the
short-lived periodical *The Bee.*

[25] James Joyce, *A Portrait of the Artist as a Young Man* (1916; rpt. New York:
Viking, 1964), p. 203.

definition of Anglo-Irish achievement—"Everything that is not God consumed with intellectual fire" (II.vi)—is also the speaker's own cry for purification. Such extremities cannot be matched; a sudden emotional trough follows:

> The purity of the unclouded moon
> Has flung its arrowy shaft upon the floor.
> Seven centuries have passed and it is pure,
> The blood of innocence has left no stain.

And then, as awareness of the assassination intensifies:

> Odour of blood on the ancestral stair!

Nauseated, he recoils from the crushing revelation of his mortal condition. All summonings of Anglo-Irish imaginative strength have failed to create a sacred ground. As the speaker contemplates the inviolable moon, self-loathing mingles with awe. "The purity of the unclouded moon . . . is pure." Not a tautology, this is the grim judgment against earth permitted by the ambiguity of "it" (1. 3). Whatever purity humankind achieves is besmirched, even the exalted Anglo-Irish genius. The tragedy of the "blood-sodden" heart is that, while it seeks purification, it also suffers the equally unassuageable need to pollute what it most loves. Thus, in the tower's history, "Soldier, assassin, executioner" have "shed blood, / But *could not cast* a single jet thereon" (III): the verb conveys nothing less than frustrated desire. "Blood-saturated" man, perpetually trying to recreate the universe in his image, must hate what he cannot obtain. As natural description merges with mythic personification, Diana, murderously innocent, flings her "arrowy shaft" in sexual challenge, tormenting men to madness. Does man murder because he cannot make love to the moon? Do all murderings but displace a greater desire, deliverance from "the crime of death and birth"? Murder becomes a quest for the apocalyptic cessation of time; for "The sun shall be turned into darkness, and the moon into blood, before that great and notable day of the Lord come" (Acts 2:20). Philosophies and psychologies unconsciously seek the same end: Swift's hatred of common humankind, Goldsmith's aversion to raw experience, Burke's metamorphosis of human institutions into permanent organic forms, Berkeley's wish that the world "vanish" (II.v).

Inevitably, the revelation involves the speaker's awareness of his tower. The visceral exclamation, "Odour of blood on the ancestral stair!" is shocking dramatically precisely because the speaker, even as he contemplates earth's impurity, has tried so desperately to believe his territory sanctified. The "bloody, arrogant" spirit of place (I) has ironically turned against its defender; the invasion, more intimately experienced than in any other 'tower' poem, systematically erodes the speaker's faith. This is why the word "Odour" is so perfect; it conveys a surreal encroachment, as if the Cloone River's "blood-dimmed tide" were swelling against the tower and its attainted possessor. Yet the speaker must accept the consequences of having made the tower his symbol: all people are Cain's kin, implicated in the fellowship of blood,

> And we that have shed none must gather there
> And clamour in drunken frenzy for the moon.
>
> [III]

Love of the moon again connotes sexual brutality. Caught between antinomies, maddened by knowledge of inexpiable sin, the speaker becomes a parody of Swift his nemesis: "drunken," not "sibylline." Behind the renewed cry for purification lies a political judgment as disturbingly honest as that in "Meditations . . ." (I). Anglo-Ireland, for all its "greatness," has finally reaped the proper harvest of "Bitter and violent men": the "blood of innocence" has been shed in payment for the accumulated guilt of a "bloody, arrogant" culture. And the speaker, like Swift and the others, although technically innocent, must share the guilt by virtue of blood-kinship. The judgment is "Bound neither to Cause nor to State" ("The Tower," III).[26] As the speaker is humbled from "Uttering" the Anglo-Irish pride of sections I and II, his vision becomes tragic.

An exquisite night-piece deflects the cathartic rage his frenzy intimates:

> Upon the dusty, glittering windows cling,
> And seem to cling upon the moonlit skies,
> Tortoiseshell butterflies, peacock butterflies,
> A couple of night-moths are on the wing.
>
> [IV]

In this fine mingling of observation and symbol, the butterflies are traditional emblems of the soul, their ascent aborted by imprisonment within the tower. But their mediatory stationing ("cling, / And seem to

---

[26] Torchiana's interpretation of the political judgment (*W. B. Yeats*, pp. 320–21) is more partisan than the one offered here: O'Higgins' assassination represents modern Ireland's "repudiation" of "all those qualities seemingly come down from the world figures of eighteenth-century Ireland to Kevin O'Higgins" (p. 321). He considers the entirety of section III a cry for wisdom and sees in that cry "the possible triumph of the intellectual imagination in the terrestrial realm, a continuous possibility despite the intermittent bloodshed and political roils since the Normans came in"

cling") points, for a vanishing instant, to a universe which harmonizes
lunar and sublunar realms. Like the image of Keats in "Ego Dominus
Tuus" ("face and nose pressed to a sweet-shop window"), the barrier of
the windowpane—demarcating the profane from the sacred—is agonizingly transparent. Here, however, there is no violent desire; instead, the
speaker's resignation to entrapment passes into disinterested love for
the butterflies as creatures. The emotion resembles that felt for the
"Magical unicorns" in "Meditations . . ." (VII.iii) and for the swan and
"mother bird" in "The Tower" (III). Even the aesthetically unattractive
moths, perhaps an ironic self-reference, seem lovely.

In the midst of this sudden calm comes a furious, horrified explo-
sion: "Is every modern nation like the tower, / Half dead at the top?"
This is the final knowledge: the tower heralds catastrophe—personal,
Irish, international. The mood rapidly shifts into bleak gloom:

> No matter what I said,
> For wisdom is the property of the dead,
> A something incompatible with life; and power,
> Like everything that has the stain of blood,
> A property of the living . . .

The judgment transcends neat historical categories to become ethical
and epistemological commentary. Redemptive wisdom is unavailable,
an unknown "something." Man's doom is natural blindness: efforts to
escape that condition can only produce a more spectacular failure, a
more elaborate turn on the treadmill. "Blood" and "power," now
synonymous with earth, operate inexorably. The savored pun on "property" (philosophic "attribute"; land, enclosed space) stresses human
limitation in terms of the territorial metaphor. As the Greek in *The
Resurrection* remarks, "Every man's sins are his property. Nobody else
has a right to them."[27] That pessimistic irony, reducing identity to
guilt, accords wholly with the speaker's vision. Yet the poem's more
generous irony, and the one which confers tragedy, is that the speaker,
beginning in proud isolation, ends in humbled consciousness of community. Unable to bless his tower, he finally blesses the moon:

> but no stain
> Can come upon the visage of the moon
> When it has looked in glory from a cloud.

(p. 321). Such an interpretation accords well with Yeatsian theory but hardly does
justice to the hellish experience the poem creates; surely there is no sense of
"possible triumph" in the crazed stupor of the stanza's conclusion.

27 *Collected Plays*, p. 367.

As the poem completes its circular form, the violent self-willed consecrations (I) and the drunken clamor (III) ripen into a disinterested
emotion of sanctity. How can man bless the infinite? Again, paradox:
but what other response is appropriate? Diana, responding to this
gesture of awed obeisance, sheathes her "arrowy shaft" to become a
mandala of light.

Viewed in relation to the 'tower' poetry generally, this small joy
which staves off utmost nihilism[28] —the joy of humility, not of self-
fulfillment—is all Yeats managed to salvage from the monumental
design which first stirred his imagination in "Ego Dominus Tuus" and
"A Prayer on Going into My House": the creation of a complete self
upon sacred, unfallen ground. Blood has washed away the "Magical
shapes" once traced upon the sand; the expectation of prophetic,
self-unifying wisdom has given place to knowledge of ignorance; and
faith in the power of language to establish boundaries has crumpled.

---

[28] Cf. Bloom, *Yeats*, p. 380.

CHAPTER

EIGHT

Coole Park
and Ballylee

I

In Yeats there is a vast difference between poems whose speakers actually consecrate their ground and poems in which, although the consecration fails, the very subject-matter acts to sanctify. "Blood and the Moon" spans the extremities: even as the speaker's fierce blessing disintegrates, the poem ennobles the tower by placing the eighteenth-century tradition squarely within its walls. The speaker's final defeat cannot obscure that radical and numinous realization of a new element in the tower's mythology; and while the dramatic action blurs the demarcation between tower and world, the poem itself clarifies the tower's sacral value. Yeats in large part made his territorial and histori-cal myths by having his speakers experience their inadequacy or obsolescence; as modernity impinged upon the West of Ireland, this tragic mode of creating myth while acknowledging its defeat became indispensable. "In the Seven Woods" shows the method of consecration in its early stages: the allusion to Tara "uprooted" enhances Coole's glory. "Coole Park, 1929" and "Coole Park and Ballylee, 1931" sing Coole's Anglo-Irish splendors for the first time; simultaneously they chronicle the collapse of traditional culture. "The Black Tower," which culminates Yeats's lifelong dedication to the heroic West, transforms the tower into the center of an epic world at the same time that its action portends the tower's demolition and the death of its chief defender.

In April 1927, after years of anxiety and financial strain, Lady Gregory sold Coole to the Irish government. Although she occupied the

house until she died in 1932, her familial guilt was great: she considered
her act the destruction[1] of a fine tradition and the betrayal of her
grandson's birthright.[2] She had signed away the principal symbol of the
literary renaissance; decreased participation in Abbey affairs, the loss of
close friends, recurrent cancer, and intermittent broodings on death
made the sale a personal and historical crisis. "I shall be sorry," she
concluded the chapter of *Coole* entitled "The Library," "to leave all
these volumes among which I have lived. They have felt the pressure of
my fingers. They have been my friends." Her drafts for the same
passage speak of departure in terms of exile and death.[3] The published
version softens into literary nostalgia the blunt pang of doomed separation. Yeats felt the irreparable division also. While the sale was still
pending, Lady Gregory told Yeats of her intention to lease Coole; by
the next day, with a striking rapidity, Yeats had decided to give up the
tower: Thoor Ballylee meant Coole.[4] Although he did not take general
leave of the tower until 1929, some of his most enduring ties to the
West were now broken. He understood that the primary work of the
literary movement was completed; the territory which had inspired it
was no longer owned. He knew, angrily, that he was being displaced by
younger writers "determined to express the factory, the metropolis,
that they may be modern."[5] The giving up of his house on Merrion
Square, the end of his senatorial duties, and increasingly long winters
spent in Rapallo and southern France for reasons of health augmented
his awareness of closure.

Yeats had written poems about every major crisis in Coole's recent
history. Now, almost inevitably, he offered Lady Gregory "Coole Park,
1929" as a preface to *Coole*.[6] A commemorative elegy like "Coole Park
and Ballylee, 1931," its mood of epochal conclusion embraces Yeats's
quiet estrangement from a significant "portion of my mind and life":
the present was suddenly sliding into the forgettable past. Yeats's

---

[1] Lady Gregory, Unpublished Journals, Book XXXV, February 28, 1927 (Berg
Collection, New York Public Library).

[2] Lady Gregory, *Journals*, ed. Lennox Robinson (New York: Macmillan, 1947), p.
47.

[3] Lady Gregory, *Coole* (Dublin: Cuala, 1931), p. 21; Lady Gregory, MS to *Coole*,
Book II (Berg Collection, New York Public Library).

[4] Lady Gregory, Unpublished Journals, Book XXXV, January 30, 1927.

[5] W. B. Yeats, *Essays and Introductions* (New York: Macmillan, 1961), p. 525.

[6] Lady Gregory read drafts of *Coole* to Yeats when he visited her in October 1926.
In November he wrote to her from Rapallo that he wanted to write an introductory poem for her book. (Lady Gregory, Unpublished Journals, Book XXXIX,
November 30, 1928). "Coole Park and Ballylee, 1931" was never intended as a
preface to *Coole*, although after the publication of *Coole* Yeats experimented with

public intent, as at the end of *The Stirring of the Bones,* was to establish Coole's fame in Irish history, so that "young men to whom recent events are often more obscure than those long past, may learn what debts they owe and to what creditor."[7] As in "Under Ben Bulben," he sought to exercise control, from beyond the grave, over the future. "Coole Park," balancing *Coole*'s modest and private focus on family, literature, local geography, emphasizes Coole's cultural importance; the naming of John Shawe-Taylor underscores the catalytic force of the Gregory tradition in securing land reform. "Coole Park and Ballylee," including the tower, extends the historical scope of celebration: Coole's evolution, as an idea of civilized perfection, spans the entire period from the Anglo-Norman conquest to the present. Yeats arranged *The Winding Stair,* moreover, to show Coole's special Anglo-Irish achievement. In "In Memory of Eva Gore-Booth and Con Markiewicz," Eva sacrifices the rich Anglo-Irish heritage of Lissadell for "Some vague Utopia"; "Blood and the Moon" gathers the Anglo-Irish tradition within the tower only by fiat; Coole alone, among all architectures in the West of Ireland, has kept that tradition intact.

As elegies presaging the oncoming desecration, "Coole Park" and "Coole Park and Ballylee" diverge sharply from the traditional country house poem. The house is not eternal; its period of creative hospitality is ended. Coole can no longer influence the present or the future, except possibly as an inspiring memory—and even this hope, intimately Yeats's, remains severely muffled. Separated from contemporary history, Coole no longer has enemies from whom the poet must defend it through moral outrage or satiric wit. His attitude consequently alters; his tone is neither so official as in "Upon a House . . ." nor so self-dramatizing as in "The New Faces" or the epilogue to *Responsibilities;* it is, in a certain way, remote—less intense, less introspective than in the days when his retreat to Coole was usually precipitated by personal crisis.

Yeats designed the remoteness in "Coole Park" to validate his praise. His speaker is a historian who once participated in the movement he commemorates—intimately familiar with Coole's rich achievement yet chiefly concerned with objective judgment and sufficiently detached from his earlier involvement to avoid the egotism which mars "The Municipal Gallery Revisited" (VI). Thus, Yeats studiously under-

---

subjoining it to "Coole Park, 1929." Cf. Marjorie Perloff, " 'Another Emblem There': Theme and Convention in Yeats's 'Coole Park and Ballylee, 1931,' " *Journal of English and Germanic Philology* 69 (1970): 223.

7 W. B. Yeats, *The Autobiography of William Butler Yeats* (New York: Macmillan, 1938), p. 323.

played his own part in the brilliant world he intended to glorify, made himself nearly anonymous, cancelled these lines:[8]

> She *taught me* that straight line that sets a man
> Above the crooked journey of the sun.

He replaced "Here I"[9] with

> *There one* that ruffled in a manly pose
> For all his timid heart . . .
>
>   [II]

The self-irony reinforces the distanced tone of critical revaluation. The speaker's only explicit affiliation—"For scholars and for poets after us" (I)—is neutral enough. Suppressing himself, Yeats could cast aside the pompous rhetoric of unearned epic convention:

> I sing miraculous intricacies
> . . . .
> I sing what seemed unnatural amities
> Of ancient passion . . .[10]

The crucial alteration to "I meditate" (I) establishes tone and structure. Like "Easter 1916" and "In Memory of Major Robert Gregory," the poem reveals the influx of new awareness. Beginning in meditative quest to understand the past, the speaker ends in oratory: only after discovering the full ramifications of his subject does he recognize his proper audience and address them directly. Through that awakening, moreover, Yeats indirectly coaxed his readers to concur with his convictions. Unlike the Jonsonian country house poem, "Coole Park" is not a discursive praise of the estate's nobility; like much of Yeats's other poetry on public themes which has wrongly been called "public poetry,"[11] its rhetorical technique is wholly subjective, a subtle persuasion by private means.

---

[8] W. B. Yeats, *The Letters of W. B. Yeats,* ed. Allan Wade (London: Hart-Davis, 1954), p. 769. Despite his critics' glosses, and his own in *Dramatis Personae* (*Autobiography,* p. 390), biographical truth and poetic function do not always coincide; see Thomas Parkinson, *W. B. Yeats: The Later Poetry* (Berkeley: University of California Press, 1964), pp. 80–81. See also the suppression of personal allusion in "A Prayer for My Daughter" (V).

[9] Jon Stallworthy, *Between the Lines: W. B. Yeats's Poetry in the Making* (Oxford: Clarendon, 1963), p. 186; see also pp. 193–94.

[10] Ibid., p. 181.

[11] See, for example, Paul de Man, "Symbolic Landscape in Wordsworth and Yeats," in *In Defense of Reading,* eds. Reuben Brower and Richard Poirier (New York: Dutton, 1963), pp. 28–29.

The speaker starts from scratch:

> I meditate upon a swallow's flight,
> Upon an aged woman and her house,
> A sycamore and lime-tree lost in night
> Although that western cloud is luminous . . .

These fragments, through which he will ultimately develop a whole conception, are auto-suggestive but opaque. Their random, haphazard order mirrors a mind groping for precise judgment; although the subsequent praise of Coole reverts to that of "Upon a House . . .," the image of the house no longer controls reflection. This "composition of place" hardly manifests the formal exactitude, the clarity of statement found in traditional Ignatian meditation;[12] it proceeds not according to known principles but, more radically, through a questioning of the landscape which, as in "The Tower" (II), is simultaneously its creation. Gradually the house comes into focus, and with it Coole's capacity to form unity out of multiplicity, its will to dominate time:

> Great works constructed there in nature's spite
> For scholars and for poets after us,
> Thoughts long knitted into a single thought,
> A dance-like glory that those walls begot.

The entire sentence, although the force of its main verb ("meditate") dissipates, articulates both the speaker's exploration and his growing sensation of magnitude. Syntactic subordination, a sign of prior design, is suppressed: individual images, thus equalized, have no hierarchical relation. With the majestic conclusion, the speaker finally unifies his musings: Coole, its eighteenth-century architecture humanized, was the womb of aesthetic beauty. The astonishingly tactful phrase "A dance-like glory" evades a realism which would have wrecked the paradoxical metaphor of gestation and gives, instead, an image of radiance so transcendent that it can only inadequately be compared with human activity.

The consciousness of definite place awakens memory; the speaker can visualize concretely the genesis of the Irish renaissance. His distanced recollection has warmth and wit:

> There Hyde before he had beaten into prose
> That noble blade the Muses buckled on,
> There one that ruffled in a manly pose
> For all his timid heart, there that slow man,

12 Cf. Louis L. Martz, *The Poetry of Meditation* (New Haven: Yale University Press, 1954), p. 326.

That meditative man, John Synge, and those
Impetuous men, Shawe-Taylor and Hugh Lane,
Found pride established in humility,
A scene well set and excellent company.

[II]

Again Yeats's syntax implies psychology. The suspension of the main
verb imitates a question: What lured such disparate men into community? The catalogue hovers in search; the particular memories are
linked only by unity of place and not, until the end, by recognition of
common experience. Thus, the final closure does more than designate
the aristocratic virtue and decorum Coole's guests found magnetic. It
marks the speaker's own discovery of these qualities; he too "finds"—
again. What he finds now, moreover, is a tentative explanation for the
movement's extraordinary accomplishment. Discovery and praise occur
simultaneously. "Pride established in humility": these abstractions define absolute virtues localized at Coole. Yeats, always sensitive to
climactic development, kept his speaker from focussing too swiftly on
Lady Gregory herself, and the suspension implies belief: what the
founders of the movement found was an ambiance of creativity as
"constructed" (I) as the house itself, a "scene well set" through decades
of devoted service to Ireland and the arts, a classical love of manhood
and charm, patient study and courtesy.

Yet no environment, however morally and aesthetically compelling,
could in itself have produced such a renaissance: the climax of the
speaker's meditation turns on Lady Gregory's incalculable directorial
influence in energizing the "scene" into actual drama. Significantly, the
illustrious creators of Anglo-Irish culture gathered in stanza II are
antithetical psychological types. Hyde's bold heroism as the darling of
the peasant Muses contrasts sharply with the bluffed assurance of the
unnamed Yeats; Synge's cool deliberation finds its opposite in the hot
romantic impetuosity of Shawe-Taylor and Hugh Lane.[13] Yet Lady
Gregory wrought such diversity into a unity; like her son in "Shepherd
and Goatherd," she transformed Coole into what Cuchulain in *On
Baile's Strand* calls "A brief forgiveness between opposites."

They came like swallows and like swallows went,
And yet a woman's powerful character
Could keep a swallow to its first intent.

[III]

13 Cf. Graham Martin, "Fine Manners, Liberal Speech: A Note on the Public
Poetry of W. B. Yeats," *Essays in Criticism* 11 (1961): 50. Martin thinks that an

This is not the arrogant power of "Bitter and violent men" but a steady, refined sensitivity to her friends' genius: the power to forestall waywardness without inhibiting creative impulse, to unify a multiplicity of talents without reducing them to drab sameness. Awed by Lady Gregory's discretionary tact, the speaker now understands why "a swallow's flight" first appeared to his imagination. The movement which she formed with such *sprezzatura* had the "purity of a natural force";[14] her artistry made base nature golden.

> And half a dozen in formation there,
> That seemed to whirl upon a compass-point,
> Found certainty upon the dreaming air,
> The intellectual sweetness of those lines
> That cut through time or cross it withershins.
>
> [III]

The image of the stable center, revised from "The Second Coming"[15] to distinguish Coole from Europe, proceeds with assured metaphysical complexity. Here in the compass-point is the earthly counterpart of the inaccessible "hidden pole" in "A Dialogue of Self and Soul" (I.i) or the "Tent-pole of Eden" in "Veronica's Napkin." In the speaker's new perception, the disparate, dissociated images of the opening stanza have now cohered into a total order.

These realizations compel the speaker to public utterance (IV). Like Eliot's protagonist at the ruined chapel in Little Gidding, he demands no merely casual homage. Endowing the ground with special meaning, he virtually creates a ritual and prescribes its decorum. With the emphatic trochaic address of "Here, traveller, scholar, poet, take your stand," he envisages a centripetal movement in which Coole again becomes the recognized center of a circle both geographic and human. "Here" means "on this ground, on these principles of aesthetic and intellectual excellence, on this conviction in the power of art to transform a national consciousness"; "take your stand"—a variant on "make a stand" or defense—enjoins future generations to consider Coole a metaphorical fortress against the the incursions of modern mediocrity.[16] In tragic paradox, the embattled defense of Coole's foundations must occur

---

understanding of the phrase "impetuous men" "depends wholly on knowledge about Lane and Shawe-Taylor the poem doesn't provide."

14 "The People."

15 Harold Bloom, *Yeats* (New York: Oxford, 1970), p. 381, has also commented on this relationship.

16 John Unterecker, *A Reader's Guide to William Butler Yeats* (New York: Farrar,

> When all those rooms and passages are gone,
> When nettles wave upon a shapeless mound
> And saplings root among the broken stone . . .

To take a stand on this antipastoral ground, seemingly inimical to creative endeavor, is to move very close to the defiant affirmation of "The Black Tower." Staring upon "the foundations of a house," as in "The Tower" (II.i), can bring impetus to renewal; what the speaker requires of future generations is the difficult exercise of imaginative memory (aided by the poem itself), the creative insight to perceive in "broken stone" the "dance-like glory that those walls begot." In a meditative transcendence of all temporal distraction,[17] Coole's greatness may be glimpsed, the magnificence of its guiding spirit internalized:

> And dedicate—eyes bent upon the ground,
> Back turned upon the brightness of the sun
> And all the sensuality of the shade—
> A moment's memory to that laurelled head.

Yet even as the speaker establishes that ritual contemplation, he knows an irreparable loss. For all its heroic resonance, his formal address to a new generation is self-consciously limited in scope; like the isolate speaker of "Blood and the Moon" as he compacts his Anglo-Irish heritage into the tower, traveler, scholar, and poet are the only ones who might conceivably care enough to honor Coole's legacy.

That knowledge is not, however, prophetic. Critics have persistently debased prophecy and sentimentalized Yeats by making his speaker a breast-beating seer who foresaw an invisible event, the actual destruction of Coole in the mid-thirties.[18] But to recognize, as Shakespeare did, that time will "root out the work of masonry" (Sonnet 55) is no

---

Straus, 1959), p. 211, interprets the travelers, scholars, and poets as the ghosts of Lane, Shawe-Taylor, Hyde, and Synge. There are several objections to this reading. (1) When Yeats summoned ghosts, he always made it plain that they were ghosts— as in "To a Shade," "Reprisals," and "All Souls' Night." (2) The reading disregards the intent expressed in "For scholars and for poets after us" (I), as well as the dogmatic tone of the injunction, "take your stand." (3) If "take your stand" were to refer to the earlier group—who have already stood their ground at Coole—the phrase would be little more than redundant.

[17] Cf. Donald T. Torchiana, *W. B. Yeats and Georgian Ireland* (Evanston: Northwestern University Press, 1966), p. 327.

[18] See, for example, A. Norman Jeffares, *W. B. Yeats: Man and Poet* (London: Routledge, 1949), p. 274; Torchiana, *W. B. Yeats*, p. 327; Perloff, "Theme and Convention," p. 223; T. R. Henn, "*The Green Helmet* and *Responsibilities*," in *An Honoured Guest*, eds. Denis Donoghue and J. R. Mulryne (London: Edward Arnold, 1965), p. 35.

great matter; Lady Gregory herself expected Coole's dissolution upon her death.[19] Yeats was too honest and too considerate to indulge in prophetic posturings; had he done so, he would have made the inevitable seem extraordinary and would consequently have exacerbated Lady Gregory's pain of dying. His speaker accepts Coole's demise with the same hard stoicism found at the end of "To Be Carved on a Stone at Thoor Ballylee." Nevertheless, the harsh evocation of architectural decay is plainly a metonymy for Lady Gregory's death. This, too, is more humane than prophecy. With great effort the speaker prepares for the unspeakable end of his deepest friendship; in a psychological displacement unusual even in anticipatory elegy, he assembles the future generation at Coole's ruin to enact the loss he feels but cannot directly express. The notion of prophecy wholly obscures this personal tension which gives the last stanza its power of superbly appropriate restraint. The passage radiates what Yeats attributed to Synge's *Deirdre,* the "civility of sorrow,"[20] the courtesy of tragic awareness.

The fascination with prophecy, finally, because it concentrates on Coole's physical collapse, distorts the tribute to Lady Gregory which the speaker's vision of ruin paradoxically involves. "When she died the great house died too," Yeats wrote to Rossi in 1932.[21] That causal connection, pointing so clearly to Lady Gregory's indomitable spiritual presence, informs Yeats's last stanza. How can Coole, animated by Lady Gregory, survive her death? The speaker's vision of Coole's fall translates into physical terms that ethical, imaginative, metaphysical proposition. Had Yeats left the house standing, he would have significantly diminished the scope and force of Lady Gregory's spirit. To turn into compliment the transience of the house is no mean feat; Yeats accomplished no less. Jonson would never have contemplated such a metamorphosis, nor had he need; yet Yeats, transforming Coole into a rubble, took the last conceivable step in the Jonsonian scheme of correspondence between self and architecture.

II

"Coole Park and Ballylee" disclaims all hope of aristocratic regeneration. Unlike "Coole Park," it is suffused by an omnipresent doom, punctuated throughout by endings: "to finish up," "drop into a hole"

[19] Lady Gregory, *Journals,* p. 15; see also Elizabeth Coxhead, *Lady Gregory: A Literary Portrait,* 2nd ed. (London: Secker and Warburg, 1966), p. 197.

[20] *Essays,* p. 239.

[21] *Letters,* p. 796.

(I), "murdered" (III), "a last inheritor" (IV), "all that great glory spent" (V), "the last romantics" (VI). Its focus is neither Lady Gregory's life nor her impending death; in stanza IV Yeats carefully avoided any narrowing reference to their friendship. Nor is Coole considered simply the source of the literary renaissance. Foreseeing its demise, the speaker pronounces whole epochs and cultural modes dead—aristocratic tradition, the passion of romanticism, significant Irish history. When, at the end of this terrible catalogue, he imagines Homer toppled, the Western world all but halts.

Yeats's most elaborate poem on Lady Gregory's estate displays at every point a handling of materials commensurate with its scope. The vision of Coole comprehends the lake and the Seven Woods, the gardens, the house, its rooms and furnishings. What contributes most, however, to the impression of a total environment is the inclusion of Thoor Ballylee and the territory which joins the tower to Coole. Yeats's inevitable linking of tower and country house in a single poem was more than a symbol of close and extended collaboration; it fulfilled ideas of cultural continuity implicit in "In Memory of Major Robert Gregory," "Meditations . . ." (I–II), "A Prayer for My Daughter" and its drafts.[22] Such a complementarity breaks dramatically with traditional country house poetry. Jonson and his successors typically acknowledge a second house, profane, which illuminates by negative comparison the virtues of the house they celebrate; its tasteless, garish structure, newly built by the newly rich, exhibits an un-Christian pride, and classical hospitality is as foreign to its culture as moderation. Yeats had tapped this convention of antithetical houses in "Upon a House . . ." and "A Prayer on Going into My House"; here, he sought a more intricate vision of his territory.

Coole and the tower mark the spatial limits of a self-coherent community whose intimate scale the word "mile" (I) measures. Raftery's "cellar" (I), where the Cloone River drops underground, is—as Yeats's architectural word implies—an additional house, the natural, chthonic house from whose eternal forms of consciousness civilization springs. Like the "hut" in "What is 'Popular Poetry'?"[23] this symbol of peasant tradition, the common substratum of the Irish experience, is properly situated between the poet's tower and the aristocrat's country house. The temporal relationship between Thoor Ballylee and Coole, involving a historical perspective on architecture wholly inimical to Jonsonian methods, embodies the concept of evolution with which Yeats had experimented in "Meditations . . ." (I–II) and elucidated in

22 See Stallworthy, *Between the Lines* pp. 38–42.
23 *Essays*, pp. 10–11.

describing Coole: "it was into such houses men moved, when it was safe to leave their castles, or the thatched cottages under castle walls."[24] Anglo-Norman castle and eighteenth-century house, both anomalies in the corrupt present, form a microcosm of Anglo-Irish history, a humane version of "Blood and the Moon" (I). While stanza I steadfastly resists allegory, it is plain that Coole, symbolically enriched by memories of peasant imagination and Anglo-Norman aristocracy, is the last, creative fulfillment of Anglo-Irish culture: turbulent energy ends in the serenity of ordered civilization.

This brilliantly achieved landscape expresses, in Yeats's most complete symbolic form, his myth of a unity of culture in the West of Ireland. Unlike "Coole Park" (I), it has the clarity of a map:

> Under my window-ledge the waters race,
> Otters below and moor-hens on the top,
> Run for a mile undimmed in Heaven's face
> Then darkening through 'dark' Raftery's 'cellar' drop,
> Run underground, rise in a rocky place
> In Coole demesne, and there to finish up
> Spread to a lake and drop into a hole.
> What's water but the generated soul?

Through visionary observation all becomes symbol: the Cloone River is the human soul's uneven earthly progress, the tumultuous flow of Anglo-Irish history, and time itself. Like Coleridge's "sacred river" Alph, it embodies "All those antinomies / Of day and night" Yeats saw in the complex unity of existence. Height, depth; contraction, expansion; speed, slowness; vision, blindness; the heavenly and the chthonic—these dynamic analogues to the theoretical opposites of *A Vision* fuse perfectly in an organic emblem of wholeness, psychic, geographical, historical. Note the claims: unlike the Cloone in "A Prayer on Going into My House," sacramentally allegorized as the Red Sea, the river here stays Irish, and Yeats's territory in the West of Ireland contains the paradigm of universal experience. Beginning at Thoor Ballylee, it culminates in Coole Lake—a place of miraculous secular glory where the divine swan, symbol of individuation and the soul's liberty, ascends from the waters of generation (II–III). That action, an emblem of Coole's greatness, blesses all human life created on the "spot" (V); there, nature and art "momently" collaborate. The proximity of lake and house is nearly as numinous as Kubla Khan's paradoxical "miracle of rare device, / A sunny pleasure-dome with caves of ice!"

24 *Autobiography*, p. 334.

No other passage validates so triumphantly the admonition of Yeats's Communicators: "we have come to give you metaphors for poetry."[25] Yet the central principle of Yeats's geometry, its cyclical pattern, is wholly absent. The river, however reminiscent of Yeatsian recurrence, represents linear time; it expresses no idea of afterlife or rebirth. Half-conscious of its own teleology, it *finishes up* in Coole Lake; beyond that, there is nothing, death, "a hole" (I), Coleridge's "lifeless ocean." Ms. Perloff's interpretation relies too heavily on the system: "the imagery of the whole stanza is based on Book III of *A Vision,* 'The Soul in Judgment,' which expounds Yeats's doctrine of reincarnation." As Mr. Whitaker has remarked, the poem "seems a vision not of the cycles of history but of a radical fall."[26]

This landscape shadows forth contrary visions of experience: a world of erratic flux and final death—and a world nevertheless imbued, "momently," with great and sacred richness. The daring rhetorical question—"What's water but the generated soul?"—absorbs the duality. What matters for the poem's progression is less the metaphor than the speaker's intonation. Two readings are possible. First, "What's water but [except] the generated *soul?*" The assured optimism here springs from the imaginative joy of deftly proclaiming his soil spiritualized. Second, "Water's but [only] the *generated* soul." These nuances make the equation limitary, ironic;[27] the speaker, conscious of an immutable divine soul beyond generation, contemptuously deems the created world insufficient. The crucial ambivalence comes not, as Ms. Perloff believes, from a "philosophical question" concerning "the nature and destiny of the soul,"[28] for the lay of the land has already resolved that issue: neither rebirth nor immortality is humanity's province. The real problem, as in "The Tower" and "A Dialogue of Self and Soul," is a choice between attitudes: either to accept and celebrate mortal things, despite their precarious beauty, or to practice a self-defensive contempt of earthly reality which, as in "Blood and the Moon" (I), may finally turn inward and corrode the mind. For a split second the speaker

[25] W. B. Yeats, *A Vision* (New York: Macmillan, 1961), p. 8.

[26] Perloff, "Theme and Convention," p. 228; Thomas R. Whitaker, *Swan and Shadow: Yeats's Dialogue with History* (Chapel Hill: North Carolina University Press, 1964), p. 221. Whitaker, however, is ultimately ambivalent about the nature of time in the poem: although he perceives the final "fall" of the river, he concludes by suggesting that "winter does lead to spring, a riderless horse may be ridden, a drifting swan may mount." As Perloff herself remarks (p. 234, n. 20), this is an "unusual reading"; the tone of the last stanza does not support such an optimism.

[27] The most striking precedent for this use of "but" is in "Ego Dominus Tuus": "art / Is but a vision of reality." See Whitaker, *Swan and Shadow,* p. 184.

[28] Perloff, "Theme and Convention," p. 229.

almost jettisons his celebratory intent. No traditional country house poem plays so loose with eulogistic decorum; but the praise of Coole gains from the hesitation. The speaker's bodily movement at the end of stanza II ("I *turned about* and looked . . .") symbolizes the end of sardonic bitterness, and the poem then summons those moments and places of consecration in Coole's history which, transforming mere mortality into an earthly "sanctity and loveliness," make living bearable. Yeats did not misuse Arnold's term when he called "Coole Park and Ballylee" "a criticism of life."[29]

Seeking memories of past glory to avoid thoughts of the "hole," the speaker journeys imaginatively back to the lake (II). Critics have generally construed the speaker's visionary memory of the "mounting swan" as actual observation and have consequently underestimated his difficulty in finding *present* reasons for joy.[30] The memory is vivid prior to verbal articulation; to achieve complete awareness he deliberately intensifies the felt discrepancy between present and past. "Dry sticks under a wintry sun" contrast with the formerly lush "wood" and "copse of beeches." Nature seems unattractively naked yet retains a coy wit which the speaker glumly admits: in reality she has only exchanged the garments of summer for the rags of winter. In these rapid vacillations in time, the conjunction "For" makes the speaker's compensatory psychology explicit: the memory of vital joy comes *because* everything is "Now" so barren. Finally, a recollected sound cancels his own self-mocking "rant":

> At sudden thunder of the mounting swan
> I turned about and looked where branches break
> The glittering reaches of the flooded lake.
>
> [II]

The tense-shift ("turned about," "break") accomplishes a virtual hallucination: the swan *is* where it was, he *sees* what he had seen. The present re-vision continues through stanza III, strengthened by dramatic gesture: "Another emblem *there*! *That* stormy white / But seems a concentration of the sky." The memory becomes so immediate that it fills the blank space of present actuality. Consciousness of winter vanishes: the lake, magically transformed by the swan's ascent, now

---

29 TS. of "My Own Poetry Again," BBC broadcast, October 29, 1937; cited by Torchiana, *W. B. Yeats*, p. 327.

30 Yeats's revision of the poem in his edition of *The Oxford Book of Modern Verse* makes the retrospective structure of the stanza even more obvious than in the *Collected Poems*. Cf. Perloff, "Theme and Convention," p. 229; Denis Donoghue, "On 'The Winding Stair,'" in *An Honoured Guest*, p. 121; Balachandra Rajan, *W. B. Yeats: A Critical Introduction* (London: Hutchinson, 1965), p. 141.

Courtesy of the Manchester University Press

"COOLE LAKE,"
by Robert Gregory

At sudden thunder of the mounting swan
I turned about and looked where branches break
The glittering reaches of the flooded lake.

glitters like the "abounding glittering jet" in "Meditations . . ." (I.ii); the flood, later so dangerous (VI), is a refulgent amplitude. Mr. Parkinson comments that Yeats, when he published the poem in *The Oxford Book of Modern Verse,* changed "break" to "broke" in order to "clear up these shifts in tense."[31] But the revision wrecks a superbly crafted moment out of time and renders awkward the transition to stanza III. Stanza II is Yeats's most extreme conjuring of a landscape into a place of revelation. The overwhelming rediscovery of the swan has all the renovating virtue of a Wordsworthian "spot" of time;[32] yet instead of remaining a past experience narrated afresh, it leaps temporal boundaries to become present vision.

[31] Parkinson, *W. B. Yeats: The Later Poetry,* p. 251, n. 32. Parkinson also argues that Yeats first had "break" in order to satisfy "rhyme requirements" (p. 145).

[32] Bloom (*Yeats,* p. 382), following Donoghue (*An Honoured Guest,* p. 121), has claimed that "All the poem's emblems are imposed, never discovered." The criticism is unjustified.

Seen in the past, the ascending swan symbolized Coole's continual transcendence of generative nature by art, "the momentary fulfilment of spirit that redeems the imperfect temporal world."[33] Although the ascent now intimates, tragically, the death of Coole and the final departure of the shaping imagination, the swan's presence casts a last grace upon estate and symbolic history alike:

> And, like the soul, it sails into the sight
> And in the morning's gone, no man knows why;
> And is so lovely that it sets to right
> What knowledge or its lack had set awry,
> So arrogantly pure, a child might think
> It can be murdered with a spot of ink.

> [III]

It is not the knowledge that humankind has a divine soul which redeems, for the habits of the soul are inscrutable: "no man knows why."[34] Even more remarkably, in a poet whom Mr. Bloom terms gnostic, neither the extent nor the limitations of human self-knowledge matter. The admission of "Blood and the Moon"—"wisdom is the property of the dead"—recurs, but without remorse. The swan redeems through its "lovely" presence; its inviolability, unlike the moon's, does not craze. Its concentrated heavenly whiteness—unlike the unity of the expanding, sometimes dark river—is an exalted simplicity. Its beauty so far transcends human contrivance and yet so fully expresses ultimate human achievement that the speaker can only respond with disinterested aesthetic excitement. For a moment, his sense of sublimity, and of his own dissociation from the creature he contemplates, paradoxically engenders in him that same transcendence. The concluding witticism, breaking the high meditation with such casual, daring tact, affirms the immunity of the swan's beauty.[35]

---

33 Whitaker, *Swan and Shadow*, p. 219.

34 Cf. Perloff, "Theme and Convention," p. 231.

35 Perloff, (ibid., p. 231) contends that these lines concern the "uncertainty" of the swan's flight to heaven; her reading is based on a draft of the stanza printed by Parkinson (*W. B. Yeats: The Later Poetry*, p. 143), not on the final text. Unaccountably, she attributes the child's uncertainty—explicit in both versions—to the swan. She argues further (p. 229) that in this stanza the speaker consciously makes a "second attempt at transcendence." This is to confuse what Yeats represents with what his speaker feels. Glossing the passage with "Nineteen Hundred . . ." (III), she claims that the attempt at transcendence fails. But one poem is not another: a "desolate heaven" is hardly equivalent to the white "sky," and there is no warrant for assuming that the swan's ascent in "Coole Park and Ballylee" ends in desperation.

The memory restores the speaker's consciousness of inestimable worth, quells the bitter pain of doom foreknown which roughens the last stanza of "Coole Park." In the subsequent celebration (11. 27–37), Coole is the human incorporation of the swan's beauty: "*Beloved books*" (IV) are as "lovely" (III) as the swan, and the speaker envisages the house and grounds with the same disinterested joy which permeates his memory. What Yeats called the "shaping joy" of tragedy[36] is the consummate achievement of this passage—an elegy on departing greatness so vivid, so abundant in its love that the ravages of time scarcely seem relevant.

The accomplishment, not simply tonal, results from the transition to stanza IV:

> So arrogantly pure, a child might think
> It can be murdered with a spot of ink.
>
>   [III]
>
> Sound of a stick upon the floor, a sound
> From somebody that toils from chair to chair.
>
>   [IV]

The word "murdered" and the suggestion that the artist can ruin his emblem with an aesthetic *faux pas*[37] return the speaker to the generated world of human limitation. The uncertain tapping of a cane is hardly a swan's "sudden thunder" (II); laborious struggle against age is not a graceful, effortless ascent. Yet the contrasts prompt neither a discontented "rant" upon the futility of existence nor a great personal grief; they disclose, instead, a new equanimity, a stoic acceptance of mortality. Death can end but not nullify Coole's magnificence. These extraordinarily private lines—Jonson would have considered them indecorous[38] —function rhetorically to make Coole's public, "established" greatness all the more resonant:

> Beloved books that famous hands have bound,
> Old marble heads, old pictures everywhere;
> Great rooms where travelled men and children found
> Content or joy; a last inheritor

---

36 *Essays*, p. 255.

37 See T. R. Henn, *The Lonely Tower* (1950; rpt. London: Methuen, 1965), p. 138.

38 Cf. Perloff ("Theme and Convention," p. 231), who claims that Yeats adhered fully to the "conventions of the estate poem." According to Torchiana (*W. B. Yeats*, p. 328), Lady Gregory "took exception to this opening line, hating any reference to her illness."

Where none has reigned that lacked a name and fame
Or out of folly into folly came.

[IV]

Personal difficulty is subsumed to communal identity, traditional power and intelligence, architectural stability. The entire progression from painful disease to health—bustling activity, families, "Content or joy"—has the rhetorical effect of a resurrection. Had Yeats omitted the opening lines of stanza IV, he could have linked the house to the swan even more closely than it is now, but he would have sacrificed the dramatic value of the speaker's own recovery. Confronting his speaker with knowledge of impending death and then alleviating its pressure, Yeats deliberately created a regenerative structure which would free his speaker to evoke Coole's glory in the fullest possible manner.

Concomitantly, Yeats defused linear time of its destructive power. Coole in stanzas IV and V enjoys a magical stasis. "All that great glory spent" (V), the culminating tragic phrase which demolishes in a flash all that seems permanent, is held long in abeyance, until abundant material for the irony has been assembled. The catalogue of Coole's magnificence (IV), containing no verbs suggesting the imminent demise, stresses continuous life. The objects and actions which the speaker envisages demonstrate Coole's creative *use* of time, not its subjugation to transience. Even the phrase "a last inheritor" meshes so rapidly with the speaker's imagining of the preceding generations ("Where none has reigned . . .") that "last" almost means "most recent"; it rings with the speaker's exultation, not sorrow, and has the same authoritative pride as Yeats's quotation from Henley: "A good poet must . . . be the last of a dynasty."[39] The speaker celebrates in Coole's tradition the same consecrative habit of mind which motivates so many 'tower' poems;[40] indeed, the swan confers a blessing upon the estate precisely because its inhabitants have sought to transcend time through aesthetic and social behavior. Their practiced commemoration of heritage radiates an affection that avoids the sterility which merely ritual form threatens. The attitudes toward literature, craftsmanship, history, and nobility clustered together in "Beloved books that famous hands have bound" (IV) are the very opposite of what Pope found in Timon's library

---

39 W. B. Yeats, *Explorations* (New York: Macmillan, 1962), p. 295.

40 Perloff ("Theme and Convention," p. 232) asserts that the details of Coole's culture are celebrated merely because they are "old." Like her contention that Yeats's language in stanzas IV and V is "matter-of-fact and denotative" (ibid.), the judgment is simply inaccurate.

(*Epistle to Burlington,* 11. 133–40). Objects have become local habitations for human emotion, nodal points of memory which bind the present to the past and provide direction for the future. The consecrative habit persistently joins place, action, and thought, nourishes upon a "spot" what Eliot called the "life of significant soil":[41]

> ancestral trees,
> Or gardens rich in memory glorified
> Marriages, alliances and families,
> And every bride's ambition satisfied.

[V]

Art and nature collaborate to form a cohesive social organism through which, in rooms made great by an august sense of human dignity, "travelled men and children found / Content or joy."

That joy, sufficiently sophisticated to satisfy world-besotted wanderers, innocent enough for children, is the human analogue of the swan's ascent, the unaccountable emotion of sanctity which is everywhere sought in *The Winding Stair* and nowhere to be "found" established except at Coole. Coole expresses, ideally, what the tower's inhabitant, in "A Dialogue of Self and Soul" and "Blood and the Moon," cannot achieve in any fully humanistic shape. But the claim for Coole's continuous joy most directly answers "Meditations . . ." (I.i–ii):

> Yet Homer had not sung
> Had he not found it certain beyond dreams
> That out of life's own self-delight had sprung
> The abounding glittering jet . . .

If Homer is eventually unseated, Coole now validates that faith in the possibility of a permanent joy amidst "levelled lawns and gravelled ways." Placing the phrase "a last inheritor" just after "Content or joy," Yeats defined Coole's true inheritance: what the "founders" (V) founded—for others to find—was not simply an Augustan equipoise but joy itself.

Their act of creation is unique in Yeats's work: paradoxically, they institutionalized the most fleeting of evanescent emotions within the walls of an eighteenth-century house and created, unlike the bitter Anglo-Irishmen of "Meditations . . ." (I.iii), a world whose original perfection did not contain the seeds of its own destruction. The lasting creative blaze which Yeats had once praised in Gregory he now attrib-

41 "The Dry Salvages," V, in *Four Quartets.*

uted to Coole's entire culture. Thus designating the joy in Coole's tradition, he quashed the nemesis of romanticism—preoccupation with the quest, the belief that illumination and joy are momentary phenomena—and synthesized, after many poems, his romantic and classical ideals. "Upon a House . . ." extols Coole's union of "passion and precision"; but that passion, although it intimates the quest for joy, is not joy itself. "Gradual Time's last gift" is not a personal elation but the more classical craft of art. In the epilogue to *Responsibilities,* Coole offers "A sterner conscience and a friendlier home"; and in "Coole Park," "pride established in humility, / A scene well set and excellent company." Here, without losing its classical ceremony and Anglo-Irish custom, Coole becomes the ground of the completed romantic quest, where "Everything we look upon is blest."

Thus, as nowhere else, the speaker explicitly names Coole a kingdom,

> Where none has *reigned* that lacked a name and fame
> Or out of folly into folly came.
>
> [IV]

The chiming accolade creates territorial demarcations which imply social, intellectual, and imaginative unities of the highest order. Unlike the speaker's sudden, flamboyant consecration of the space between Thoor Ballylee and Coole, this consecration is a hyperbole treated as if no exaggeration were involved. Yet, as so often, the speaker fails to sustain his consciousness of glory. Self-irony sunders spatial unity; an ageing Yeats transmuted his periodic migrations to the Mediterranean into a metaphor of alienation:

> Where fashion or mere fantasy decrees
> We shift about—all that great glory spent—
> Like some poor Arab tribesman and his tent.
>
> [V]

After such concentration on Coole and the West of Ireland, the geographic dislocation is startling, uncomfortably comic. Coole no longer exercises its benevolent sovereignty. Pathetically obedient to the tyrannical dictates of undirected impulse or, worse, deranged imagination, the speaker is exiled from "gardens rich in memory" to the mental deserts of Lockean blankness. Unhappily rootless, he is barred from a consecrated "spot" which has become the center of European tradition.

Once again, however, the speaker recovers, this time from self-pity. As in "Coole Park," he turns to public speech. The valedictory fuses in tragic joy the proud summation of extended achievement with the knowledge of death and cultural obsolescence.

> We were the last romantics—chose for theme
> Traditional sanctity and loveliness;
> Whatever's written in what poets name
> The book of the people; whatever most can bless
> The mind of man or elevate a rhyme;
> But all is changed, that high horse riderless,
> Though mounted in that saddle Homer rode
> Where the swan drifts upon a darkening flood.
>
> [VI]

The forceful self-identification—"We"—may include the founders of the Abbey, the self-sustaining community in the West of Ireland, or the entire span of Anglo-Irish tradition. Its ultimate range is immense; twenty years ago Mr. Ellmann observed that Yeats "would no doubt have said that the first romantics were Homer and Sophocles."[42] The radical, presumptive redefinition of romanticism, calculated to forestall specious categorizations and to ridicule modernism, is the fruit of Yeats's efforts, in the fumbling early drafts of "Coole Park," to create in Coole a heroic magnitude. Recalling the implied epic of stanza I, it welds together aristocratic, peasant, and poetic imaginations, affirms their source in oral culture, and asserts the poet's province. The idea of poetry and sensibility is so extensive that it embraces everything the speaker values. The reiterated "whatever" suggests illimitable imaginative freedom; "chose for theme" taps the bardic vocabulary of epic invocation. Subject-matter must be "special":[43] a rhymester's tinkerings are elevated only by the purpose of the poetry, to "bless / The mind of man" by delineating secular glory.

For all these marks of epic context, the climactic introduction of Homer must always shock. The allusion is not of the same order as Jonson's in "To Penshurst":[44]

> Thou hast thy walkes for health, as well as sport:
> Thy Mount, to which the Dryads doe resort,
> Where Pan, and Bacchus their high feasts have made,
> Beneath the broad beech, and the chest-nut shade . . .
>
> [11. 9–12]

[42] Richard Ellmann, *The Identity of Yeats* (1954; rpt. London: Faber, 1964), pp. 3–4.

[43] See *Essays*, p. 499.

[44] Cf. Perloff, "Theme and Convention," p. 234.

This is significant decoration, an imagistic flourish welcomed by an audience delighted by classicism. As the reference to Juno in "Meditations . . ." (I.iv) indicates, Yeats knew how to import mythological figures to grace an estate with Saturnian blessedness; but he saw, too, that the convention had staled. Thus he went straight back to Homer, the putatively historical man who had made the myths. What Jonson paraded as literary allusion, Yeats insisted that his readers take as reality: his speaker all but sees "that high horse riderless." The incredibly daring transposition of Homer from his proper geography is Yeats's most elaborate Hellenizing of the West of Ireland: the *force* of the image comes less from the toppling of Homer than from the fact that Homer is at Coole to be toppled at all. This is Yeats making a credible myth of "Traditional sanctity and loveliness" in the only way available to him: to name the myth and then deny, just as rapidly, its present continuation. Homer's presence extends the historical myth of the Anglo-Irish aristocratic tradition back to its epic source and transforms the territory between the tower and Coole into a realm paradoxically beyond history. Homer, Coole, Western civilization fall simultaneously, and the making of that disastrous collocation is an astounding praise. The point of greatest doom is the point of greatest celebration; and the fall of culture, which Yeats once dated just after the Renaissance and then attributed to the Enlightenment, is now his speaker's actual experience.

This epic monumentality would seem rhetoric were the image less precise. Homer's "high horse"—as arrogant as the swan—is the winged Pegasus of imaginative power. Pegasus, however, was Bellerophon's horse; there is no iconographic tradition of Homer on horseback. Yeats revised the myth purposefully: Pegasus, by stamping his hoof, created the "blushful Hippocrene" upon Mount Helicon, sacred to the Muses; who else should ride that horse but Homer? Coole Lake becomes the Hippocrene, the sacred waters of the imagination. The sacramentalizing equation gains intensity from the superb collocation of Homer with the swan: "Though mounted in that saddle Homer rode / Where the swan drifts upon a darkening flood." The reference of "Where" is deliberately vague. Did Homer ride around the lake? Or did he also ride *on* it? Or, because "high" Pegasus has wings and "mounted" recalls "the mounting swan" (II), did Homer ride *above* the lake? Water, earth, and air were Homer's epic province. Only the celestial realm of fire, where all images are purged into the ineffable, lay beyond his reach. And rightly so: "What theme had Homer but original sin?" and, in the speaker's view, earthly redemption? Like Gregory's riding, Homer's unified the entire sublunary universe.

The swan's descent duplicates Homer's fall, the end of poetic imagination. The speaker "sees" both events; tactfully, the verse renders neither, eschews histrionics which would have disrupted the spacious tranquillity of the closure. The last line is a kind of after-image: as the waters of imagination become the murderously "innocent" waters of destruction, the "swan drifts" calmly toward the inevitable doom foreseen since stanza I. Because of that final loss, Ms. Perloff argues that the speaker's "efforts to mythologize the landscape fail. . . . The poem records the experience of a man who tries to read spiritual meanings into the landscape but fails and must accordingly come to terms with the temporal reality of human loss."[45] The false dichotomy between spiritual and temporal denies symbol. The landscape remains spiritualized throughout, yielding the speaker signs of utmost loss which are no less potent than those of utmost creativity. What kind of failure to mythologize the landscape can there be when the territory between the tower and Coole has been made to incorporate personal, Anglo-Irish, and the Western experience alike? What failure can there be when Homer has been summoned to grace Coole's demise with epic dignity? In this, Yeats's last poem about Lady Gregory's estate, Coole assumed its fullest proportions to become a symbol perfected in death: a microcosm of all the world that mattered.

III

I am old, I belong to mythology.
—Prologue, The Death of Cuchulain

As Yeats lay dying in southern France, he imagined himself dying in the West of Ireland, within the tower he had made his symbol. The pull of place was strong; he needed to end "where his breath began."[46] What he dramatized in "The Black Tower" was the experience of dying; what he defined was the meaning of his death. There is no cause to apologize for the poem:[47] Yeats's shrewdness of design and skill in dramatic monologue, his sense of form and rhythm, his power to pack great themes into little room—these, the dying body could not impair.

Mr. Wilson has called the tower a Plotinian symbol of the "intellective soul."[48] The identification, theoretically valid, is far from central

[45] Ibid.

[46] "In Memory of Alfred Pollexfen."

[47] Cf. Bloom, *Yeats*, pp. 465–66.

[48] F. A. C. Wilson, *W. B. Yeats and Tradition* (London: Gollancz, 1958), p. 224.

poetic meanings. The tower is Yeats's corporeal body and nothing less, although it is also more. It is the "divine architecture of the body"[49] blackened by years of war against experience, "black" because it is the doomed tomb of the living in which, from birth, "the dark grows blacker," "black" like Tamburlane's cloak in sign of defiant wrath.[50] It is invaded by an enemy who holds the power of life and death: life, if the speaker surrenders his identity; death, if he refuses to capitulate. From the outset the speaker defies the insidious ultimatum. That the choice is already made, however, hardly obscures the psychological fact that he is committing a heroic suicide—like Cuchulain in *On Baile's Strand,* like Roland refusing to blow his great ivory horn for help.

Yeats at the end was not prepared to yield time dominance. In his suicide he asserted his will. He had admired his grandfather Pollexfen for having deliberately "*Laid* his strong bones down in death"; he had sung The O'Rahilly, who, dying in Easter Week, had written his epitaph with his own blood; he had celebrated the stern self-control of the ancient hero who had stepped into his coffin, "stopped his breath and died."[51] And in "Vacillation" (III) he had bluntly admonished himself to

> call those works extravagance of breath
> That are not suited for such men as come
> Proud, open-eyed and laughing to the tomb.

"The Black Tower," though it shows no gaiety, is Yeats's personal adherence to the stiff heroic code. His speaker has finally become a swordsman—not a poet gazing with timid envy upon soldiers ("Meditations . . .," V), nor a man afraid to use Sato's blade ("Meditations . . .," III; "A Dialogue of Self and Soul," I), nor a man studying from a distance the "Rough men-at-arms" who have made his tower's history ("The Tower," II.ix).

The logic of his suicide is sacrifice, a homage to the ancient Irish heroic dead who, buried upright in their cairns,[52] inspire the final act of service at which "The Curse of Cromwell" (III) hints in far less demanding terms. In this extreme allegiance, Yeats proclaimed his nationality. With the great Anglo-Irish culture dead, he now reverted, for his last defiance against a corrupt modernity, to the imaginings of

49 W. B. Yeats, *Mythologies* (New York: Macmillan, 1959), pp. 332–33.

50 *I Tamburlane,* IV.ii.119–22. The allusion to Browning's "Childe Roland to the Dark Tower Came" is obvious.

51 "In Memory of Alfred Pollexfen"; "The O'Rahilly"; "In Tara's Halls."

52 See Stallworthy, *Between the Lines,* pp. 228–29.

Courtesy of M. Frances MacNally

THOOR BALLYLEE
seen from the southeast

There in the tomb the dark grows blacker,
But wind comes up from the shore . . .

his youth—and to the sole mythology of Irish history he had not yet
incorporated into Thoor Ballylee: Celtic combat, Celtic glory, Celtic
disaster. The appropriation was plausible. The tower had been erected
by Anglo-Normans—not quite Celtic, but close enough to satisfy a
dying man who needed a model of heroic nobility almost barbaric in

order to perform, as he once wrote of Gregory, a "good death."[53] Into the tower Yeats gathered his troops, his emblems and themes. The bedraggled, starved compatriots whom the speaker marshalls are Yeats's Irish body, a compound version of the "last romantics," the vanishing body politic that has kept faith with Ireland's heroic past and believed in its resurgence. With him would die this remnant.

The values Yeats ascribed to his death inhere in his manner of telling. For all that bespeaks an intimate dread behind the unflinching pride, "The Black Tower" is not personal utterance. The antiphonal voices which chant this haunting poem of doom are all larger than those of either Yeats himself or his typical speaker in the 'tower' poems. "The Black Tower" is a fragment of epic. What "Coole Park and Ballylee" accomplishes for Yeats's territory through swift allusions to Raftery and Homer, this poem achieves through the very form of its drama. More than any earlier work, it begins in the middle. You can intuit the preceding sequence of defeats, delivered with a Cromwellian ferocity, which has left Thoor Ballylee the sole bastion of traditional Irish culture; you know the crumbling of its stone which will follow: over the whole an inexorable fate descends. Yeats wanted that distance from event which epic confers: the poem translates the private experience of dying into a heroic vision, which is then filtered through the distinctively Yeatsian prism of communal legend into ballad form, the peasant's version of courtly *geste*. This amalgam of genres, bundling together Yeats's favorite masks of poet, aristocrat, and peasant, renders formally the cultural "equality" of noble and beggar-man which the poem indirectly celebrates. The fusion produces not only the impersonal monumentality of a drama which seems already received into the public consciousness, but also a very strong narrative element which verifies the speaker's epic stature. The refrain in particular, as an omniscient choric meditation on the speaker's situation, augments that sense of a narrated action.[54] It establishes the crucial collocation of tower and tomb; it elevates the speaker's resistance into patriarchal fury; it describes with macabre vividness the chosen doom, and places that event within the historical and cosmic cycles of decay and regeneration.

But the poem is also a dramatic monologue, a form inimical to authorial commentary. The refrain, while it keeps by convention its objective character, is simultaneously an internal continuation of the

---

53 "Reprisals."

54 Stallworthy (*Between the Lines*, p. 242) has also commented on the narrative impetus of the poem; John Unterecker, *A Reader's Guide to William Butler Yeats* (New York: Farrar, Straus, 1959), p. 292, construes the refrain as a "chorus."

speaker's thought—language not addressed to the enemy, language which transmits his most private feelings. Making the most public element in ballad embody interior monologue, Yeats carried to conclusion the experiments with subjectivized refrains which he had begun in the earliest ballads of *Crossways* (1889). This deliberately incongruous merging of objective and subjective elements results in a strange, eerie resonance. Two voices consider the same event from radically different perspectives, experiential and omniscient; both say the same thing: *"There in the tomb the dark grows blacker."* The dying warrior shares the commentator's omniscience; the commentator, the warrior's tragedy. The conjoined voice, reverberating from a disembodied source, is that of the individual self amplified through the megaphonic mask of a transcendent impersonal self-consciousness. It is that of subjective epic created by the speaker as he experiences it: cold, austere, intensely passionate.

When does this poem occur? Like the speaker's hovering double-voice, the poem's temporal referent is uncertain. On the one hand, the poem *enacts* a medieval drama, perhaps the Celtic resistance to Anglo-Norman invasions; on the other, the action is wholly present. It is not the narrative of a historical event or fiction, as it would have been if Yeats had written the refrain in the past tense. Nor does the poem filter a contemporary event through the lens of another historical epoch, although you can hardly ignore Yeats's choice of a medieval scenario for his death. The poem is a paradox: a present medieval event. The anomaly is part of Yeats's self-definition: it brandishes with pride the speaker's absurd adherence to a heroic code which the debased twentieth century has scrapped; it flaunts, with a hatred of contemporary poetics no less ornery than the prologue to *The Death of Cuchulain*, the absurdity of writing heroic poetry in modern times.

The poem's unlocalized time militates against any efforts to allegorize into modern contexts the final conflict between the invisible enemy and "the men of the old black tower." Mr. Stallworthy has claimed that the enemy is England and/or the Third Reich. Mr. Wilson thinks that "what Yeats has in mind here is the insidious spiritual propaganda of communism." Mr. Torchiana associates the enemy with the Irish political party Fianna Fail and its leader de Valéra, who in 1922 had refused to take the oath of allegiance to the British crown and then, in 1927, accepted it only "with mental reservations."[55]

---

[55] Stallworthy, *Between the Lines*, pp. 227, 242; Wilson, *Tradition*, p. 227; Torchiana, *W. B. Yeats*, p. 329. Henn (*The Lonely Tower*, pp. 338–40) joins Ellmann (*The Identity of Yeats*, p. 209), Whitaker (*Swan and Shadow*, pp. 259–60), and Bloom (*Yeats*, p. 466) in resisting the temptations of political allegory.

These interpretations, all plausible in light of Yeatsian attitudes and twentieth-century realities, do not accord with the experience of mysterious warfare which the poem renders. To specify particular historical conflicts may offer readers a certain safety from calamity, but the poem does not give evidence to warrant such labelings.

The poem defines the enemy in its own terms. Its form makes them faceless. They reject the heroic code, "bribe," "whisper," appeal to low instincts. Like Henry V in Yeats's mythology of Shakespeare, they are political pragmatists, mechanists; they have neither historical imagination nor any sense of allegiances binding through time; they slide with public opinion, which has conveniently "forgotten" the speaker's "own right king" and dismissed him as an obsolete fiction. These anti-heroic qualities the speaker deftly exposes as he mimics the enemy's demand for surrender and then retorts with terse, sardonic mockery:

> If he died long ago
> Why do you dread us so?

This is the crux of the matter. The invaders conquer in fear. Like the demagogues reviled in "The Leaders of the Crowd," "They must to keep their certainty accuse / All that are different of a base intent." The very existence of a last heroic enclave, revealing their diminished stature, threatens their precarious self-identity: to assert their masculinity they must co-opt or destroy. The possible return of the vanished, dead king challenges their legal authority. Most important, the belief in that return maintained by "the men of the old black tower" endangers the enemy's psychic universe, calls into question the most fundamental premises governing their behavior—not because the belief may prove justified, but because it is belief. It is the evidence in minds of things unseen, a wholly foreign mode of thought which presumes the validity of myth, spirit, imagination. What if the cosmos is more complicated by invisible forces than their dwarfed, materialistic mentalities can comprehend? This is the self-doubt, the dread of the ineffable, which the usurpers seek to overcome by compelling the speaker to break faith. If the enemy represents an "atheistic rationalism,"[56] it is a rationalism the dictates of whose limitary logic its proponents cannot fully accept; and in shrinking from "uncontrollable mystery," the strong, who possess all physical power, become weak.

Against this overwhelming aggression of fear, the speaker retaliates with his last possessions: faith, and nothing. That "nothing" is a real property, as in the *Anima Hominis:* "I shall find the dark grow

---

[56] Stallworthy, *Between the Lines*, p. 234.

luminous, the void fruitful when I understand I have nothing . . . ."[57]
Here, "nothing" is less the precondition of revelation than of heroic
courage. In stanza I, as at the end of "The Tower," he arrogantly names
all his deprivations and then, having no more to lose, claims his fearless
self-sufficiency. Maintaining fealty to the gigantic shadows whose skele-
tons loom within his mind, within his tower, within their tomb, he
incorporates their prowess. Dead, they live in him; dying, he joins them,
knowing that their ghostly clatter is his own death rattle. "Upright,"
like the "upstanding" fishermen in "The Tower" (III), they inspirit
him. Mr. Whitaker has remarked that "stand . . . upright" suggests "not
merely placement but also the act of rising again."[58] Even as the "faint
moonlight" *drops,* signaling the end both of his life and of the last
heroic epoch, it illumines the dead; in imitative response, he stands *up.*
To his retainers, imaged "stretched in slumber," he cries: "*Stand* we on
guard oath-bound!" The command parallels the implicit ascent of the
dead.

Despite the intimations of cyclical recurrence and resurrection
carried in the refrain, the speaker's belief in his dead king's return is
highly problematical. The poem offers a rare extrapolation from the
Yeatsian theory of history: a myth of messianic deliverance. Mr. Wilson
traces it to Plato's *Statesman:*

> When it [the world] must travel on without God, things go well
> enough in the years immediately after he abandons control, but as
> time goes on and forgetfulness of God arises in it, the ancient
> condition of chaos also begins to assert its sway. At last, as this
> cosmic era draws to its close, this disorder comes to a head. . . .
>   The God looks upon it again . . . and anxious for it lest it sink
> racked by storms and confusion, and be dissolved again in the
> bottomless abyss of unlikeness, he takes control of the helm once
> more. . . . and, so ordering and correcting it, he achieves for it its
> agelessness and deathlessness.[59]

Mr. Keith, discussing the Arthurian parallel of this myth of restored
order, identifies the soldiers in the Black Tower as "men who believe in
the eventual return of King Arthur to lead the Celts to glory."[60] There
is no doubt that the speaker, adamantly refusing to deny Irish great-

---

[57] *Mythologies,* p. 332.

[58] Whitaker, *Swan and Shadow,* p. 260.

[59] *Statesman,* 273c-e; Wilson, *Tradition,* p. 226.

[60] W. J. Keith, "Yeats's Arthurian Black Tower," *Modern Language Notes* 75
(1960): 121.

ness, gives the myth credence. But does he believe in the actualization of the myth? Does he believe that the king *will come?* Through this central question Yeats defined the nature of his faith:

> The tower's old cook that must climb and clamber
> Catching small birds in the dew of the morn
> When we hale men lie stretched in slumber
> Swears that he hears the king's great horn.
> But he's a lying hound:
> Stand we on guard oath-bound!

Why does the speaker disbelieve the cook? reject with snarling brusqueness the very return he so desires? He plainly considers the cook's claim a threat to his heroic defense. Paradoxically, the king's coming would vitiate his strength; the messiah, as supreme deliverer, appropriates all power to himself and leaves man dependent, weak. To the speaker, the cook is the specter of betrayal from within the tower; an unwitting traitor, faithful to his king, who interprets the myth literally and thus invalidates it by diminishing the power of defiant resistance gained from the king's absence. The speaker thinks the cook obsessed, the victim of either specious optimism or a despairing need for signs of deliverance when there are none. The cook, hardly an emblem of the "poetic imagination,"[61] is a type of Doubting Thomas: he cannot believe in his king without evidence. His mentality exactly reverses that of the enemy, who find all evidence for disbelief, yet suspect irrationally that the belief may be true.

Yet the stunning complexity is that you cannot know whether the cook hears an actual sound or a hallucinatory buzzing; nor are you meant to.[62] And what if the speaker himself actually thinks the cook is telling the truth, but still derides him as a "lying hound"? This is the

---

[61] Ellmann, *The Identity of Yeats*, p. 209.

[62] Cf. Stallworthy (*Between the Lines*, p. 236): "we are secretly inclined to believe the cook, and, I submit, it is intended that we should"; "If we were not to believe him he would not be there" (p. 242). But in dramatic monologue, all reality is filtered through the speaker's consciousness; it has no objectively or externally validated existence. The actual truth of the cook's belief is irrelevant; what matters is the kind of psychological and dramatic tension which his belief creates within the speaker—and the reader. Unterecker (*A Reader's Guide*, p. 293) takes a position exactly the opposite of Stallworthy's: "The old cook of the last stanza is, of course, a 'lying hound' when he swears that the 'king's great horn' is already sounding; for that horn cannot sound till the moon blacks out completely and the elemental transformation takes place." Asserting as objective fact what cannot be known, Unterrecker violates the poem's form. The additional danger in his reading is that it substitutes Yeats's cosmology for Yeats's drama as an explanation of the poem.

explosive interior crisis which both the ambiguity of his response and the form of dramatic monologue suggest. In denying the cook's experience, the speaker is wrestling free of his own worst temptations—not simply an easy faith, but hope and fear, all that endangers detachment. These emotions would keep him from facing "the greatest obstacle he may confront"—the immitigable end—"without despair."[63] The cook represents, very nearly, Yeats's desire for the life he could not have. If salvation from death were available, then heroic suicide, the true test of his allegiance, would be impossible. Like Cuchulain having lost his son, the speaker can perform his terrible bidding only when there is nothing, when the king is absent. The mood is that of "Nineteen Hundred and Nineteen" (I.v): "all triumph would / But break upon his ghostly solitude." But the nihilism of "The Black Tower" is redemptive: the most extreme negation is also complete self-affirmation. How else to be indomitable but in defeat? Thus the speaker's wholly paradoxical faith: the king exists; he must not come; long live the king. The king is a numinous image; were he real, he would have no power to inspirit the mind. He is not the absconded god whose absence is deleterious, but a figure who can compel a creative obeisance precisely because he does not appear. His charisma is very Irish: he is impotent to aid his oath-bound servants. The speaker believes in his unseen presence because Irish greatness, despite all evidence, must exist. He believes what is absurd, and believes it *as* an absurdity. Unlike the cook, he requires no proof, no personal benefit to confirm his faith. The burden of proof is his: dying for the king, who cannot save him, he will prove the king's power. His faith has the chill discipline of total disinterest, and total vision:

> *There in the tomb the dark grows blacker,*
> *But wind comes up from the shore:*
> *They shake when the winds roar,*
> *Old bones upon the mountain shake.*

Simultaneously, the moon vanishes and the sight of the eyes goes blind. Yet he hears "the dead upright," their presence created by the once menacing wind, now an emblem of his own revivifying imagination. Stone cairn and tower are identical: they are his bone-house, the "soil" in which his soul has worked. The coexistence of the self and its architecture is nowhere else achieved with such certitude and imperceptible skill. Compare "Meditations . . ." (VI) and "Blood and the Moon" (IV):

[63] *Autobiography*, p. 234.

My wall is loosening . . .

Is every modern nation like the tower,
Half dead at the top?

These symbolic equations are constructed through explicit language; their speaker is conscious of his tower as a symbol; both analogies result in negative self-definition. The intermediary link between these equivalences and the wholly self-affirming collocation in "The Black Tower" is "Coole Park" (IV): the destruction of Lady Gregory's house is the ultimate expression of her creative, spiritualizing presence. In "The Black Tower" Yeats earned the reward of all his discipline: the poem achieves an analogy between self and stone which transcends symbolic relation to become an absolute identity, and that identity embodies not the self-deriding agony of fragmentation but the fullness of his human nature. A week before he died, after fifteen years' work setting his pen to the hardest stone, Yeats had no need to designate architectural detail, nor to declare possession of a world, finally epic in shape, which he had made the intimate emblem of his historical experience. He wrote with the absolute conviction that his chosen symbol had become himself, and with the knowledge that "old forms, old situations" had yielded him the "original relation" to his Irish acre of stony ground he had so passionately sought. Through the plenitude of his gift, Thoor Ballylee is simply his presence. As his speaker enters into its blackness, seeing nothing standing there, he enters mythology.

Index

Italicized page numbers indicate major discussion of the work.

tan," 24; objects to Yeats's reference to her illness in "Coole Park and Ballylee," 238n; and peasantry, 22–24, 26n; rage at Dublin's ingratitude toward Hugh Lane, 44; self-isolation, 39; sells Coole, 223–24; sense of symbolic space, 7, 13, 96, 239; takes Yeats to Italy, 5, tours Synge's *The Playboy of the Western World*, 43; writes for Catholic audiences, 24; 3–8, 22–24, 27–30, 39, 42, 43–45, 51–57, 60n, 61, 63–67, 74n, 75, 80, 82, 87, 87n, 90, 92, 93, 100, 114, 114n, 123–26, 132, 142, 149, 152, 153, 159, 160, 161n, 162, 176, 201n, 224–44 (passim), 253. *See also* Coole *and commentaries on poems about Coole*

—*Coole*, 224–25

"Coole" (holograph MS., Berg Collection, New York Public Library), 7, 28, 44, 162

Cuchulain of Muirthemne, 24n, 26n, 27, 160

Gods and Fighting Men, 160

Mr. Gregory's Letter-Box, 4n

Hugh Lane's Life and Achievement, 44, 45n

Journals, 4, 8, 43, 153n, 159, 224, 231

"Journals" (unpublished TS., Berg Collection, New York Public Library), 2–5, 28n, 29n, 93, 96, 153, 159, 160n, 162, 201n, 224

Kiltartan Poetry Book, The, 161n

Our Irish Theatre, 4, 24, 43

Poets and Dreamers, 27

Visions and Beliefs in the West of Ireland, 28n

Gregory, Margaret (Robert Gregory's wife), 87n, 115, 116n

Gregory, Richard (18th c.), 6, 7

Gregory, Richard (Lady Gregory's grandson), 124–25

Gregory, Robert (18th c.), 4, 6

Gregory, Robert (Lady Gregory's son), 6, 38, 55, 57, 75, 76, 77, 87n, 92, 100, 112, 114–40 (passim), 143, 147, 166n, 169, 178, 213, 236, 240, 243, 247

Gregory, Sir William (Lady Gregory's husband), 6, 43, 61

Hegel, G. W. F., 181

Henley, William Ernest, 29, 49, 148n, 239

—"When You Wake in Your Crib," 148n

Herbert, George, 53n, 107

—"Church-Porch, The," 107

"Vertue," 53n

Herbert, Mary, Countess of Pembroke, 52, 85, 135n

—"Astrophel" (or "The Lay of Clorinda"), 135n

Herrick, Robert, 71, 77

Homer, 21, 112, 164–65, 172, 174, 188, 196, 202, 232, 240, 242–44, 247

Horace, 53, 68

Hyde, Douglas, 22–24, 227–28, 228n, 229n

—"De-Anglicizing of Ireland, The," 24n

Hyde-Lees, Bertha Georgiana (Mrs. W. B. Yeats), 94, 96–97, 104, 128, 176

Hynes, Mary, 21, 111, 187–90

Ignatian meditation, 227

Ireland, history of heroic age, 16, 19; bardic colleges, 20, Anglo-Norman invasion, 27, 214, 225, 248; Elizabethan plantations, 34; Battle of the Boyne, 171; famine, 43; emigrations, 75; Young Ireland movement, 2; Land Wars, 58; death of Parnell, 1, 28n; Land Conference (1902), 23, 225; riots over Synge's *The Playboy of the Western World*, 44; Land Act (1909), 58–59; Easter Rising, 93, 155–56, 186, 245; "German Plot," 138; election of December 1918, 138; Black and Tan mercenaries, 12, 115, 117–18, 152, 153–54, 186; Treaty of 1921, 152, 158, 202, 248; civil war, 6, 12, 158–59, 166n, 176–77, 184, 186, 201; Irish Republican Army (IRA), 138, 158–59, 163, 201; Anglo-Irish aristocratic houses burned, 12, 158–59, 162–63, Kevin O'Higgins assassinated, 12, 201, 202, 218, 220n

Johnson, Lionel, 45n, 128, 128n, 130–32, 134, 136

—"Friend, A," 45n

Johnson, Samuel, 71

Jones, Inigo, 79n

Jonson, Ben, 5, 29, 30, 31, 36, 42, 52, 64–68, 69–86 (passim), 87, 89, 96, 97, 108–10, 115, 120, 125, 127, 127n, 130, 137, 141, 143, 146, 147, 149–51, 162, 163n, 167, 198, 226, 231, 232, 238, 242–43

—*Alchemist, The*, 64, 64n

"Come Leave the Loathed Stage," 71

Conversations with Drummond of Hawthornden, 69

Cynthia's Revels, 73n

Discoveries, 69, 72

"Epistle to Elizabeth Countess of Rutland," 76–77

"Epistle. To Katherine, Lady Aubigny," 29, 71–72, 76, 149–50

"Eupheme," 71

Every Man Out of His Humour, 68

"Execration upon Vulcan, An," 70, 141n

"Expostulacion with Inigo Jones," 79n

"Inviting a Friend to Supper" (Epigram CI), 67

"My Picture Left in Scotland," 71

"Ode. To Sir William Sydney, on his Birthday," 70, 130

"On Lucy Countess of Bedford" (Epigram LXXVI), 70

"On My First Sonne" (Epigram XLV), 76

THE JOHNS HOPKINS UNIVERSITY PRESS

This book was composed in Baskerville text by
The Composing Room from a design by Victoria
Dudley. It was printed on S. D. Warren's
60-lb. 1854 paper, regular finish, and bound in
Columbia Mills Llamique by the Maple Press Company

Library of Congress Cataloging in Publication Data

Harris, Daniel A 1942–
    Yeats: Coole Park and Ballylee.

    Includes bibliographical references.
    1. Yeats, William Butler, 1865–1939—Criticism and
interpretation. 2. Yeats, William Butler, 1865–1939—
Homes and haunts. I. Title.
PR5907. H33   821'.8   74–5185
ISBN 0-8018-1576-2